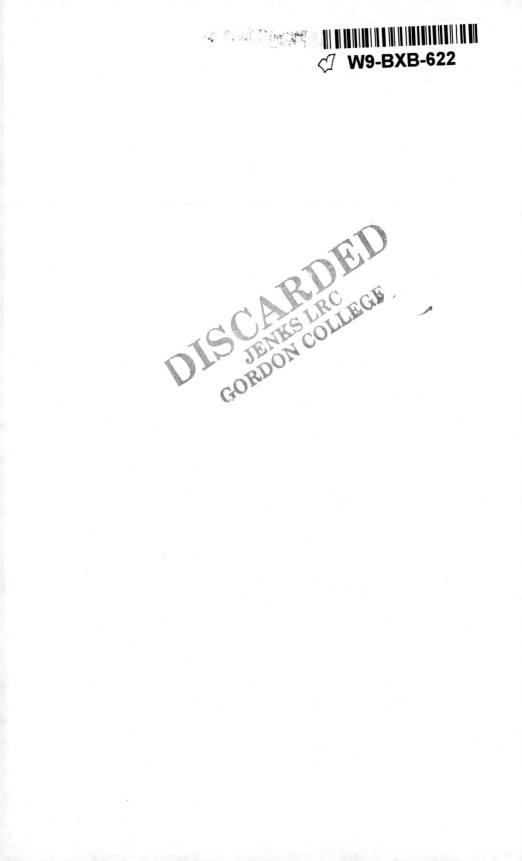

W9-BXB-622

Procedures of Power and Curriculum Change

Studies in the
Postmodern Theory of Education

Joe L. Kincheloe and Shirley R. Steinberg
General Editors

Vol. 35

PETER LANG
New York • Washington, D.C./Baltimore • Boston
Bern • Frankfurt am Main • Berlin • Vienna • Paris

David W. Blades

Procedures of Power and Curriculum Change

Foucault and the Quest for Possibilities in Science Education

PETER LANG
New York • Washington, D.C./Baltimore • Boston
Bern • Frankfurt am Main • Berlin • Vienna • Paris

Library of Congress Cataloging-in-Publication Data

Blades, David W.
Procedures of power and curriculum change: Foucault and the quest for
possibilities in science education / David W. Blades.
p. cm. — (Counterpoints; v. 35)
Includes bibliographical references and index.
1. Science—Study and teaching—Methodology. 2. Curriculum planning—
Methodology. 3. Foucault, Michel—Contributions in education. I. Title.
II. Series: Counterpoints (New York, N.Y.); vol. 35.
Q181.B5566   507'.1'2—dc21   96-54295
ISBN 0-8204-3325-X
ISBN 1058-1634

Die Deutsche Bibliothek-CIP-Einheitsaufnahme

Blades, David W.:
Procedures of power and curriculum change: Foucault and the quest for
possibilities in science education / David W. Blades. –New York;
Washington, D.C./Baltimore; Boston; Bern; Frankfurt am Main;
Berlin; Vienna; Paris: Lang.
(Counterpoints; Vol. 35)
ISBN 0-8204-3325-X
NE: GT

Cover design by James F. Brisson.
Cover illustration: Detail, Eugène Delacroix, *Jacob Wrestling with the Angel*,
c. 1858, Church of Saint-Suplice, Paris.

The paper in this book meets the guidelines for permanence and durability
of the Committee on Production Guidelines for Book Longevity
of the Council of Library Resources.

© 1997 Peter Lang Publishing, Inc., New York

Printed in the United States of America.

Dedication

*This book is dedicated to my life partner Edith
and my four sons Jesse, Daniel, Samuel, and Joshua.*

*They gave me the courage to look into the Chasm
and the desire to return to the Kingdom.*

Table of Contents

Preface and Acknowledgments   xi

Introduction   1

**Chapter 1 Modernity, Crisis and Curriculum
               Change in Science Education**   7

Introduction: Narratives of Change   7

Modernism and the First Crisis in Science Education   9

    The First Wave of Science Education Reforms   12
    The Great Conversation   16

The Second Crisis in Science Education: A Question From
   a Generation   21

    The Drift From Science   21
    The Growing Ecological Crisis   29

Responses to the Second Crisis in Science Education   33

    The Challenge of Renewal in Science Education   33
    The Rise of STS Science Education   35

**Chapter 2 The Genesis and Evolution of Science
               10, 20, and 30**   41

Introduction: Science Education as Curriculum-Discourse   41

Vision and The Genesis of Science 10, 20, and 30 in
   Alberta   43

    The Genesis of Science 10, 20, and 30   47

The Development of Science 10, 20, and 30 as a
   Technical-Rational Act   49

Controversy and Crisis in the Evolution of Science 10, 20,
   and 30   55

Controversy in the Science Education Curriculum-
    Discourse   59
Structuralistic Explanations of the Evolution of
    Science 10, 20, and 30   69

The Griffin Arises: The Reconceptualization of Science
    10, 20, and 30 in the Alberta Science Education
    Curriculum-Discourse   72

What is the Meaning of Educational Change?   78

The Barren History of Curriculum Change   83

    The Determined Hope of Structuralism in Educational
        Discourse   84

Rethinking Curriculum Change   85

**Chapter 3 Foucault's Invitation to Research
            Power**   91

Introduction: Beyond Modernity in a Curriculum-
    Discourse   91

Re-Searching Power   93

    Researching Possibilities for Curriculum Change   93

Foucault's Rethinking of Power   98

    The Influence of Foucault's Project   101

The Archaeology of Power in a Curriculum-Discourse   104

    Collecting Documents   104
    Archaeology as a Trachealizing Act   106

An End and a Beginning   118

**Chapter 4 Procedures of Power in a Science
            Education Curriculum-Discourse**   121

Introduction: Wrestling an Angel   121

Allegory and Post-modern Dis-covering   123

    Paradox and Possibilities in Post-modern Writing   123
    Allegory and Metaphor in Post-modern Writing   127

The Quest   130

Procedures of Power in a Curriculum-Discourse   133

    Destining Who Can Speak in a Curriculum-Discourse   134
    Destining What Can be Said in a Curriculum-
        Discourse   150

Characteristics of Power in a Curriculum-Discourse   158

    The Adaptability of Power   159
    The Great Anonymous   162
    Effecting an End to the Quest   167

Is Change in a Curriculum-Discourse Possible?   171

    At the Edge of Modernity   172

**Chapter 5 Possibilities for Change in Science
         Education**   175

At the Chasm of Despair   175

Locations of Hope for Change in Science Education
    Curriculum-Discourses   177

    The First Book: Foucault's Pedagogy   177
    The Second Book: Heidegger's Warning   189
    The Third Book: Nietzsche's Challenge   204

Towards a Post-Modern Science Education Curriculum-
    Discourse   213

Notes   221

**Appendix A A Summary of Topics in Biology 10,
         Chemistry 10, and Physics 10**   237

Appendix B A Brief Biography of Michel Foucault   240

Appendix C General Map of the Kingdom   243

References   245

Index   281

Preface and Acknowledgments

To guide their planning most teachers are expected to use (and some actually do) 'curriculum guides', those sometimes ponderous, official documents that list the concepts to be taught and, if the teachers are lucky, some ideas on how to teach these concepts. Those who have been teachers long enough typically encounter several new or revised versions of these curriculum guides during their career. I experienced my first 'new' guide, for 10th grade science, during my sixth year as a high school science teacher. Glancing through the guide, I was surprised with its similarity in tone, direction, and topics to the previous curriculum guide. The more experienced teachers in our school laughed when I shared my amazement, informing me that curriculum change was a cyclical process involving the predictable repetition of topics every ten to fifteen years. The end result, they assured me, was little—if any—change.

That experience, and several others shared in this book, began a question destined to haunt my thinking: Is change in science education possible? Ill formed at first, through further studies I came to realize the depth of the question I posed, and the great difficulty finding an answer. This book is the result of the journey I have taken to find possibilities for change in science education; whether an answer can be found in the pages that follow depends very much on the conversation that results from the reading. This sounds evasive, I admit, but as you will see there are good reasons to avoid any premature closure to questions concerning curriculum change.

When I set out to discover possibilities for curriculum change I was not prepared for how my search would come to challenge the very foundations of my being. At times the journey was difficult and without the kind and generous help of family and friends I may not have traveled far. I acknowledge, with heartfelt gratitude, the following who accompanied me in my quest:

Wallie Samiroden, with the Department of Secondary Education at the University of Alberta in Edmonton, Alberta, Canada was always available to help, encourage, challenge, and discuss ideas. Words do not exist that can express my gratitude for all he has done for me and my family. Heidi Kass, with the same Department, was the first to invite me to be involved in the science education discussions in Alberta that were destined to become the subject of this book. Her guidance, many contacts in the education community, inspiration, and friendship to me and my family made my foray into the Alberta science education discourse possible.

Making sense of this discourse was difficult and I will always be grateful to Terry Carson, also with the Department of Secondary Education, for alerting me to the works of Heidegger. It was reading Heidegger that led me to consider post-modern insights to curriculum change and, eventually, the works of Foucault. Terry's friendship and conversation, in particular our memorable trip from Dayton, Ohio to Louisville, Kentucky, was critical in helping me realize a vision of possibilities for curriculum change. This vision was enhanced through discussions with John Hoddinott and Daiyo Sawada, both at the University of Alberta and William Doll, Jr. at Louisiana State University.

The Department of Secondary Education proved to be a rich location as the ideas presented in this book developed. In particular I extend my thanks to Ken Jacknicke, Wytze Brouwer and Larry Beauchamp for their interest in my studies and insights. I owe a special debt to Ted Aoki for his thoughtful comment that I might find the works of Nietzsche useful; he was right. The implications of Foucault's work to curriculum change was discussed with friends over coffee; those conversations are part of my journey and helped to hone the fundamental ideas presented in this book. I especially wish to thank for their patience and responsive listening Carl Leggo, Keith Roscoe, Kalafunja O-Saki, Rillah Carson, Heather Ryan, Dennis Sumara, Laura Ho, Barb Keppy and Betty Kifiak.

Without the assistance of my associates at Alberta Education this book would have never been written. They sought to change science education in the Province with Alberta with a true vision for a scientifically literate population; I owe them much for their willingness to share their experiences. In particular, I am grateful for the friendship and enthusiastic support of Raja Panwar, Oliver Lantz, Bev Romanyshyn, Keith Wagner, Bob McClelland, Janice Leonard, and Jim Dinning. Kathy Austin of Gage Publishing was always helpful and provided very useful insights to the events in Alberta.

I deeply appreciate the encouragement to complete this book I received from faculty, support staff, and students at the University of Saskatchewan, Saskatchewan, Canada. My colleagues Glen Aikenhead, Reg Fleming, and Alan Ryan at the University of Saskatchewan and Peter Fensham at Monash University in Australia kept me inspired through their keen interest in my work as I wrote the final chapter.

I am honored this book appears as part of the *Counterpoints: Studies in the Postmodern Theory of Education* series published by Peter Lang. Shirley Steinberg, who edits the series with Joe Kincheloe, has been wonderfully supportive from the very start. The publishing staff at Peter Lang, especially Nona Reuter and Christopher Myers, have been very patient with the book development and my many questions; I have appreciated their advice in helping this book reach publication.

Poet and songwriter Leonard Cohen and his representatives at Stranger Music have been generous and kind in granting permission for me to use the lyrics from two of Mr. Cohen's songs that appear in his album, *The Future*. Mr. Bing Masley was equally as generous with his consent for me to share a poignant and timely cartoon he published in *The Medicine Hat News*. The complete text of the poem, *"pity this busy monster,manunkind,"* by e. e. cummings appears with the kind permission of Liveright Publishing Corporation. A more detailed citation for each of these works appears in the appropriate section of the endnotes.

The unwavering support of my immediate and extended family, especially their interest in my ideas and the discussions that arose through letters and over dinner, encouraged my journey and the ideas presented in this book. Special gratitude belongs to my wife Edith for her constant belief in the importance of my quest, excellent editing, loving encouragement, and willing involvement in every phase of the production of this book. Together with the love, humor, and support of my sons, I confess that while the words of that follow are mine, the journey was truly a team effort.

Introduction

I was born only a few years before the former Soviet Union launched the first artificial Earth satellite, *Sputnik*. This abrupt initiation of the space age during the so-called 'cold war' was destined to play a major role in the development of my generation. The tacit faith that science and technology could solve world problems was our inheritance and subsequent education as fear of the apparent technological superiority of a foreign power catalyzed renewal in North American science. The legacy of these reforms was an invitation to children world-wide, through the new and predominantly American and British science education teaching materials and methods, to become involved in a science-related career. Many would accept this invitation, although haunted by a sense of hesitation about the modernistic claims of a better life through science and technology. Growing up in the fifties, sixties, and early seventies the promises of science and technology seemed contradictory: How could we reconcile the development of antibiotics, television, and transistors with DDT, nuclear weapons, and napalm? Yet we clung to the belief that problems facing our world might be solved through science and technology. Some of us became educators, investing our hope in the education of the next generation. But at the sunset of the twentieth century optimism seems shallow and fears have returned. A deep suspicion about the claims of modernity has arisen from our experience and echoes in the voices of our children. Faced with global concerns of rain forest depletion, water and air pollution, and dwindling natural resources for a growing population we are beginning to realize the promises of modernity are barren and our trust in a technological salvation betrayed.

From a dawning sense of crisis the last modern generation asks a truly post-modern question: Where is hope? Like the generation before us, our search has led Western countries once again to curriculum reform in science education; perhaps if our children understand the nature, activities, benefits and dangers of science and technology, and the relationship between science, technology and society (STS) the next generation may find a hopeful future.

It would be comforting, perhaps, to present a discourse that reveals solutions to the problems of changing a secondary school science education towards an STS approach. Such a presentation could examine organizational hierarchies, lines of communication, and places where breakdowns in the development of a curriculum change attempt led to ineffectiveness. The formula of change could be our currency; we could deal in certainties, in new methods and techniques. I could form an explanation about the process of curriculum change that could be generalized and applied to other settings and situations considering curriculum change. Such a work could conclude with a new theory of curriculum change; the task of changing any curriculum could be presented as a sequence of steps to be followed carefully that in turn ensure the change takes place as planned. Books elaborating these steps might be written and workshops given to administrators, teachers, and government officials on how to correctly manage the business of changing a curriculum. But the belief that curriculum change is essentially a technical problem to be solved is seductive and misleading. As we shall see, technical approaches to curriculum change slip easily, comfortably, and surely towards a siren, only to be shipwrecked, discouraged, and even left hopeless.

Our peril in assuming a technical stance towards curriculum change springs from the assumption we act freely when proposing solutions to problems of curriculum change. As Sartre (1969) points out through the character Mathieu in *The Age of Reason*, freedom is often very remote. "We are," the philosopher Abraham Hershel (1955) reminds us, "free at rare moments. Most of the time we are driven by a process; we submit to the power of inherited character qualities or the force of external circumstances" (410). Hershel's observation suggests that the formation of a discourse that is one's own, brought forth by unique experiences and the convergence of events in space and time, also reflects the evolution of the many discourses we unconsciously—and consciously—participate in and belong to. These larger discourses may define how we speak, what can be said, and what is left unspoken, limiting our freedom to speak.

In the chapters that follow, I argue that attempts to change secondary school science education curricula are defined and thus limited by the positivistic, technical-rational assumptions of the discourse of modernity. So enframed, curriculum change seems destined to technicality, to a view of change as a problem to be solved once all the factors are elucidated; a search for a correct method and generalizable technique. The barrenness of this technical-rational approaches to curriculum change is revealed in the first two chapters through an account of the attempt from 1980 to 1990 to develop new, STS secondary school science education programs in the Canadian province of Alberta. Why explore the genesis and evolution of these high school science programs in this part of Canada? The province of Alberta was one of the first regions internationally to attempt large-scale renewal of science education towards an STS approach. A study of the struggle to change the secondary school curriculum in this region provides timely insights for others anticipating or considering changing secondary school science education towards an STS approach. The attempt to change science education in Alberta suggests technical-rational approaches to curriculum change will continue to be futile. Despite the demonstrated failure of such approaches to curriculum change, however, technicality seems to be deeply entrenched in curriculum studies precisely at a time when a growing chorus of voices are calling for change in science education.

This call presents a dilemma: restricted by the tradition of modernity to approaching change as a technological problem the question, 'How is curriculum change in science education possible?' urgently demands a post-modern response. This response involves thinking and speaking about curriculum change in ways not thought or spoken before, an attempt to break free from the defining frames of modernity. As the twentieth century comes to a close, this call to find a post-modern response to questions about curriculum change from within our modern situation is charged with urgency and great difficulty.

Fortunately we are not alone in our struggle to find post-modern ways of speaking and thinking. The recent work of some philosophers directly challenge the prevailing technical-rationality of modernity. One of these philosophers, Michel Foucault (1926–1984), provides by example a way to understand how modernity works and where possibilities for change may lie. Foucault presents his project as an attempt to discover "those systems which are still ours today and within which we are trapped. It is a question, basically, of presenting a critique of our time" (Foucault 1989a, 64). These systems are able to exist within the social body, Foucault claims, through a multiplicity of force relations which he calls *power*.

In this book I demonstrate how Foucault's concept of power provides a useful way to understand the enframing activity of modernity in curriculum change attempts and where hope and possibilities for curriculum change in secondary school science education may exist. My hope and tactic through the presentation of the text that follows is that a Foucauldian interpretation of the procedures of power in a particular attempt to change science education towards as STS approach opens a conversation of critique that is capable of revealing possibilities for curriculum change in science education.

Of course, this approach cannot be presented as a formula of how to find these possibilities or a meta-theory for analyzing power in every curriculum-discourse. To avoid such modern destining I have tried to form the discourse that follows into a post-modern presentation. This presentation may be unfamiliar to many readers and before embarking onto the chapters that follow a few words are in order. I have endeavored to avoid presenting a new theory of curriculum change or a stance that the procedures of power that I describe operating in Alberta represent a set of generalizable factors to consider when initiating change elsewhere. To do this I have presented the text that follows in a narrative style that develops on three levels. The first level is the narrative of the recent attempt to change the secondary school science curriculum in Alberta, set in the context of the response of STS science education to the second crisis in science education in Western democracies since World War II. The second narrative is my own story of how the ebb and flow of science reforms came to affect my life and how I became directly involved in the science education curriculum change attempt in Alberta. With this narrative I share how I was a participant in the attempt and how I came to interpret the events in Alberta in conversation with Foucault's work. This interpretation in turn forms the third narrative: The struggle to find hope and possibilities for change in secondary school science education. Each narrative level interrelates and intertwines, demonstrating that curriculum change is not a straight-forward process or series of steps to follow but is part of a life journey that is not separate from the discourses that define who may speak and what may be said.

Locating freedom from the defining discourses of modernity is the central purpose of this book. Through an archeology of power in a particular curriculum-discourse via layers of narrative, I explore the nature and activity of our modern enframing, the 'destining of technicality', to use the words of the philosopher Martin Heidegger (1977), leading to a consideration of possible locations for change in a curriculum-discourse. One key location for change rests with the readers of this book. I extend an invitation to enter into an on-going, hopeful conversation of critique with the text that follows. Foucault (1982) defines critique as "seeing what kinds of self-evidences, liberties, acquired and non-reflective modes of thought, the practices we accept rest on" (33): a 'dis-covering' of the way we think and act. This critique, claims Foucault, can lead to change since "the moment one begins to be unable, any longer, to think things as one usually thinks them, transformation becomes simultaneously very urgent, very difficult, and altogether possible" (34). In the spirit of this hope, I challenge readers through our conversation together to reflect on their own situation, to discover how modernity enframes a particular curriculum discourse and where possibilities for freedom may exist.

Before we begin this conversation of critique I have two requests. First, I ask readers to avoid forming opinions or conclusions too rapidly, so that our conversation may remain open. A certain patience is needed as the narratives unfold and then recollect forward, as philosopher Søren Kierkegaard (1983) would describe it, through the allegory presented in the final two chapters. At many places in this book the organization and presentation might seem odd, unfamiliar, and uncomfortable. In fact, this is my hope and intention: That the discomfort of a post-modern presentation will provoke conversation while discouraging modernistic appropriations of what I am about to share. Second, I ask readers to remember that throughout the narratives that follow and in our conversation together in no way do I suggest that I have somehow found a pathway to post-modernity or that I am recommending a route anyone else may follow. No, I wish to avoid this telling slippage back to modernity and so I ask, as did Foucault in the introduction to one of his works, that readers "do not ask me who I am, and do not ask me to remain the same" (Foucault 1972, 17). Let us leave such defining to others and choose instead to enter into a conversation of critique over the enframent of science education curriculum-discourse and through our conversation locate hope and possibilities for change.

Chapter 1

Modernity, Crisis and Curriculum Change in Science Education

Introduction: Narratives of Change

When I teach I am always impressed with the ability of stories to capture the attention of my students. The words, 'Let us begin with a story' are almost magical in the way the teaching relationship with students transforms from didactic to communal. One purpose of forming stories, or narratives, suggests education philosopher Maxine Greene, is to engage in a journey of consciousness, an attempt to "go beyond, to reach towards imagined possibility" (Greene 1987, 11). In other words, story telling is more than entertainment but an invitation to reflect together through the communion of story so that our shared wisdom might reveal possibilities otherwise covered by the business of living.

Finding these possibilities involves people telling stories that reflect upon life. The public nature of this telling means that sharing stories is a type of political action since, as educator and curriculum theorist Bill Pinar observes, "we are not the stories we tell as much as we are the modes of relation to others our stories imply" (Pinar 1988, 29). Educator Tom Popkewitz (1988) explains this further by reminding us that

> while we are immersed in our personal histories, our practices are not simply the products of our intent and will. We take part in the routines of daily life, we use language that is socially constructed to make camaraderie with others possible, and we develop affiliations with the roles and institutions that give form to our identities. We speak not only as ourselves but, as Foucault reminds us, as part of discourses of power as the social complexities and subtleties of intellectual life are inter-related with institutions. That which is seemingly normal and natural about our participation in the world are the very acts about which we need to become curious and critical. (379–380)

The telling of stories can thus reveal who we are and why we act and speak the way we do, a critical examination of how we live in the world and how else we might be. In this way, forming and sharing narratives can become a call to action through a commitment to change present situations. This call not only involves the individual sharing a story but includes those listening or reading the stories as they add these stories to their own. What can emerge from such sharing of story is a conversation of critique about our normal, comfortable, and natural participation in the world.

This conversation of critique helps, in the words of curriculum theorist Madeleine Grumet (1987) "mark the territory that is to be the ground for meaningful action, thus establishing the perimeter of our freedom as well as our containment" (320–321). The nature and activity of our modern containment, or enframement, and possibilities to move beyond this entrapment are the focus of this book. To understand this enframing, I begin in this Chapter the three narratives outlined in the Introduction. Each narrative is a story of a struggle for change. At the personal level, I will share how, like Grumet, I became "impatient with a kind of subordination I was experiencing, as if my whole life would be filled with stern and critical fathers, making sure I did not stray from a beaten path they had laid down" (10). In successive chapters I share through the narrative of events in my life how this impatience led to an archeology of self that suggests possibilities for change. A second narrative that is wider in scope also begins, although briefly, in Chapter 1. In the chapters that follow this narrative tells and then later re-visits the story of the genesis and evolution of a set of new secondary school science education programs in the Canadian province of Alberta. Finally, I begin in Chapter 1 to deconstruct and lay bare some aspects of the 'Great Conversation' of Western modernity. Intimately linked to the other two, this largest of all narratives forms a nexus of relations explored in the pages that follow. The relentless and effective ability of the Great Conversation in setting the boundaries of our freedom requires critical examination if change in science education is to have any hope of success. Two events in space exploration are symbolic of our modern situation in the Great Conversation. We now turn to the first of these events and thus begin the weaving of three narratives that explore our modern situation.

Modernism and the First Crisis in Science Education

The sober desire for progress is sustained by faith—faith in the intrinsic
goodness of human nature and in the omnipotence of science.
—Eric Hoffer, *The True Believer* (1951, 8).

On July 20, 1969 Neil Armstrong, the 38-year-old commander of
Apollo 11, slowly descended a ladder and extended his foot to touch
the powdery surface of the moon. As Armstrong placed the first
human footprint on an extra-terrestrial body, he captured the hopes of
the world in the historic phrase: "That's one small step for man, one
giant leap for mankind."[1] A staff reporter covering the *Apollo* project
for the *New York Times* recalls how humankind seemed on the brink
of interplanetary travel: "The moon, long the symbol of the
impossible, was now within reach, the first port of call in the new age
of spacefaring" (Wilford 1971, 20). This was not idle speculation.
The director of the George C. Marshall Space Flight Center, Werner
Von Braun, felt the *Apollo 11* mission reinforced the "utter
conviction that tomorrow's knowledge and technology will provide
the means to attain the goals" of interplanetary flight, "sooner than
thought" (Von Braun 1970, x). The very day of the lunar landing a
senior administrator of the National Aeronautics and Space
Administration (NASA) declared that "the triumph of *Apollo* is
nevertheless only a beginning" towards establishing a lunar base
"within the next decade" (Mueller 1969, 14). Not even a year after
Armstrong's historic first step onto the lunar surface, some science
writers were predicting Americans and Russians would make over 50
voyages to the moon by 1975, leading to a permanent lunar base.[2]
These writers confidently forecast that by 1990 there would be space
flights to Mars and established lunar science research and astronomy
stations that would employ a permanent and growing population on
the moon.

I had just completed my freshman year of high school when I
joined a world community of 500 million temporarily linked through
the medium of television to watch the historic lunar landing. "No
one," commented one major newspaper editorial, "could watch the
televised pictures of earthmen walking on the moon without a
tightening in the throat, a tear or two of emotion, and a surge of
vicarious pride in being a member of the human race."[3] As we

watched the almost unreal unfolding of events culminating with Neil Armstrong and Buzz Aldrin walking on the moon, we felt the power in U.S. President Johnson's optimism that America could now "do anything that needs to be done."[4]

For many around the world, the mission to the moon dramatized the possibility that technological solutions exist to world problems. In Israel, Prime Minister Golda Meir spoke of the "great future ahead of us" and Pope Paul VI called for the application of the effort and thinking behind the *Apollo* mission to be now applied to "true progress toward the temporal and moral good of humanity."[5] The Foreign Minister of France at the time suggested the historic event "opens for all humanity prospects of a considerable extent," agreeing with the President of Poland that "the flight will serve peace and all mankind [*sic*]."[6] For many, the *Apollo* landing signified hope for new prosperity and opportunities resulting from the commercial application of space technologies. In the summer of 1969, I knew I wanted to be part of these new challenges, part of the journey of humankind to the stars. I also knew, after considerable personal agonizing, what would be my career: I would help humanity, I would find solutions to the world's problems; I would become a scientist.

I had been practicing. When I was only seven my father gave me a microscope. It was a kit with prepared slides, some preserved specimens, a needle probe, and a wonderful optical instrument that opened views of worlds beyond my dreams. I vividly remember the first specimen I examined with my new microscope: a prepared slide of the hairs of a silverberry plant, stained all shades of the rainbow. Spellbound, I was speechless at the view. A few years later my father brought me a telescope. Late into the night I would gaze at the phases of Venus, the blueness of Rigel and the redness of Mars. I made detailed maps of the moon, longing and expecting to travel there someday. When I entered high school my father brought me a chemistry set. Though we had to evacuate the house when I produced too much sulfur dioxide gas during an experiment, he never complained; well, not *too* much. His love of learning, fascination with all things scientific, and faith in scientific research as the foundation to material progress became my inheritance.

I was not alone. My best friend Rob and I planned joint biology ventures that would make us rich, Larry had chemistry equipment that was the envy of us all, Karl built electronic equipment in his basement, and Fraser launched insects into the sky with a rocket set. By the end of our freshman year, all of us wanted to be scientists. Our generation, at least the boys I knew, continued to build our lives on what historian Paul Johnson calls the 'foundation stone' of modernity: The fundamental conviction that "science and technology seems to make all things possible for humanity" (Johnson 1991, 360). In the summer of 1969, the *Apollo 11* achievement seemed evidence *prima facie* of the unlimited potential of humanity through science and technology.

Ten years before the Apollo mission, the United States Academy of Sciences held a ten day meeting held at the U.S. Oceanographic Research Institute in Wood's Hole, Massachusetts to "discuss how education in science might be improved" in the primary and secondary schools of the United States (Bruner 1960, vii). Stimulated by funding support from the U.S. National Science Foundation (NSF), initiatives to renew topics and structure of American school science education programs was well under way before the Wood's Hole Conference.[7] Wood's Hole, then, was a retrospective appraisal of the process and direction of the new American science education programs and an exploration of how continued renewal in science education might proceed: This was a curriculum conference.

Attendance at the Wood's Hole conference reflected a movement in post-World War II American education towards a focus on the knowledge content and structure of high school subjects. Of the thirty-four men attending Wood's Hole, only two represented the field of education. The unchallenged suppositions of the meeting at Wood's Hole reflected the modernistic primacy of progress through the applications of scientific thinking. Leading researchers in behavioral cognitive science, such as Robert Gagné, Lee Cronbach, and Jerome Bruner, met with university natural scientists, psychologists, mathematicians, historians, and representatives from other disciplines to consider the following questions about school science education:

What shall be taught, when, and how?
What kinds of research and inquiry might further the growing effort in the design of curricula?

What are the implications of emphasizing the structure of a subject, be it
mathematics or history, emphasizing it in such a way that seeks to give the
student as quickly as possible a sense of the fundamental ideas of a discipline?
(Bruner 1960, 3)

Bruner's report on discussions at the Wood's Hole Conference, *The
Process of Education* (1960), quickly became an influential text that
had a powerful effect in shaping the research and direction of the
field of curriculum.[8] The meeting at Wood's Hole clearly supported
the direction and approach of the American science education reform
initiatives. At this conference participants enthusiastically endorsed the
movement to allocate decisions about the content, approach, and
structure of school science education to "those with a high degree of
vision and competence in each of these fields," which Bruner
identified as "the best minds in any particular discipline" (19); that
is, outstanding university and corporate researchers. Bruner argues
these researchers should continue developing school programs that
emphasize "the fundamental structure of whatever subjects we choose
to teach" (11). Bruner is clear on the reason for this approach to
curriculum change: The new school programs would help all students
achieve the "full utilization of their intellectual powers" (11) so that
the United States "will have a better chance of surviving as a
democracy in an age of enormous technological and social
complexity" (11). Somewhat ironically, Bruner suggests only a few
sentences later a rather undemocratic focus in science education with
his plea that new curriculum directly appeal to the "top quarter of
public school students from which we must draw intellectual
leadership in the next generation" (11).

The First Wave of Science Education Reforms

The move towards school science programs designed by scientists
grew from a widespread post-World War II sentiment in the United
States of a need to revise school science programs towards
encouraging school graduates to pursue science-related careers.
During the forties it became obvious that American science education
was "at too great a variance with modern concepts of science and too
far removed from the educational needs of contemporary society to
meet the needs of the period ahead" (Marshall 1962, 2). Part of this
variance was the effect of World War II on science and technology.

Stimulated by the war, America had transformed from an "agrarian society to a scientific-technological society," leading to a "demand for men and women trained for scientific and technological vocations" (Hurd 1964, 7). After the second world war the U.S. was in such rapid need of a trained scientific community that American science education in the early fifties is described by science educator Paul Hurd as a time of "confusion and crisis" (Hurd 1961, 108). The rapid growth of science and technology during the years immediately following World War II exasperated this sense of crisis. New discoveries, techniques, and innovations in science and technology contrasted dramatically with an increasingly irrelevant school science curriculum that dogmatically portrayed science as a static body of knowledge oriented towards a society that existed in the past.

Wartime innovations, such as RADAR, proved the importance of scientific developments to national security. This lesson was not lost in America. Spectacular successes in atomic energy and electronics led to the popular public myth that if one were to take a team of great scientists, put them into a well-equipped laboratory, provide them with a clear objective and essentially unlimited amounts of money, they could do anything. In Canada, the federal government acted on this belief through large investments involving high technology; specifically atomic energy and the ill-fated military aircraft programs of the fifties. Similar projects were the focus of government spending in the U.S. with the important addition of education. Post-war concerns in the U.S. about the spread of communism and fear of scientific and technological progress in the Soviet Union encouraged government agencies, including the military, to invest in educational research. Almost immediately upon inception by government statue in 1946, the U.S. Atomic Energy Commission (AEC), together with the U.S. Office of Naval Research, began funding projects cryptically termed "mission-oriented basic research" (B. Smith 1990, 49) that included curriculum renewal efforts in college science education. Public criticisms of American public schooling, such as American Admiral Hyman Rickover's claim that American education was 'soft', prompted academics, supported with government funds, to form in the early fifties the school science education curriculum committees destined to be enthusiastically endorsed at the Wood's Hole Conference.

On Saturday morning, October 5, 1957, a sleepy Western world woke to the headline, *"RUSSIA LAUNCHES FIRST SATELLITE."*[9] Washington was quick to congratulate the Soviet Union on the remarkable achievement of producing the first human-made satellite, called *Sputnik*; although the chief of American naval operations quipped the Russian satellite was a "hunk of iron almost anybody could launch."[10] Disconcerting to readers in North America was the announcement by the Russian news agency *Tass* that the Soviet Union planned to send up within a year *several* more artificial satellites that would pass directly over North America.[11] The following day American papers reported the agreement of British experts that the new technology could be used as a 'spy in the sky'. An essay in the *New York Times* introduced another area of concern: The rocket technology to place a satellite in orbit meant Russia also must have intercontinental missile capabilities.[12]

One editor of a major newspaper bluntly acknowledged the launching of *Sputnik* "shocked the complacency of nations where science is an accepted part of life, and whose attainments therein have been taken for granted as setting the pace for the rest of the world" (Dalgleish 1957a, 6). The solution to this situation, according to the editor, was to make much larger sums of money available to national research centers, the actual amounts to be worked out by "those who know the field" (6). U.S. President Eisenhower claimed to be "undisturbed" by the launching of *Sputnik*, although some journalists in the United States suggested the President could not "bring himself to admit that it was under his administration that the United States fell behind" (Deane 1957, 1–2).

The launch of *Sputnik II* by the Soviet Union on November 4, 1957 brought an end to the President's public blasé attitude towards Soviet achievements in space technology. Carrying a dog as passenger, *Sputnik II* seemed to give credence to Russian boasts that a trip to the moon by Soviet cosmonauts was imminent. Claims by the Soviet Union the following day that *Sputnik II* was launched "by a new source of power"[13] led to an immediate emergency meeting of the United States Cabinet. A poignant editorial comment in the November 6, 1957 issue of the Canadian newspaper, *The Globe and Mail*, captures the mood of both Canada and the United States at this time:

The two Sputniks buzzing about the earth may be taken as a judgment upon us. A judgment, and perhaps a final warning. If we of the West are going to survive in the world, if we are even to hold our present level of power and wealth, *we have got to care very deeply about education and the people associated with it*. We have got to care as much as the Russians, and indeed we may have to care more. For they seem, in a good many ways, to be ahead of us. (Dalgleish 1957b, 6, emphasis mine.)

From crisis came commitment. Four days after *Sputnik II* began orbiting the Earth, President Eisenhower announced a massive 'overhaul' of the American science-defense infrastructure that included plans to stimulate school science education in the United States. In the wake of the Soviet launches, the United States government passed the National Defense Education Act (NDEA) in 1958. The NDEA provided massive funding for education with the result that "millions of dollars were devoted to the cooperative involvement of scientists, educators, and learning theorists in the development of science curriculum materials" (Helgeson, Blosser, and Howe 1977, 1). By 1960, ninety-three percent of all post-War U.S. government funding of educational initiatives came from the Department of Defense, AEC and NASA, illustrating how issues of national security influenced the direction and approach of American science education reform in the late fifties. The goal of this investment of funds and personnel in science education was the production of top-notch, career scientists through studies of the traditional disciplines of biology, chemistry, and physics.[14] Even though American science education in the fifties and sixties was oriented towards the recruitment and selection of an elite corps of students that were invariably a "homogeneous group of white males" (Champagne and Hornig 1986, 2), the support and endorsement of these initiatives in science education by leading academics at the Wood's Hole Conference guaranteed few would question this approach to science education curriculum development.

The launching of the two *Sputnik* satellites led to an unparalleled degree of activity in efforts to reform school science education, beginning with the United States and Britain. Through extensive financial support of the NSF in the United States and the Department of National Defense with the passing of the NDEA, millions of dollars were invested in the production of various new science programs for American elementary and secondary schools. The various acronyms used to describe these programs have lead some science educators to describe the sixties as the era of the 'alphabet soup' science education reforms.[15] In Britain the 'cold war' climate heightened concerns that science education was not producing enough scientists, keeping pace with scientific discoveries, or responding to the general social changes in Britain. These concerns led to the development in the early sixties of the British Nuffield Science Foundation programs. These programs, similar to the American science courses, were also "designed largely by academic scientists" (Matthews 1989, 3) with the focus on "being able to create little scientists" (3).[16]

During this time of intense curriculum development in the U.S. and Britain, Canada tended to play the role of spectator, choosing to import to its school systems with little or no modification the American science education programs developed in the early sixties such as BSCS, CHEM Study, and PSCS.[17] The acceptance of these new science programs in Canada confirmed "the widespread assumption that Canadian schools were carbon copies of their counterparts to the south" (Tomkins 1977, 10). Canadians were not alone as spectators during the first round of curriculum reforms in science education. Many countries adopted science education curriculum reforms originating from Britain and the United States: British curricula were adopted in the latter sixties by countries such as Malaysia and Nigeria while the new American science programs were imported by a wide diversity of countries such as Australia, Turkey, Israel and Japan.

The Great Conversation

The British and American science programs that were exported to Canada and other countries world-wide display in orientation, spirit, and approach what the Editor-in-Chief of the 1952 version of *Encyclopedia Britannica* calls in the introduction to this work, "The Great Conversation" (Hutchins 1952, 1). According to this Editor-in-Chief, the dominant element of this Great Conversation "is the Logos" (1), where

> nothing is to remain undiscussed. Everybody is to speak his [sic] mind. No proposition is to be left unexamined. The exchange of ideas is to be the path to the realization of the potentialities of the race. (1)

Belief in the value of inquiry and enunciation to human progress echoes in the most ancient philosophies. Modern expressions of this spirit formed during the European Enlightenment[18] (ca. 1350–1650) through the "precepts of Bacon, the conceptions of Descartes and the discoveries of Galileo" (Aiken 1956, 129) and the discoveries and innovations in science and art during that era. The modern legacy of the European Enlightenment is a "logocentric metaphysics of presence" (Madison 1988, x) that has come to dominate Western thinking for the past three hundred years. Foundational to this metaphysics of modernity is the belief that a rational subject can truly come to know objective reality and this knowledge can be used to further human progress towards, in the words of seventeenth century scientist Francis Bacon, "the effecting of all things possible" (Bacon 1942, 288). How is this knowledge achieved? The successes of the scientific revolution amidst the European Enlightenment directed the focus of the Great Conversation towards science: Knowledge of the objective world is possible through reasonable, logical, experimental inquiry. Human progress, asserted the eighteenth century philosopher Auguste Compte, will come once people extend "to social phenomenon the spirit which governs the treatment of all other natural phenomenon" (Compte, quoted in Zeitlin 1987, 65). In his *Cours de Philosophie Positive* (Course of Positive Philosophy), Compte argues for a 'positive philosophy' based on the activity and principles of scientific inquiry:

> Under the rule of the positive spirit, again, all the difficult and delicate questions which now keep up a perpetual irritation in the bosom of society, and which can never be settled while mere political solutions are proposed, *will be scientifically estimated*, to the great furtherance of social peace. (Compte, quoted in Zeitlin 1987, 65, emphasis mine.)

Compte's assertion of the primacy of scientific knowledge above other ways of knowing became a modern, public belief during the nineteenth century as "men and women could see wealth increasing on all sides, while science and technology seemed to make all things possible for humanity" (P. Johnson 1991, 360). A tacit faith in the primacy of science and technology to human progress became a common theme in popular fiction as writers anticipated the twentieth century; for example, Jules Verne's *Twenty Thousand Leagues Under the Sea* (1870), Henrik Ibsen's *An Enemy of the People* (1882), Conan Doyle's *The Sherlock Holmes Mysteries* (1891), and Bernard Shaw's *Major Barbara* (1905) were in harmony with the spirit of Victor Hugo's recommendation for social progress in his classic, *Les Misérables*: "Science is authority rightly understood. Man [*sic*] should be governed only by science" (Hugo 1887, Volume I, 45). During the first fifty years of the twentieth century astounding scientific discoveries, such as the structure of the atom, existence of hormones and antibiotics, and Rh factors in human blood—and spectacular inventions through scientific research, such as RADAR, digital computers, electron microscopes, transcontinental telephone service, airplanes, television, and electrocardiograms—seemed to confirm the optimistic faith of modernity that through science and technology our species might be able to accomplish almost anything, solve any problem. In the early fifties few in the Western world would have doubted the accuracy of philosopher Bertrand Russell's assessment in 1952 that one hundred fifty years of modernity have proved scientific inquiry to be an important "source of economic technique capable of transforming human life" (Russell 1952, 9).

This modern, logical positivism permeates the science education curriculum reforms of the late fifties and early sixties. Tacit faith in science and technology to solve problems and guarantee progress led the attention of funding agencies to fall naturally towards the scientific community as key players in the design and development of new school science programs. Bruner's *Process of Education* (1960) provided a modernistic approach to curriculum reform that guided the majority of the nationwide curriculum development projects of the sixties. Three key assumptions were foundational to the activity of the science education reform of that era:

1. *Assumption of expertise:* Bruner's proposal to base the design of school science programs on the structure of academic science disciplines reflected the assumption by funding agencies such as the NSF that the design of science education curricula was itself a type of scientific activity best left to scientists.[19] To encourage children to experience biology as a biologist, chemistry as a chemist, or physics as a physicist, experts in these science disciplines became school curriculum writers and advisers during the fifties and sixties. The publication of Bruner's *The Process of Education* celebrated and

promoted this use of non-education specialists in curriculum reform. In Chapter 2 we will see if this assumption of expertise still guides attempts at curriculum reform in school science education.

2. *Assumption of curriculum:* I first encountered the new American science programs during my sophomore year of high school. The new science courses, we were told, were so new and revolutionary all our school could provide at this moment were mimeographed handouts of the BSCS text and laboratory manuals, although we were promised the new textbooks and films were on their way (they arrived later in the year). It was enough. Intrigued with the physiology, anatomy, and ecology of organisms I devoured the unusual applications of Greek and Latin sounds familiar to the practicing biologist. My success in learning to speak the language of biology led me, and many of my classmates, to consider a career in science. Our teacher, unfamiliar with the new materials, simply acted as a guide to our explorations. In that classroom the authority for our studies came from the authors of the BSCS materials; to us the new biology curriculum *was* the textbook and laboratory manuals we were using.

This perception of the science curricula as materials-in-use with authority located somewhere distant to the classroom was accurate. For example, in a U.S. National Science Teacher Association (NSTA) position paper on post-World War II science education curriculum reforms science educator Paul DeHart Hurd (1964) describes the new science curricula as programs that were constructed, organized, and then implemented in schools. The focus of this curriculum activity was the development and publication of science education textual materials: textbooks, films and laboratory kits. These materials, claims curriculum theorist Elliot Eisner (1979), were developed with the assumption that "nationally known scholars would be able to provide teachers with a higher quality of materials than teachers could create on their own" (38).

3. *Assumptions of method:* Through his work on the nature of science education and direct involvement in the development of the BSCS program, educator and curriculum theorist Joseph Schwab was seen during the science education reforms as a "spokesman [*sic*] for the importance of discipline-based teaching of science in schools" (Westbury and Wilkof 1978, 24). In his influential essay, *Education and the Structure of the Disciplines* (1978), Schwab argues for a school science education curriculum that is, "from the start, a

representative of the discipline" (Schwab 1978, 269). Schwab continues in his essay to recommend a science curriculum based on Compte's structuralistic approach to knowledge and philosophical stance of positivism, leading naturally to the consideration of curriculum development in science education as a scientific problem. This view was not unique; as we have seen, the Wood's Hole conference endorsed a positivistic, scientific approach to curriculum building in science education.

The three-fold strategy in the early sixties of replacing science programs rather than revising previous curricula, looking to professional scientists rather than educators for the authority and leadership of the reforms, and infusing federal funds to support the new initiatives initially seemed successful. Student enrollment and achievement in high school science programs increased in schools that adopted the new science programs (Kyle, Shymansky, and Alport 1982), although large-scale assessments of school science education was not conducted in the U.S. or Canada during the early sixties. The glowing optimism surrounding the *Apollo* moon landing at the end of that decade provided a modern reassurance of the primacy of science and technology to human progress, confirming the direction and intent of the new school science programs. Exposed to these new science curricula in our senior years, one goal of the reforms seemed to be realized: many of my classmates announced at our high school graduation their intention to pursue science-related careers.

I traveled in a slightly different direction. Inspired by my high school science teachers, I decided my future lay in teaching high school biology. Embarking on a career as a high school science teacher, I eagerly anticipated my university science courses. Part of my education degree involved learning how to plan lessons that reflected Schwab's focus on the discipline of a science field. I worked hard to find the best way to deliver to my students the content, structure, and approach of various science disciplines, especially biology. I wanted them to love and experience science as I had. After four years of university study in sciences and one year of education courses, I felt ready to teach! I knew my science, I could plan lessons, I was ready for the classroom. I was not prepared, however, for the single, sincere question Albert was to ask.

The Second Crisis in Science Education: A Question From a Generation

Crisis, even if it does not comprise the totality of human life, nevertheless belongs necessarily to human life; and has a necessary function to fulfill in it.
—O. F. Bollnow, *Crisis and New Beginning* (1987, 5).

It was, as I remember, a hot Friday afternoon. I was teaching a rather obscure concept in a senior chemistry class when Albert raised his hand. "Sir," he asked sincerely, "why are we learning this crap?" Phrased poorly, I had to admit it was a good question. I turned to the blackboard and stood facing the notes and diagrams I had so carefully crafted during the past fifteen minutes. Why were my students learning this, I wondered. I could honestly see no connection to their lives, no use, no real reason a student in high school should learn what I had just been teaching. "I suppose..." I responded slowly, "so you can continue in your science studies at university." I could tell neither of us felt comfortable with my answer! The lesson concluded and students were dismissed, but Albert's question stayed after class. I recognized, for the first time in my life, that Albert had given a voice to a 'dis-ease' that had been steadily growing within my thinking. Vaguely aware something was amiss in science education, I embarked on further studies to learn more about the curriculum I inherited and had so faithfully represented in my classroom.

The Drift From Science

In the summer of 1984 I began graduate studies of curriculum. There was considerable excitement among educators in Canada that year over the publication by a governmentally-supported agency, the Science Council of Canada (SCC), of the results of a four-year study of school science education in Canada. One essential purpose of this study was the assessment of post-*Sputnik* science education curriculum reform in Canadian science education. From 1979 to 1984 the SCC reviewed school science curricula across Canada through case studies, textbook reviews, interviews, document analyses, examination of government guidelines for science education, and consultation with interest groups throughout the country.

The SCC review reached a rather blunt recommendation: "Renewal in science education is essential. Now" (Science Council of Canada 1984a, 2). Many concerns surfaced as a result of the SCC study, including a lack of Canadian content in science education, missed opportunities for all students to study science, the entrenchment of science programs that present an inaccurate view of the activity of science and the failure of science courses to relate science to technological or societal issues.

There were similar studies in the late seventies and early eighties in the U.S.; so many, in fact, that that era has been described by some educators as the 'decade of reports' in the U.S.[20] Three major studies of science education in the U.S. by the National Science Foundation during the years 1969–1977 provided "substantial evidence that serious attention needs to be paid to improving the quality" of pre-college science education (H. Smith 1980, 55). A review of American post-*Sputnik* science education assessments by the National Science Foundation Panel on School Science (1980) concluded that "the whole educational system is in trouble" and that science education in particular has displayed "considerable slippage" in instructional quality and student academic performance during the seventies (84).

I was shocked by these studies of science education and in particular by the SCC studies. In my movement from high school student to classroom science teacher I simply assumed the high school science I experienced as a student would remain valuable to *my* students. Indeed, my instructional approach was based at that time on the models of my past science teachers and university professors of science. But the evidence from the science education assessments spoke clearly, challenging my conceptions of what it means to teach children science. This was only the beginning of the conceptual challenges I would encounter. As I explored curriculum issues in science education, I found more voices calling for reform in science education.

The Voice of Students
As the so-called 'baby boomer' generation graduated from high school, colleges and universities in America enjoyed an overall increase in student enrollment from the late sixties to the mid-seventies. The number of students studying science at a post-secondary institutions rose steadily until the mid-seventies, when most

institutions began to experience a steady and rather disconcerting decline in the number of students actually graduating from post-secondary institutions with a science-related degree.[21] Institutes in other countries, such as Britain, reflected the trend in America, prompting science educator David Stenhouse (1985) to suggest an alarming international pattern among in Western democracies:

> All the educational might and ingenuity of the most powerful Western democracies has been lavished, since about 1960, on the development and improvement of education in the various sciences—and what has been the outcome? Recruitment to science has suffered not only a relative but also in many cases an absolute drop. The young adults who were expected to provide the scientific work force and the spearheads of original research for the 1980s and beyond have been voting with their feet; they have gone into the humanities, and the social sciences, and 'business studies', and so on, rather than the basic sciences. (3)

The drift from a career in science was reflected in the lives of my close high school friends. Although many had announced at our high school graduation that they were pursuing careers in science, most of us drifted to other areas. Rob dropped out of university to manage a lumber store. Larry became a manager trainee at a Bank, Fraser worked for a telephone company and I, although still somewhat involved in science, had become a teacher. Of my closest high school friends, only Karl had chosen a career related to science with his rather timely employment in the field of computer software design.

Part of the 'drift from science' by my classmates and other students in the Western world during the seventies and eighties may have been due to the inability of the science reforms of the sixties to make a significant impact on school science instruction. Already by 1973, Canadian educator Hugh Stevenson complained that the real legacy of the sixties reforms was the realization that "we did not learn how to make the fundamental changes that led to genuine reform" (52). An architect of the reforms in American high school biology, Paul Hurd (1991b) agrees with Stevenson's assessment, observing that "despite the turmoil over the science curriculum during the past decades, not much has happened" (35). In fact, only 22–25 percent of the boards of education in the U.S. ever adopted the new science programs;[22] ironically, adoption of the programs tended to be higher among countries outside of the U.S., such as Canada. Even in those regions where the programs were adopted, follow-up studies revealed that the majority of high school science teachers were ill-equipped to teach them. What did appear in American and Canadian schools during the seventies were science courses that emphasized the structures of the scientific disciplines and relatively advanced theoretical concepts explicitly designed to increase the supply of trained scientists, engineers and technicians. Often missing from these courses was the enthusiasm and deep understanding of the values, nature, and processes of science characteristic of the first versions of new science programs. It seems *the vision of the new programs never reached the classroom*; instead the new programs became absorbed into a prior tradition of science education at the secondary level being important only to those who intended to study those subjects at post-secondary institutions.

This focus on specialization and recruitment in science education, suggests science educator Glen Aikenhead, allowed high school science to continue to be dry, socially and culturally sterile, content-laden courses of study that, not surprisingly, held little or no appeal to students (Aikenhead 1980, 1983). A review of American science education in a 1992 issue of *Scientific American* reports that teachers came to interpret the new, post-*Sputnik* science programs as a focus on the mastery of science content, leading to the development of science lessons that consisted of mainly rote memorization of words towards the goal of passing examinations (Beardsley 1992). The result, suggests the article, is that many young persons become 'turned off' science before graduating from high school because of programs which they perceive as boring and intimidating (103).

By the late seventies and early eighties, the failure of educational reform in science education in America became apparent through studies that revealed students attitudes towards science sharply decline when these students enter high school. In a comprehensive review of the results of the Third National Assessment of Science Education in the United States (1978), Yager and Yager (1985) note that in general "students have better perceptions concerning science, science classes, science teachers, the value of science, and what it is like to be a scientist in grade three than when they are in grade eleven" (356). In a follow up study, Yager and Penick (1986) reached the disturbing conclusion that "the more years our students enroll in science courses, the less they like it" (360). International assessments of student achievement in science education reported a similar trend world-wide, with very positive attitudes towards science among children in sharp decline by the time these student are in their senior year of high school.

Ironically, the lack of relevancy of the science reforms of the late fifties and sixties to students in the seventies and eighties and declining attitudes towards science as children progress through grade levels may be due to the focus of those programs on attracting young persons to science careers. Working with science educator Heidi Kass, I found that for many high school students science careers

> tend not to be viewed as particularly prestigious. For the training involved, being a scientist is perceived as a somewhat low-paying career with few, if any, perks. Scientists may have somewhat poor working conditions, e.g., smelly laboratories, tramping through the bush alone, and often somewhat little real power or influence, since research funding dictates that they work for the interest of business, e.g., consultants for pulp mills. "What is so great about being a scientist anyway?" Is a question increasingly asked by young persons today. (Kass and Blades 1992, 2)

Compounding this lack of interest in a science related career is the belief held by young persons that high school science courses are difficult and the misperception among students in Western democracies that anyone willing to study high school science courses such as physics must be a 'nerd, brain, geek' or some other derogatory label.[23]

Postulating a relationship between the drop in student attitudes towards science and declining numbers of students graduating from post-secondary institutions with degrees in science-related fields may be simplistic. Students are part of general society, their voices reflect and are mixed in the chorus of the general public. Even before *Apollo 11* left on its historic voyage in 1969, public belief in the modern assumption of the value and centrality of science and technology to human progress had begun to change.

Changing Public Perceptions of Science
In the heady optimism of the summer of 1969, some critics "persisted in saying the *Apollo* program cost too much, [and] that the money and talent could be more usefully directed to fighting disease and poverty" (Wilford 1971, 21). Concerns about scientific endeavors

were not new. Popular works such as Louis Stevenson's *Dr. Jekyl and Mr. Hyde* (1886), Orson Wells' *The Time Machine* (1895), Aldous Huxley's *Brave New World* (1932) and George Orwell's dark *1984* (1948) express deep reservations about modern faith in science and technology. Mary Shelly's classic tale, *Frankenstein* (1831) is one of the earliest criticisms of scientific research in the modern era. Bent on creating a living being just to see if it could be done, the words of the young Dr. Frankenstein are hauntingly contemporary:

> Had I the right, for my own benefit, to inflict this curse upon everlasting generations? Now, for the first time, the wickedness of my promise burst upon me; I shuddered to think that the future ages might curse me as their pest, whose selfishness had not hesitated to buy its own peace at the price, perhaps, of the existence of the whole human race. (Shelly 1988, 189)

Doubts about the unbridled growth of science first entered American post-World War II public discourse with the publication in 1962 of *Silent Spring* by Rachel Carson and in 1965 Ralph Nader's exposé, *Unsafe at Any Speed.*[24] Perhaps for the first time the North American public became aware that the technological benefits of science also produce risks. In his analysis of American science policy since World War II, historian Bruce Smith (1990) suggests the inability of Americans to win the war in Vietnam (1965–1973) was part of the public drift from science as the Western world realized the "most powerful and technologically advanced nation on earth was unable to subdue a technologically backward enemy" (76). Commenting in particular about the situation in the United States, Smith observes that the sixties and seventies

> were a time of conflict, divisions, shifting attitudes and loyalties, and wrenching social change. The policy conflicts and underlying differences in values shook all institutions and all settled habits of thought. Society's support for science had been placed on the assumption that progress in the various scientific disciplines would ultimately lay the foundation for a better life for all Americans. Social improvements of all kinds would follow when the nation's collective intelligence was brought to bear on the most pressing problems. But as Americans lost confidence in this premise, as their optimism about the future became tinged with pessimism, the foundations of society's support for science—and scientists themselves—eroded. (77)

Problems world-wide with poverty, racism, civil unrest and the widespread abuse of drugs during the sixties did not diminish as the Western democracies entered the seventies; the hope of *Apollo* was followed by growth in public sullenness and rising anti-science sentiment.[25] In a 1971 address to the International Conference on Education in Chemistry Yale Professor of Chemistry Richard L. Wolfgang observed a change in public attitudes towards science:

> Science has never been fully accepted by humanity. It has been tolerated because of the material benefits it can provide. But now it is being increasingly questioned whether these practical benefits of science are indeed benefits. (Wolfgang, quoted in Layton 1973, 1)

This erosion of faith in science and technology to human progress within Western democracies is partially due to the very public displays of scientific activity in the latter half of the twentieth century. Through the medium of television we have been able to witness the spectacular side of science and technology, such as the landing of men on the moon, and the tragic. On January 28, 1986 I brought a television to my classroom so my sophomore science class could watch the launching of the U.S. space shuttle *Challenger*. Shuttle flights had become so routine by this time that, in the words of one reporter, "we had been encouraged in the belief that boarding a shuttle is like catching a bus" (Webster 1986, A6). This particular shuttle was unique, however, in that for the first time a civilian passenger, a school teacher, would be riding along. This teacher was to relay science lessons about space from the orbiting shuttle to an estimated 2.5 million children as part of a NASA education initiative called *Project Classroom Earth*. I had coordinated the start of my science unit on space to coincide with the shuttle launch and the broadcasts by the space-bound science teacher, Christa McAuliffe.

What began as another U.S. space triumph became one of the worst disasters in space exploration as the shuttle exploded in full view of live television coverage seconds after lift off, killing all seven astronauts aboard. The horror and deep sadness felt by my students and I is not easily captured by words. The same *New York Times* columnist who covered the *Apollo* mission summarized the mood of many at that time with the observation that "the almost casual acceptance of technology exploded Tuesday in a fireball" that has shaken us "into an appraisal of the bargain modern society makes in relying too much on advanced technology" (Wilford 1986, A7). The columnist's prediction that "seeing the *Challenger*, with its crew of seven on board, blow up in the sky in the full view of everyone at Cape Canaveral and all the others watching on television will leave an indelible impression in the world's memory" (A7) was correct, at least for me. As I write these words I can still see the white fireball as the shuttle exploded, feel the horror anew, and recall how my faith in technology and science was challenged by the sudden, terrible destruction of a system I thought foolproof.

During my graduate studies the summer following the *Challenger* disaster my belief in the benefits of technological achievements and the enterprise of science was challenged further when a college professor remarked far too casually to me that objectivity is a myth. Completely unnerved by this claim, I countered with my long-held belief that the scientific method is a truly objective, altruistic process. The professor challenged my claim, initiating a discussion on what he termed 'the dark side of science'. My classmates were able to quickly list modern examples of this dark side: scientific experiments in concentration camps by Nazi doctors, the decision to use tactical nuclear weapons on the population of Hiroshima, environmental consequences of DDT use, invention of napalm, the Volta river project in Ghana, the Love Canal disaster at Niagara Falls, birth defects due to the use of thalidomide, and the breakdown of the American nuclear reactor at Three Mile Island were but a few of the examples listed. In his penetrating analysis of our modern situation, sociologist Shiv Visvanathan (1987) reminds us that only in the 'laboratory state of modernity' (37) could these developments take place.

My college studies that summer were difficult. Personal forays into the history and philosophy of science forced me to agree with geneticist and environmentalist David Suzuki (1992) that while some scientists may work in the pursuit of truth and benefit of humankind, most "exhibit the entire range of human foibles from idealism to greed, zeal, and bigotry" (D12). I had always believed in, and taught to my students, the social primacy of the pure, rational scientist's ability to solve world problems. But the foundations of my modernistic world view began to crumble as I began to realize that scientific investigation is not necessarily a pure, objective, straightforward act but often a complex interplay of personal choices dependent on subjective interpretations.[26] Through graduate studies I came to reluctantly agree with science educator and physicist Wytze Brouwer that "in the final decades of the twentieth century we find ourselves nearing the end of a long tradition in which science has been viewed as completely rational, objective, and philosophically neutral quest for knowledge about the natural world" (Brouwer 1985, 13). My studies about the dark side of science and the myth of objectivity in scientific research pushed science to the edge of the pedestal it once occupied in my world view. My growing concern over planetary ecological degradation finished this movement, pushing science off.

The Growing Ecological Crisis

One of my favorite weekend pastimes growing up beside the ocean was building driftwood rafts with my friends. We would pretend to be pirates, floating our galleons into the bay where we would swim and dive for shells. During breaks from classes in my summer graduate program I decided to revisit these same spots, only to find the beaches so polluted that swimming is forbidden by law. The clean sand and driftwood I remember a few decades ago is now accompanied with such filth and debris that walking beside the ocean in certain places is hazardous and disgusting. My testimony is not unique. Suzuki (1989a) reminds us that

> within the lifetime of our elder citizens, the planet has changed almost beyond recognition. Their childhood recollections are not simply the musings of old folks for the good old days, but they constitute a living record of the cataclysmic degradation that has taken place around us in the span of a single human life. (127)

This witness to destruction is part of a dawning public realization that the environment is under siege and our quality of life endangered. "Everyone," suggested one newspaper columnist, "is now more aware of the staggering array of global concerns facing us all. If global warming doesn't get us then the ozone hole will. If we don't poison our environment with toxic wastes then we will suffocate in a rising tide of unmanageable garbage" (Wilson 1991, A16). Reflecting a growing public concern about global ecology, feature issues devoted to ecological concerns seem to dominate the popular press as the eighties came to a close.[27] The Southam Environmental Project (1989) insert found in many newspapers in 1989 summarizes the tone of the popular press in the observation that "the destruction we have wrought since the Industrial Revolution is not so much to the Earth, but to the conditions on Earth that support human life. There is very little time left" (1). In the best selling novel *Jurassic Park* (1990), author Michael Crichton uses the character of Dr. Ian Malcolm to echo this perspective: "Let's be clear. The planet is not in jeopardy. We are in jeopardy. We haven't the power to destroy the planet—or to save it. But we might have the power to save ourselves" (369).

There may be very little time left to act. Suzuki (1989b) reminded readers in a newspaper column a few months after the publication of the Southam Environmental Project Insert that some scientists estimate that we have little more that a decade or two to turn the present eco-crisis around. This gloomy picture was supported in 1990 by the President of the Royal Society of Canada, Digby McLaren. In his preface to the to the Royal Society of Canada's book on global change, *Planet Under Stress* (1990), McLaren declares that

> the human animal that has moved out of ecological balance with its environment. Humankind is a wasteful killer and a despoiler of other life on the planet. This normal and apparently acceptable behavior has been licensed by a belief that our use of the Earth's resources is God-given, and encouraged by an economic system that emphasizes short-term profit as a benefit. We are only slowly learning to put a real cost on the resources we consume, and the wastes we produce. Humankind is now dominant in effecting perhaps irreversible change on the Earth's surface, and I suggest that we do not know enough to decide how to run this planet. (xiv)

Few would argue with the assessment of the United Nations' World Commission on Environment and Development (1987) that "over the course of this century, the relationship between the human world and the planet that sustains it has undergone a profound change" (22). Radical scientist James Lovelock is considerably more blunt. In his controversial proposal the Earth can be viewed as a single organism he calls 'Gaia', Lovelock (1991) presents a chilling metaphor: "As a vast collective, the human species is now so numerous as to constitute a serious planetary malady. Gaia is suffering from *Disseminated Primatemaia*, a plague of people" (155–156).

There is little agreement about what can be done to preserve the conditions needed for the survival of our species on Earth, what Lovelock euphemistically terms 'healing Gaia'. The United Nations promotes through the International Union for Conservation of Nature and Natural Resources and the World Wildlife Fund the concept of "environmentally sound sustainable development" (United Nations Environment Program 1990, 3) or planetary management through science and technology. The belief that economic, social, and ecological problems can be addressed through government use of science and technology is an expression of modernistic faith in a technological salvation to the problems facing our species, what I call 'technoptimism' (Blades 1990). This technoptimism is widespread. Consider, for example, the pamphlet by the Canadian government, *Science and Technology in Canada* (Government of Canada 1988). According to this pamphlet, in order to "provide new jobs....solve environmental health, and safety problems....create new products and educate our children for the future" then Canadians must "be players in the international field of science and technology" since "the quality of our lives in the future *depends on science and technology*" (2, emphasis mine). International business consultant Frank Feather would agree with the tone and encouragement of the Canadian government. In his book *G-Forces* (1989) Feather suggests that "it is time for some straight talk and fresh ideas about the exciting prospects for the future of the world" (ix). In complete contrast to what he calls the doomsday predictions of some scientists, Feather outlines thirty five global forces of change and technological innovation, or 'G-forces,' which he insists offer the opportunity for humankind to achieve its "collective destiny" (1) through a "combination of global, futuristic and opportunistic thinking skills that are *applied* in understanding and reinventing the world" (9, emphasis his). Some might argue the fact that we've been able to clothe, feed, and house the majority of the world's population indicates our resourcefulness, ingenuity and unlimited potential to manage our affairs and, by extension, the entire planet. From this perspective, dire prophesies of looming ecological disaster represent a lack of faith in the abilities of our species to solve monumental problems.

It is precisely this technoptimism that worries American futurist Jeremy Rifkin. In his provocative book, *Algeny* (1983), Rifkin argues that humans have relentlessly fashioned from the crust of the Earth a "new home for themselves" (6). This industry has led, claims Rifkin, to a "shortage of raw energy and resources necessary to maintain that home" (6). The result, claims Rifkin, is that humankind now faces two crises simultaneously: "The earth is running low on its stock of burnable energy and on the stock of living resources at the same time" (6). Rifkin is not encouraged by recent developments in biotechnology, which he argues springs from the same modernistic attitudes that have led to our present environmental situation. To Rifkin, the brave new world promised by the technoptimists is not really new nor is it a world he wants for his children.

The voices of technoptimists contrast with those who sense environmental concerns are inevitable symptoms of modernism. For many, hope lies in finding a new way to live in the world, not in a modernistic faith that some technological solution exists. Instead of working towards the total management of our planet, suggests environmentalist Max Oelschlaeger (1991), we need to reconceive our existence as "interwoven, harmoniously coexisting in mutually supporting system" of the wilderness that is Earth (18). Oelschlaeger's idea of wilderness is close to Lovelock's view of the Earth as a living organism. It is modernistic arrogance, argues Lovelock, to suppose we will ever be capable of managing the vast complexities of our planet. The concept of sustainable development is, according to Lovelock (1991),

> the greatest of errors. Consider how the well intentioned application of the principles of human welfare and freedom that moved us all in the second half of the 20th century has failed our bright expectations. (175)

Our hope for the future lies, claims Lovelock, in "establishing a basis of a new civilization in harmony with Gaia" (180), although he is short on advice on how this new relationship might begin or what shape it may take. Suzuki (1989a) agrees, reminding readers that "the only way to get off our destructive path is to develop a radically different perspective on our place in nature" (183). Suzuki advances the position that hope lies with the education of our children who

> have most at stake since they will inherit the world we leave them; since they have not invested time and effort in the status quo, they are still receptive to

possibilities and options. So we must fight to save as much wilderness as possible while simultaneously working to ensure our children are different from us. (183)

The dilemma, suggests Suzuki, is that while the "most important issues that the next generation will have to contend with will result from science and technology" for many children today "the way science is taught in school turns them off, and too many have stopped taking any science courses midway through high school" (190). As discussed earlier, this crisis in science education is well documented. Public suspicion of the claims and activity of science and technology and questions about which direction to take in dealing with environmental degradation has led voices within the Great Conversation to speak once again of renewal in science education. The impetus for change in science education this time, however, is far more than the threat of the technological superiority of a foreign power. If estimates are correct, our children and perhaps our grandchildren may be the last generations capable of finding a way to live with changes to our planet's systems. The crisis facing humankind is how to find possibilities for global survival in the midst of declining faith in the premises of modernism precisely at a time of exponential growth in the knowledge, complexity, and activity of science and technology. I submit that in this crisis it is not an exaggeration that renewal in science education is essential to the survival of humankind.

Responses to the Second Crisis in Science Education

The standard-bearers of the new reform movement insist this time things will be different.
—Tim Beardsley, Staff Writer for *Scientific American* on the 'second wave' of science education curriculum reforms (1992, 100).

The Challenge of Renewal in Science Education

In a speech to the first International Cell Biology Congress (1979) U.S. Senator Edward Kennedy suggested that from precedents in scientific achievements:

> One lesson is clear. The public must participate in the resolution of issues in which science impacts on society. They must be in on the takeoff as well as the landing. They must help formulate the key public policy questions which must be answered, and they must participate in the commissions and other groups convened to resolve these issues. (Kennedy 1979, 17)

Growing concerns over ecological degradation and rapid increases in science and technology has made Kennedy's case for public involvement in science more compelling than ever. The Committee on High-School Biology Education (1990) of the U.S. National Research Council reminds us that

> population growth has placed new strains on the environment—massive pollution of air and water, deforestation and extinction of species, global warming and shifts in climate, and alternations in the ozone shield. We are engaging in the greatest uncontrolled experiment in human history, and the outcome if far from clear....What is certain, however, is that these issues are here to stay; and a necessary step to their resolution in a democratic society will be increasing the scientific sophistication of elected officials and the public. (5)

The ability of citizens in a democracy to form decisions about science based on an understanding of the characteristics and limitations of science and the relationship of science to society is described as 'scientific literacy' by science educators world-wide.[28] By the mid-seventies assessments of science education in the U.S. and Canada revealed that post-*Sputnik* science education reforms had not encouraged the scientific literacy of students; indeed, quite the opposite. The U.S. National Commission on Excellence in Education publication, *A Nation At Risk* (1983) and the U.S. National Survey of Science and Mathematics Education (1985–86) results "implicate America's education system for contributing to the public's science illiteracy" (Goodwin 1988, 52). In fact, some educators estimate that only seven percent of the American public "can be considered scientifically literate" (O'Neil 1992, 2). This picture is not improved in other countries. International assessments of school science achievements during the years 1970–71 and 1983–84 reveal a need to "raise the general level of science literacy" world-wide (Keeves 1992, 20). The deplorable lack of science literacy among the general citizenry and the inability of existing science education curricula to make a significant impact on this literacy, combined with the almost overwhelming problems the next generation of adults must face, has led to the declaration of a crisis in science education among Western nations for the second time since World War II.[29]

What is not clear at present is what direction reform in science education might take. Educators could hardly be blamed for feeling nostalgic about the single, driving purpose of the post-*Sputnik* reforms and the vast amounts of financial support available. Those days are clearly over: grim economic realities world-wide and current issues in science education reform have made changing science education a more complex and difficult task than in the late fifties and sixties. Consider *only a few* of the questions raised by educators about the direction of reform in school science education:[30]

How might a renewed science education increase students' attitudes towards science and scientific literacy?

Should science continue to exist as a separate school subject, or should integration with other school subjects become a focus of renewal?

How can young women be encouraged to consider careers in science related fields?

Should science education continue to focus on career training?

What is the role of the scientific community in determining the direction of science education reform?

Should environmental education be emphasized in school science or become a new course of study?

Is the history and philosophy of science an appropriate foundation for a renewed school science education?

The Rise of STS Science Education

In the midst of uncertainty and increasing voices in discussions about the direction of the second major science education reform since World War II, a theme has emerged. At the 1975 annual meeting of the NSTA Stanford Professor of Education Paul Hurd announced in his keynote address that the science curriculum projects of the sixties have proved to be "too restricted, fragmented, and hierarchical to focus on the science-based social problems with which students must deal as citizens" (Hurd 1975, 30). Hurd then proposed a major shift in the focus of science education towards interdisciplinary studies based on understanding the relationships between science, technology and society, a view of science education that came to be known as STS science education.

The purpose and focus of this STS approach is to "reach the larger audience of students with non-science careers and goals" by adopting a flexible pedagogy which considers the "humanistic and societal issues of science along with the facts of science" (Duschl 1988, 51). The consideration of these issues, many directly created by technological advances, allows students in STS science education the chance to debate and consider the role of science and technology in the society they will form and presently influence. With an emphasis on science for all students and not just the elite few headed for science careers, STS science education represents a radical break from the approach of post-*Sputnik* science education curricula. Instead of a focus on the structure of a particular science discipline, STS science education exposes students to science through familiarity with its social applications by organizing science courses around contemporary social issues instead of the concepts of science themselves (DeBoer 1991). What should result from this radical STS approach to science education are programs of study that are more relevant to students since their studies of science address the issues they face now and must deal with in the future as members of a democratic society. Many science educators agree that such integrated, relevant studies of the relationships between science, technology and society is essential to helping the present generation of children develop the skills, attitudes, and thinking abilities needed to deal with the crises facing our species as we enter the twenty-first century.[31]

By the mid-seventies and early eighties elective science courses that adopted a partial or total STS perspective appeared world-wide. The Netherlands was one of the first countries in the world to produce an STS science course through the Physics Curriculum Development Project (PLON), which produced a STS physics course that existed in the Netherlands from 1972–1986. *ALCHEM*, a locally developed secondary school curriculum in chemistry developed from an STS perspective was available in the Canadian province of Alberta from 1972–1977. In 1983 two STS projects, *Science in Society* and *Science in a Social Context* were introduced in Britain by science education associations. The Association for Science Education (ASE), the main professional science teacher association in the United Kingdom, set up a Science and Technology in Society (SATIS) project in 1984. This program was destined to become very widely distributed, partially due to the introduction of the British national curriculum in 1987. A key resolution of this national curriculum was the requirement that all children in Britain "take science and technology up to the age of 16" (Central Office of Information 1988, 3). As early as 1977, students in the Australian state of Victoria could elect to enroll in the STS science course, *Physical Science, Society and Technology*. An architect of this STS science course, science educator Peter Fensham (1993) reports this course was a response to the 'Science for All' movement in the state of Victoria, which led to an effort in 1988 to reform all secondary school science courses in Victoria towards an STS approach. The U.S. has lagged somewhat behind other countries in developing STS courses, but American agencies such as the National Science Foundation (NSF), the American Association for the Advancement of Science (AAAS) and the National Science Teacher Association (NSTA) support or currently sponsor curriculum reform projects that develop an STS perspective in science education.[32]

An STS approach to science education seems to have wide support internationally. Already by the late seventies, reports Canadian science educator Jim Gaskell (1980), "scientific and technological literacy and science and society are 'in' concepts in science education communities around the world" (26). Two thirds of the delegates at 1985 conference of the International Organization for Science and Technology Education (IOSTE) reported on movements to reform science education in their countries towards an STS perspective, some twenty-two countries in all (Fensham 1988b). American science educator Robert Yager (1992) observes that currently the reform of science education towards an STS perspective "is a focus in nations on every continent" (iii). Articles appearing in the International Council of Associations for Science Education 1992 Yearbook reports on struggles to reform science education towards an STS perspective in countries such as Korea, Israel, Australia, the United Kingdom, the Netherlands, the United States, and among countries of the continent of Africa. There seems to be enough interest world-wide in an STS approach to science education that some educators suggest STS represents an emerging new paradigm in science education (McFadden 1990; Pedersen 1992), although Fensham (1988b) tempers such optimistic assessments with the reminder that "the main stream of high-status science education in most countries is, however, still only marginally touched by the STS movement" (376).

Not so in Canada. Some secondary school science courses oriented towards an STS approach already appeared in Canadian provinces as early as the seventies. By the close of the following decade most provinces were at various stages of initiating science education reform towards an STS approach. These reforms were stimulated by the Science Council of Canada's scathing assessment of science education and the background discussion papers generated by the Council study, especially Canadian science educator Glen Aikenhead's monograph, *Science in Social Issues: Implications for Teaching* (1980).

One of the major recommendations of the Science Council study was a reorientation of science education towards "an emphasis and focus on the relationships of science, technology and society in order to increase the science literacy of all citizens" (Science Council of Canada 1984a, 7). The Canadian province of Alberta became the first region internationally to adopt an STS approach to *all* secondary school science courses in that province, non-academic and academic. As we shall see, this initiative, which also included the development of an entirely new set of general, integrated STS science courses called Science 10, 20, and 30, began during the early eighties and was given a legal mandate by the Government of the Province of Alberta in 1985. What happened to these new courses is one of the narratives presented in the next chapter. Other provinces were soon to follow in the footsteps of Alberta, keeping Canada in step with other Western countries until practically every province was considering adopting an STS approach to science education by the end of the eighties, many waiting to see how the curriculum reforms fared in Alberta.

It was during these attempts at major curriculum reform in science education—for the second time since World War II—that I completed my graduate studies in 1986. My new understanding of science as a human activity and interest in possibilities in curriculum change in science led me to revive considerably my approach to teaching high school science! My students were challenged to ask deep questions about the activity of science, the role of scientists in society, and the relationships between science, technology, and society. I became more of a mentor to these children, guiding their discovery of science. Lectures gave way to a more activity-based approach and topics began with an exploration of Albert's question, still reverberating in my life: Why are we learning this? I began to wonder, though, about the possibilities of curriculum change in science education. I felt the changes I had experienced in my own classroom were significant indicators of the possibility of change in science education. After a long and difficult struggle, I felt it was time for me to leave my career as a high school teacher for further studies in education. In the summer of 1988 my family and I moved to Edmonton, the capital city of the Canadian province of Alberta, so that I could begin further studies at the University of Alberta. As I drove the moving truck that held all of our material possessions towards Alberta I had no way of knowing that during my time at the University of Alberta I would also become directly involved in changes to high school science in that province.

While other provinces in Canada and countries world-wide were still considering an STS approach to school science education in the early and mid eighties, extensive planning on the organization and content of STS science courses by science educators and government officials in Alberta was in progress by the time I moved there. The reformation of science education in Alberta is significant because to date this region has made one of the first and longest efforts internationally in attempting to effect change in secondary school science education towards an STS perspective.

Given the demonstrated difficulty in changing science education since World War II, a cynic might ask why we might be hopeful during this latest round of reform towards an STS approach. After four decades of involvement in attempts at change in science education, Paul Hurd (1991b) sadly notes that attempts at change "have done more to stabilize an obsolete curriculum than to provide insight and guidance for realizing a new vision of science teaching" (35). In a latter essay he argues that "clearly, attempts to revise, reorder, restructure, reshape, and other forms of tinkering with curriculums now in place in schools will not prepare young people for adapting to the sweeping changes now taking place in our contemporary society" (1994, 103). Hurd's sobering assessments presents a disturbing and difficult question: *Is change possible in science education?* Given the current crisis in science education, faltering conversation of modernity, and the scarcity of time left for humankind to deal with environmental issues, this question on the possibility of change is critically important. Through the chapters that follow I intend to address this question directly through an examination of the significance of the recent attempts to change high school science education in Alberta. Our conversation on the topic of curriculum change in science education continues in Chapter 2 with the genesis and evolution of Science 10, 20, and 30.

Chapter 2

The Genesis and Evolution of
Science 10, 20, and 30

Introduction: Science Education as Curriculum-Discourse

The word 'discourse' can be defined as a collection of what is said, written, or thought, usually presented through words or symbols for purposes of communication. A discourse is not a random collection of words and symbols; each discourse "order and combine words in particular ways and excludes or displaces other combinations" (Ball 1990, 2). Rules define this formation and the presentation of a discourse. For example, rules guide how to ask a question, make a pun in English, or how a government agency prepares a science education document. Of course, rules vary with the discourse. I am restricted through tradition, grammatical rules and the like on how to present the text before you. A different set of rules might govern our discourse if you and I were to visit at a local tavern! Most of the rules that determine discursive practice are anonymous, an inheritance determined in time and space through historical formations and a myriad of influences such as social, economic, and geographical factors (Foucault 1972).

The previous chapter reported the support at Wood's Hole for basing the reform of high school science curriculum on the structure of science disciplines. In a paper with science educator Heidi Kass I argue that

> in such a context, questions involving the form and nature of curricular knowledge were rarely regarded as matters for debate. Relationships between school curricula and various science disciplines tended to be viewed as straightforward and largely self-evident by both teachers and the public. (Kass and Blades 1992, 3)

The assumption science education should reflect science disciplines effectively defined "who may speak and what can be said and asked"

(3) in science education reform during the fifties and sixties. This framework for discursive practice set the boundaries for the planning of events designed to have educational consequences for science students; that is, the *curriculum* of science education. This 'curriculum-discourse' is reflected in texts produced during the post-*Sputnik* reforms, such as school textbooks, films, studies of school settings, and teacher workshop packages. Texts also arise from more recent attempts at curriculum change in science education. In this chapter recent texts provide the basis for an exploration of the events and implications of the genesis and evolution of the high school science programs Science 10, 20, and 30 in the Canadian province of Alberta.

Attempts to portray developments in this science education curriculum-discourse face dilemmas of exclusion and inclusion: Which texts are important to the genesis and evolution of a discourse? Which are marginal? From which points in space and time should texts be chosen? The act of choosing makes an objective position impossible; any view of the science education curriculum-discourse in Alberta is necessarily a personal interpretation. A further complication in portraying a curriculum-discourse needs to be confessed. Any presentation of a curriculum-discourse itself forms a text that must also be part of that discourse. In our case, Chapter 2 contributes yet another text to the very curriculum-discourse it tries to portray. Since speaking adds to a curriculum-discourse, the possibilities for re-presenting a discourse are infinite. Now, with infinite possibilities for speaking about the genesis and evolution of Science 10, 20, and 30 in Alberta, Chapter 2 could become very large! For the sake of our conversation and your patience, I have chosen what I believe are key texts to prepare a brief summary of the events in Alberta.

Of course, this presentation must be personal and limited, but it is also accurate and important for two reasons. First, it is important since any discourse on attempts at curriculum reform provides a context for discussions on the possibilities of curriculum change. Given the urgency of curriculum reform in science education and the hope of STS science education, examining how the curriculum reform towards an STS perspective fared in Alberta may well prove instructive. Second, the account I share is accurate because, through a rather odd set of events, I became directly involved in the curriculum change attempt as an author and through the employment with government agency responsible for education in the Canadian province of Alberta, Alberta Education. Through the collection of documents and my contacts with Alberta Education personnel, I was able to develop a narrative of the evolution of Science 10, 20, and 30 that was reviewed and verified by my colleagues at Alberta Education.

In the chapters that follow, I disclose through a continuing narrative how I struggled to make sense of the evolution of the Science 10, 20, and 30 programs of study. Grounded in the particular experience of events in Alberta, the disclosure of this struggle to understand what happened in this particular science education curriculum-discourse leads to critical questions about the possibility of curriculum change in science education from within our modern situation.

Vision and The Genesis of Science 10, 20, and 30 in Alberta

> In Alberta, our science programs are being completely redesigned to meet the expectations of the policy statement on Secondary Education (1985) and the requirements of tomorrow's society.
> —Alberta Education, *Science, Technology, Society and the Curriculum* (1989b, 5).

Responsibility for the education of children is allotted to provincial governments by the Constitution of Canada, not unlike how education is primarily a State responsibility in the U.S. or in Australia. Secondary school education in the Canadian province of Alberta is divided into two equal halves: Junior High School, from the seventh grade to the ninth grade and Senior High School, which consists of a sophomore, junior and senior year. Successful completion of secondary schooling in Alberta depends on the accumulation of a certain number of credits earned with each passing grade in a high school course. Courses with a value of 5 credits usually have 100 hours of instructional time, those with 3 credits 70 hours of instructional time. Courses offered in secondary school are called 'Programs of Study' by the government agency responsible for education in the province, Alberta Education.

During my first semester of studies at University I had the opportunity to attend a guest lecture by an official from Alberta Education. This official began with a review of the Science Council of

Canada study and the need for renewal in secondary school science education. His points were familiar to me and I remember being distracted until he began outlining how Alberta Education was in the midst of a complete re-working of the topics, organization and focus of high school science programs towards an STS emphasis. After the presentation I met the official and decided out of general interest to pick up a copy of the Interim Draft by Alberta Education (1988a) of the structure and content of a set of new science courses to be introduced in Alberta high schools, Science 10, 20, and 30.

At first glance, the proposed changes to high school science education seemed merely organizational. Previous academic high school science programs in Alberta adopted the traditional pattern and content of science education that arose from the American secondary school science programs developed during the fifties and sixties: Beginning in their sophomore year, students in Alberta could choose sequences of courses based on the traditional science disciplines of Biology, Chemistry, or Physics. These courses were similar to their American post-*Sputnik* counterparts in structure, content, and purpose: These programs existed, according to one official at Alberta Education, to help students develop the "conceptual frameworks and skills necessary for more advanced study in the specific fields of biology, chemistry, and physics" (Campbell 1986, 2). Figure 2.1 illustrates the organization of these high school courses in Alberta:

Figure 2.1 High School Science Programs of Study in
Alberta Prior to 1988

Biology 10	⟶ Biology 20	⟶ Biology 30
Chemistry 10	⟶ Chemistry 20	⟶ Chemistry 30
Physics 10	⟶ Physics 20	⟶ Physics 30

Alberta Education proposed to replace these science-discipline specialist courses at the 10 level (sophomore year) with a single, required science course called *Science 10*. This single course substitute was proposed as a way to provide a smooth transition from junior high school to senior high school studies in science that would prevent premature student specialization that invariably selected against physics. From Science 10 students interested in a science-related career could enroll in courses which involved study of the science disciplines at advanced levels (for example, Chemistry 20 and 30), while students not intending to pursue a science career but still needing advanced academic credits in high school science could elect to enroll in the academic general science courses of Science 20 and Science 30. Figure 2.2 illustrates the proposed changes to the senior high school science program:

Figure 2.2 Proposed Changes to the High School
Science Programs of Study in Alberta

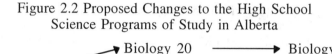
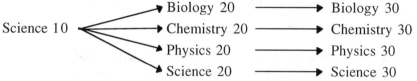

Looking over the Interim Program of Studies for Science 10, 20, and 30 I realized my initial impression of these changes to high school science education in Alberta was wrong. Rather than attempting to lure students to consider science-related careers or developing courses that emphasized the fundamental structure and content of a particular science discipline, these new courses were to be developed with the goal of providing a "science education for all students, under the umbrella goal of scientific and technological literacy" (Alberta Education 1988a, 1). In response to the second crisis in science education since World War II, Alberta Education was preparing to develop a whole new set of courses (Science 10, 20, and 30) that stress "the relationship between science and technology; an understanding of the relationship between science and its social context; the development of lifelong interests, intellectual curiosity, and the appreciation of science" (Alberta Education 1988a, 2). In addition, all the remaining courses in the science disciplines at the 20 and 30 level (such as Biology 20 or Chemistry 30) were to develop the same STS orientation as Science 10, 20, and 30. Clearly, Alberta Education was planning a massive overhaul of the content and direction of high school science education in Alberta.

The proposed topics of the new Science 10 course demonstrates the extent of the changes being considered. Instead of selecting concepts from the previous Biology 10, Chemistry 10, and Physics 10 courses,[1]

Science 10 was to be an entirely new program of study designed to "broaden the basis of science education by integrating into the science program accurate representations of the nature of science, the nature of technology, and their interactions with each other and with our society" (Alberta Education 1989b, 5). A summary in Table 2.1 of the topics in Science 10 presented in the 1988 *Interim Program of Studies* for Science 10 (Alberta Education 1988a) reveals the integrated, STS nature of this new course.

Table 2.1 Summary of Proposed Topics for Science 10, 1988

Unit	*Topics*
1: Body in Balance	Reciprocal relationship of science and technology in the context of technological applications in medical science for the diagnosis, monitoring, treatment and maintenance of human body systems homeostasis.
2: Formation of Scientific Models	The generation and role of theory in science in the context of understanding major forces in nature; the use of models to support or illustrate theories (e.g. plate tectonics, weather forecasting, etc.); the importance of theory and models in scientific prediction.
3: Importance of Water	Understanding the interrelationships of science, technology and society in the context of the chemical structure of water, water quality studies, and water quality management issues.
4: Personal Energy Systems	Understanding the importance of measurement and quantification in science and society in the context of input, conversion, and output in energy systems; the importance of energy efficiency, personal energy consumption, and energy needs in lifestyle choices.
5: Product Evaluation	Examining the nature of science through a scientific investigation of consumer products that includes a study of experiment design, organization, interpretation of data, assessment of research, considerations for further work and communications and conventions in science research.

The initiative from Alberta Education to develop current, relevant, integrated STS science education programs seemed to be a practical response to the crisis in science education. In the fall of 1988 Alberta Education personnel presented an outline of new science programs to high school science teachers at a conference held in the province. Part of my responsibilities at the University included teaching undergraduate education courses with high school science teachers seconded to the University as instructors in the undergraduate teacher education program.[2] These seconded teachers and professors at the University suggested attending the science teacher conference would provide an excellent way to capture an overview of the changes to science education in Alberta. This proved to be good advice. At the conference I attended presentations by Alberta Education personnel on the new science programs. I was struck by the infectious excitement of their presentation. While many Canadian provinces and countries in the world were talking about renewal towards an STS approach in high school science, changes to the entire high school science program seemed to be actually going ahead in Alberta.

Later that evening I had the opportunity to visit with many of the people involved in the Alberta Education presentation. Most of the Alberta Education personnel I met were high school teachers on leaves of absence to work full-time for Alberta Education on the changes to secondary school science programs. It did not take much prodding to have them share what they described as their vision for science renewal. As our evening progressed, I realized that even before the results of the Science Council of Canada (SCC) study had became public (1984) educators in Alberta had anticipated and responded to the emerging crisis in science education curriculum-discourse.

The Genesis of Science 10, 20, and 30

The vision for science education renewal in Alberta was born during the early eighties amidst discussions in Canada and world-wide about the content and organization of an STS approach to science education. Already by the mid-seventies locally developed programs in Canada such as *Science, A Way of Knowing* (Aikenhead and Fleming 1975) and the popular introductory senior chemistry course, *ALCHEM*, (Author Group 1972–1977) offered programs of studies in

science from an STS approach. In his survey of the development of
the STS approach, Australian science educator Peter Fensham (1988b)
notes that the *ALCHEM* course, developed by science teachers in
Alberta, included many of the features that were to be later considered
to be a part of an STS approach; Alberta was thus one of the first sites
in the world where STS science programs were developed. The
discussion papers generated as part of the Science Council of Canada
(SCC) study (1980–1984) stimulated conversation among educators
in Alberta about nature of science, technology, and the societal issues
as they relate to science and technology. In 1983 a Supervisor of
Science Education with one of the large school districts in the
province of Alberta and the Associate Director of Mathematics and
Science at Alberta Education published a widely-distributed paper on
how the nature of scientific inquiry might be emphasized in schools
(Galbraith 1983). This paper led to further calls to revise science
towards an STS approach among various groups interested in science
education in the province. A year later the call for renewal in science
education by the SCC provided impetus for curriculum change in
Alberta. The Alberta government responded to the calls for change
with a discussion paper that further supported the adoption of an STS
approach to science education in Alberta.[3] Two educators at one of
the universities in Alberta took this one step further by proposing that
the best vehicle for STS science education in Alberta would be a
"unified science approach for grades 7 to 10" with "specialization in
the traditional physics, chemistry and biology content areas be
restricted to grades 11 and 12" (Butt and Mokosch 1984, 37). In
their paper the educators recommend Alberta Education develop a
"separate science program route" (37) for the "academically
capable but non-science oriented students" (37).

The opportunity for Alberta Education personnel to develop just
such a program came quickly. In September, 1984 the head of state
for the province, the Premier of Alberta, announced that Alberta
Education would conduct a review of all secondary education in the
province based on widespread public input. The review discovered the
general public also supported renewal in school science education
(Government of Alberta 1985, 8). Alberta Education personnel
assumed the responsibility for making the major decisions about the
content and orientation of a new senior science education programs.
One Career Associate with Alberta Education,[4] recalls that the initial

decision-making process: "What they did is put together a group of people to look at the courses in depth."[5] Composed of mainly school science teachers, this group presented to the Minister of Education in Alberta a position paper on science education renewal arising from their "observations of many classrooms, discussions with teachers and administrators and gleanings from professional literature and reports" (Alberta Science Education Consultants Council 1985, 1). This paper, together with submissions from various interest groups,[6] recommended renewing high school science towards an STS approach and reorganizing the high school science program to include general science courses at the 10, 20, and 30 levels.

In June, 1985 the Alberta government policy statement based on their review of secondary education, *Secondary Education in Alberta*, (Government of Alberta 1985) gave legal impetus for the adoption of the proposed changes to high school science education in Alberta. The plan to develop and then implement Science 10, 20, and 30 into the schools of Alberta was now official government policy.

The Development of Science 10, 20, and 30 as a Technical-Rational Act

> Curriculum development is a practical enterprise—not a theoretical study. It endeavors to design a system to achieve an educational end.
> —Ralph Tyler, *Specific Approaches to Curriculum Development* (1981, 18).

Prior to 1985 renewal in high school science education existed within the Alberta science education curriculum-discourse essentially as a vision for change. This vision added an exciting dynamic to this curriculum-discourse as fundamental questions were discussed: Should all students in high school study science? How can students develop the science literacy through science education to be prepared for the challenges of the next century? What innovative, radical forms might science education become?

With a legal mandate to develop general, yet academic science programs for high school the curriculum-discourse of science education in Alberta became more centered on questions of content and program structure. The vision focused on issues of practical concern: What will the new high school programs look like? How many credits should the new courses have? Alberta Education had a structure in place for dealing with these questions. Through the formation of 'Program Sub-Committees', curriculum change is approached at Alberta Education as a rational, sequential process. This process follows the steps of: needs assessment, initial proposals, course outlines, content standards, piloting of the new program, subsequent revision as needed, implementation in schools and evaluation of program success (Alberta Education 1986a, 3–10; Palmer 1989a, 10). In this pattern the word 'curriculum' is interpreted to mean "an organized pattern of proposed study which identifies what is, and to whom it is, to be taught" (Tri-Partite Committee on Inservice Education 1980, 5); that is, curriculum guides and supportive textual materials that are designed, implemented, and evaluated. You will recall from Chapter 1 (pages 18–20) the definition of curriculum as textual materials was one of the key assumption of the American science education curriculum reforms of the sixties.

This similarity in assumptions is not coincidental; the science education reforms of the sixties and the attempt to renew science education in Alberta closely follow a model of curriculum change that was made popular in 1949 by University of Chicago educational theorist, Ralph Tyler. According to Tyler's *Basic Principles of Curriculum and Instruction* (1949), curriculum change can be thought of as essentially a scientific problem involving the identification of learning objectives, selection and creation of appropriate learning experiences, organization of learning experiences to achieve maximum effect, and evaluation of the curriculum on a continuing basis to ensure necessary revisions and improvements. Fractionating the process of curriculum change into manageable steps, suggests Tyler (1981), allows the change to be carefully monitored and controlled, ensuring success.

Foundational to Tyler's model is the conviction that a theory of curriculum change determines curriculum practice. From this position, discourse on curriculum change is occupied with matters of technique and management, concerned with questions about the correct instruments and organizational strategies required to ensure successful implementation of the curriculum change. Educator and educational philosopher Ted Aoki (1988) argues this approach to curriculum change originates from human interest in "intellectual and technical control of the world" (409). As we have seen in the previous chapter, belief in the possibility of this control through a rational, systematic, scientific approach is part of Great Conversation of modernity.

Published just before the start of the massive attempts at curriculum reform in science education, Tyler's technical-rational approach[7] to curriculum change proved to be a timely, practical, and natural expression of the expectations of modernity in curriculum-discourses. During the decades that followed, Tyler's technical-rational model of curriculum change came to dominate curriculum-discourse in North America. For example, consider how in 1964 the National Science Teacher Association (NSTA) in the U.S. describes the task of curriculum change in science education as "primarily one of selecting and organizing ideas" (33) exactly along the steps suggested by Tyler. Giroux, Penna, and Pinar (1981) note that Tyler's 1949 book on curriculum change "became widely used in college courses on curriculum and also played an influential role in the theoretical development of the field itself" (4). An entire genre of texts extending and refining technical-rational approaches to curriculum change were spawned from Tyler's little book, although they often extrapolated and added to Tyler's original work far beyond what Tyler intended in his rationale. In her text, *Curriculum Development: Theory and Practice*, educational theorist Hilda Taba (1962) advocates a "systematic approach to initiating curriculum change" that adds the importance of diagnostic psychological testing to Tyler's original model. Elementary educator Bruce Joyce (1969) advocated building "curriculum systems" (176) into a school that involve a set of tasks which essentially are an elaboration of Tyler's model for curriculum change. The influential writings of educational psychologists Robert Gagné and Leslie Briggs (1974) elaborate on some of the psychological considerations involved in the choice and detailed sequencing of learning objectives as suggested by Tyler's model. These and many more examples agree with the opinion of curriculum specialists Daniel Tanner and Laurel Tanner (1980) that Tyler's model of curriculum change was paradigmatic in defining the curriculum-discourses of the fifties, sixties and seventies.

Extensive building and elaboration of Tyler's original work led to the popularization of curriculum change as a technical-rational model that follows the somewhat cyclical process of curriculum design, development, implementation, and evaluation.[8] Based on the premise that theory directs practice, technical-rational approaches to curriculum change support a process where "the output of a 'curriculum-development system' becomes "input into an 'instructional system'" (M. Johnson 1981, 76). This output-input practice of curriculum change invariably seems to lead to the assumption of responsibilities for curriculum development, implementation, and evaluation by a centralized agency, most often government Ministries of Education. A technical-rational approach to curriculum change is clearly reflected in the Alberta Education monograph *Who Decides What Students Should Learn in School... and How?* (Palmer 1989a). This publication suggests curriculum reform should follow a logical progression which begins with a provincial needs assessment and initial centralized development of a program of study by Alberta Education and then progresses through a series of field evaluations which lead inevitably to the authorization, implementation and maintenance of the intended change. Eventually the curriculum must be replaced and so the process begins anew. The very titles of Alberta Education personnel suggest a strongly centralized, technical-rational orientation towards curriculum change in Alberta's provincial government: Program Managers, Program Developers, Implementation Consultants, Implementation Agents, and Subject Coordinators have worked within divisions of Alberta Education labeled 'Curriculum Design' and 'Curriculum Support'.

Given the predominance of technical-rational approaches to curriculum change in education-discourse, it seems perfectly natural that curriculum renewal of science education in Alberta was a technical-rational act. An Action Plan was developed at Alberta Education that predicted "a general science course will be implemented in September 1988. Courses for Grades 11 and 12 will follow" (Alberta Education 1986b, 3). That year Phill Campbell was hired by Alberta Education as Program Manager for Senior High School Sciences. In his paper, *Proposal for Change—Senior High School Science*, Campbell (1986) outlines how high school science education could move toward "a more contemporary and integrative focus" (2) through the introduction of the Science 10, 20, and 30 sequence and a re-working of the content and orientation of the science discipline courses at the 20 and 30 level. To engineer these changes several curriculum design committees were struck, each charged with the task under Campbell's leadership to:

1. Select content statements, curriculum specifications, and criteria for resource selection.
2. Select initial learning resources for field testing.
3. Develop curriculum guides and other related documents. (Alberta Education 1987a, 1)

This was the task facing the Science 10, 20, and 30 Sub-Committee when they first met at Alberta Education offices on February 3–4, 1987. Composed of experienced high school science teachers and Alberta Education personnel, many former high school science teachers themselves, this committee met nearly every month in 1987. By May, 1987 the fundamental ideas and topics that will form the content and credit value of the Science 10, 20, and 30 programs of study were identified (Alberta Education 1987b, 4). Since Science 10 was to replace studies in Biology, Chemistry, and Physics by sophomore students, some committee members felt Science 10 should function to introduce these science disciplines, however Campbell was able to successfully argue for an integrated, STS approach to Science 10, 20, and 30 (Alberta Education 1987c, 3). An STS emphasis in the development of all high school science programs became official policy that year.[9] The structure of changes to high school science, including replacing science discipline courses at the 10 level with Science 10 was further supported by the Alberta government with the June, 1987 publication of the new graduation requirements for senior high school (Alberta Education 1987e). At that time, all high school science courses, including Science 10, 20, and 30, were designated a value of 5 credits; that is, they were all considered full courses in science education that could be used to meet graduation requirements. As we shall see later and in Chapter 4, credit allocations became important in the evolution of the science education discourse in Alberta.

Through the Sub-Committee meetings two problems in the development of the senior science program emerged. First, textbook resources to support the topics and integrated, STS nature of Science 10, 20, and 30 simply did not exist. The Sub-Committee decided to employ the services of a publishing company to produce text materials custom designed for the new Science 10, 20, and 30 programs. Some Sub-Committee members expressed concern about having enough time to produce and disseminate such a text by the pilot of the new programs, now scheduled for the fall of 1989 (Alberta Education 1988b, 3). Campbell (Alberta Education 1988c, 3) suggested at this time that the limited time for producing a custom text should not pose a problem since feedback in the pilot stages of the curriculum implementation would give a publisher nine months to publish the text! On May 13, 1988 the Sub-Committee for Science 10, 20, and 30 chose Gage Publishing (Canada) to custom design textbooks and teachers' guides for the Science programs.

The second problem was a consequence of the Alberta government including a set of new 'Career and Life Management' (CALM) programs into high schools. These courses, mandatory for all high school students, focused on health and career-related issues, decision making and topics related to citizenship. Despite a general agreement such programs were a good addition to high schools, accommodating the new CALM programs required adding credits into a high school schedule already very tight; room simply did not exist for the CALM programs. Representatives of instruction in the fine arts also began to complain at this time that the changes in science education would force students to study more science than ever, resulting in "less time for fine arts options" (Bexon 1989, D6). This 'credit crunch', as it came to be known at Alberta Education, led to the decision by Alberta Education personnel to accommodate secondary school fine arts electives and the new CALM programs by cutting the credit value of the science discipline courses at the 20 level to 3 credits from their original 5. Science 10, 20, and 30 and all science discipline courses at the 30 level were, however, to retain their original 5 credit value.

Meanwhile, the Science 10, 20, and 30 Sub-Committee met through 1987 and 1988 to finalize the Interim Program of Studies for Science 10, 20, and 30 and to complete the specifications for textbook development. To help in the final selection of the content of the new science programs, draft outlines of Science 10, 20, and 30 were sent to high schools throughout the province with questionnaires that solicited feedback on the design and content of the new programs. According to the Alberta Education Career Associate who categorized and summarized feedback returned by teachers, this so-called validation process was used to finalize the Interim Draft of the new science programs.[10]

By the fall of 1989 the organization and content of Science 10, 20 and 30 programs of study was complete. Alberta Education personnel were also pleased to note that the "intent of the program [STS emphasis] was coming through in the resource" (Alberta Education 1988d, 3); that is, sample chapters by authors contributing to the custom-designed textbook for Science 10 (to be followed at a later date by textbooks for Science 20 and 30) were developing well. From 1985 to the fall of 1988 Alberta Education personnel had followed a traditional, technical-rational approach to curriculum change. A committee had formed that met on a regular basis to select the learning objectives and content of a new curriculum. From design came development as curriculum guides and instructions for a custom-designed textbook were written. The new Science 10, 20, and 30 programs, and changes to science specialist courses at the 20 and 30 levels, seemed on the verge of becoming the one of the first system-wide adoption of an STS approach to high school science in North America. At the conference of Alberta science teachers I attended in the fall of 1988 I was struck with admiration over the curriculum development in science education to date and I readily agreed with Alberta Education personnel that the implementation of the new programs would likely proceed as smoothly as the development. Imagine! In one year students in Alberta would begin to pilot the new integrated, STS Science 10 program, realizing a vision for science renewal that began years before! The confidence and excitement these colleagues from Alberta Education displayed that evening in Banff was understandable; but their predictions of an easy implementation of Science 10 was to prove very, very premature.

Controversy and Crisis in the Evolution of Science 10, 20, and 30

La théorie, c'est bon, mais ça n'empêche pas d'exister.[11]
—Advice to Freud by Charot, French psycho-analyst (quoted in Gay 1988, 51).

I found the changes to high school science education in Alberta fascinating, but lost track of the developments in the evolution of the new programs as I began a new semester of studies at the University. With the advice of professors in my department, I began to study the implications of the works of contemporary philosophers, especially

Heidegger, to issues of curriculum change. My office partner and I spent many, many hours discussing an essay by Heidegger, *The Question Concerning Technology* (1977). Our discussions led me to explore the writings of other philosophers until I was thoroughly submerged.

As I dove further and further into depths of philosophy, destiny intervened in the guise of opportunity. A professor of science education and research in our department was working at that time as a special adviser to Gage Publishing, the company responsible for producing the custom textbook for Science 10. I was invited to write my impressions of the Science 10, 20, and 30 initiative, which this professor then sent to the editor with Gage Publishing responsible for the development of textbooks to support the new science programs. The editor liked my ideas and writing style and, in February, 1989, I was offered a contract to write the introductory chapter for *Visions 1*, the new textbook resource designed for the Science 10 program.

I had begun keeping a personal journal of my experiences since coming to the University. In my journal I note that I discussed taking on this contract with a professor in my department. This professor thought the offer was a wonderful professional opportunity that would be a learning experience; a prophesy that proved to be very accurate, indeed! I accepted the contract and, in addition to my studies, I began to address the question: What might the introduction to an integrated, STS, academic science course look like? A journal entry records that by writing the introductory chapter of *Visions 1* "I became immersed in the curriculum change" (Journal entry, March 25, 1986). With this entry I became both participant and observer in the Alberta science education curriculum-discourse.

This involvement was developing into a study of the genesis and evolution of the new programs, although I did not realize this at the time. By becoming a member of the team writing the textbook to support the new Science 10 program, I was *de facto* a participant in the science education curriculum-discourse. Through regular journal entries and subsequent collection of documents about Science 10, 20 and 30 I also became an observer and recorder of the events in the science education curriculum-discourse. At the beginning of this study my journal entries were anecdotal since I had yet to appreciate my location as observer and participant in the curriculum-discourse. As events unfolded in this discourse, however, my research became a more focused project as I endeavored through interviews to understand the perspective of those involved in the curriculum-discourse. The purpose of these interviews, journal records, document collection and the development and goals of this participant-observation research project is explained in Chapter 3. As my study progressed I realized that to increase my understanding of the events in the evolution of Science 10, 20, and 30 I would need to adopt the perspective of those directly involved in the design of these programs of study by becoming part of their day to day experiences. I did not have to wait long for exactly such an opportunity.

Around the same time I was offered a chance to write the opening chapter for *Visions 1*, my office partner showed one of his friends a copy of the essay I had written about the new science programs. This person coordinated at Alberta Education a small group responsible for assessing whether curriculum documents, such as Alberta Education Programs of Study, matched expectations for childhood development. After reading my essay, my office partner's friend advised me of a new opening with Alberta Education in the area of assessing curriculum documents for someone with curriculum experience. The position sounded challenging and flexible enough to allow my continued studies at the University of Alberta; on April 18, 1989 I started working part time for Alberta Education as a Curriculum Validator.

Lunch meetings and coffee breaks at Alberta Education provided excellent opportunity for a novice to gain an appreciation of the inner workings of a government ministry. In this way I was able to move from "the status of stranger to friend" (Lather 1986) in my research act. Through lunch meetings and the myriad of documents that passed my desk at Alberta Education almost daily, such as newspaper clippings, internal memos, copies of Alberta Education news releases, and minutes of meetings, I began to form and re-form views of the organization I worked for. I was most impressed with the dedication of the people I worked with at Alberta Education; everyone I met seemed to genuinely care about the welfare of children in Alberta and expressed in words and deeds strong commitment to make the education system in Alberta the best possible. I began to realize that Alberta Education *per se* does not really exist; for example, a document is not authored by 'Alberta Education' but by people who work within an institution called Alberta Education. We will examine this important distinction in Chapter 3.

A rather dark, somber mood prevailed among my colleagues at Alberta Education who were working on the new science programs. Various documents circulating our Branch revealed the new science programs, and in particular Science 10, were in deep trouble. Since I was a science educator with curriculum experience, members of Alberta Education involved in the development of the new science programs kept me abreast of recent developments. I listened with a sense of dismay to how events had conspired to defeat the optimism they had shared with me only a few months before at a conference. Their clear frustration left me wondering what had gone wrong.

My casual study and general interest in the evolution of Science 10, 20, and 30 became a more serious research project with the recent turn of events against the new programs. I began collecting every document related to Science 10, 20 and 30 I could find through a somewhat archeological process that would have been impossible without the generous assistance of my colleagues at Alberta Education. In no time I amassed a ponderous collection of documents. To make sense of such documents, educational research theorists Matthew Miles and A. Michael Huberman (1984b) suggest that a "simple graphic structure" (24–25) can help "assemble the key events during a particular time" (26). I decided to follow this sage advice and prepared an 'events matrix' from the documents I had gathered. An events matrix is a spreadsheet-like graphic that organizes information into time periods on one side and events along the other side. In a large room, I placed all the documents I collected into categories based on their source, such as reports in the popular press, comments from professional organizations, such as the Alberta Medical Association. A complete list of the categories I used is given in Chapter 3 (see page 105). The documents in each category were then arranged in chronological order in a row and I recorded the main points of each document in the rows. Finally, the rows of documents were matched chronologically into a fairly large events matrix based on time and document category. I used this matrix to prepare a detailed chronology of the events in the science education curriculum-discourse of Alberta. When I shared my account of what happened to the Science 10, 20, 30 program with people closely involved in the evolution of these courses, I found the account I had prepared was reliable. As Miles and Huberman (1984a) had predicted, the preparation of an events matrix produced a "narrative, a story arranged in proper time sequence" (122) that allowed key events, people and issues to appear. These events, people, and issues become the subject of our discourse on curriculum change as we continue our story of the evolution of Science 10, 20, and 30.

Controversy in the Science Education Curriculum-Discourse

The first public murmurs of discontent about changes to the high school science program in Alberta after the Banff conference came from high school science teachers. In an article in the *Alberta Science Teacher* Ian Wereley (1989), a high school physics teacher and co-founder of the Alberta Association of Physics Teachers, argues the reduction of Physics 20 to 3 credits from 5 is a "serious threat to physics teaching in Alberta" (16).[12] Concerned that high school physics "will not be afforded any coherent treatment in this Science 10 program" (17), Wereley suggests the decrease of instructional time for Physics 20 does not allow enough time for students to develop the knowledge and skills needed to continue their studies in the successive course of study, Physics 30. Wereley calls on physics teachers throughout the province to send a "clear, unequivocal message to those who dictate curriculum content and emphases" (18) that the changes proposed by Alberta Education are unacceptable in their present form. This call was answered: scores of letters were written to Alberta Education by high school teachers expressing concern over the proposed changes to the senior high school science program (Alberta Education, 1989a).

As a new year began, secondary school teachers began to organize their protest against the proposed changes to the high school science program. In Edmonton, the capital city of Alberta and one of the two large cities in the province, Members of the Edmonton Regional Chemistry Council declared their concern over the reduction in credits for the 20-level discipline science courses at a January 12, 1989 meeting. At this meeting the suggestion was made that all high school science teachers in the Edmonton area should meet to discuss the proposed changes. Two weeks later over 75 science educators, along with representatives from Alberta Education and post-secondary institutions, attended a meeting on January 26, 1989. The President of the Edmonton Regional Chemistry Council reports that expressions of concern at that meeting and subsequent feedback through questionnaires indicates the majority of science teachers in the province "are opposed to a compulsory general science course and to a decrease in credits from 11 to 8 in the discipline streams."[13]

Soon other voices were to join the science education curriculum-discourse. Olive Elliott, the education columnist for Edmonton's major daily newspaper, *The Edmonton Journal*, reported the objections of the Edmonton Public School system to the mandatory nature of Science 10. In her column Elliott also made public the results of the questionnaire distributed at the January 26 meeting of Edmonton science educators, observing that "teachers are primarily concerned with the reduced emphasis on the specialized sciences" (Elliott 1989, C2). Even before the Alberta science teacher conference in the fall of 1988, the Dean and Associate Dean of the Faculty of Science at the University of Alberta in Edmonton felt concerns over the proposal to cut the credit value of Biology 20, Chemistry 20, and Physics 20. The Faculty of Science had formed in 1988 an ad hoc Committee to study and keep abreast of changes to the high school science programs. The Associate Dean of the Faculty of Science of the University of Alberta reports that members of this committee initially supported the idea of a general Science course at the 10 level, since this put "more physical science in the high school program"[14] but when the Interim drafts of the new program began circulating among the Faculty in the fall of 1988, some members of the committee "were very concerned" with the proposed Science 10, 20, and 30 programs.[15] In an interview I record that, when asked about the nature of these concerns, the Associate Dean replied,

Well, it [proposed Science 10, 20, and 30 program] had very little science, it was a kind of pop science, program emphasis on technology-social science approach, but not much in the way of integrated science. Our understanding initially was Science 10, 20, 30 would be an integrated science of biology, chemistry and physics so students would get more of the physical sciences because of what was happening in the high school system; to meet the minimum 11 credits they were taking either Biology or Chemistry or likely just Biology to get the minimum credits [to graduate] and never physics. (quoted in Blades 1994, 63)

The Interim Draft of Science 10, 20, and 30 clearly demonstrates different programs of study than the Dean, Associate Dean and other members of the Faculty of Science at the University of Alberta expected. In February, 1989 the Faculty of Science at the University of Alberta declared Science 30 *unacceptable* for admission to science courses in their faculty, destroying the academic acceptability of Science 30 at the University of Alberta. The professional newspaper for teachers in Alberta, the *ATA News*, reports the other major universities in Alberta responded in their own unique way. The University of Calgary in Alberta's other major city of Calgary *accepted* Science 30 for entrance requirements, except for admission to the Faculty of Engineering. The third university in Alberta, the University of Lethbridge, was recorded as 'undecided', although the Vice-president of the University of Lethbridge was reportedly unhappy with both the interim drafts of Science 10, 20, and 30 and the "lack of meaningful input [into the program] from the science people in universities" (Newbold, quoted in DeLuna 1989a, 6). Responding to a request from Alberta Education to review the drafts of Science 10, 20, and 30 the University of Alberta Faculty of Science ad hoc Committee on the Proposed Revision to the High School Program (1989) presented a scathing condemnation:

> The proposed Science 10-20-30 is not a good general science curriculum. It is a sequence of relatively isolated topics devoted to a selective technological application of science and the current social issues of this technology. The result is social science masquerading as science...Social science must not unduly dilute the science in these courses...we are concerned with the "watering down" of science in the school system. This dilution will result in a generation of individuals who will be deficient in basic knowledge skills at a time when the impact of science on everyday life is increasing greatly in both positive and negative ways. We believe it to be the very antithesis of the goals of secondary education. (2–4)

In the midst of this growing discontent, Alberta Education personnel were still predicting Science 10 would be implemented September, 1990, with the cautious addition that "controversy may delay the program of study" (Alberta Education 1989c, 3).

This prophesy was well founded. By March, 1989 the President of the Alberta Teachers' Association Science Council publicly complained in the *ATA News* that the new science courses disadvantage Alberta students intending post-secondary study in science (DeLuna 1989b, 6). That same month high school science teacher Frank McGeachy (1989) published a stinging editorial in the official publication of the Alberta Science Teachers' Association, *Alberta Science Teacher*. Describing the Science 10, 20, and 30 programs as a "Reader's Digest" science curriculum (2), McGeachy claims the implementation of these programs will lead to no less than the "death of science in Alberta" (2). In the same issue of the *Alberta Science Teacher*, science educator George Armstrong (1989) argues the removal of Physics at the 10 level and the drop of science discipline courses at the 20 level to 3 credits is the deliberate sabotage of the high school science program by Alberta Education! Armstrong chides that "perhaps the greatest single triumph that can be credited to the planners of the new curriculum is that the present program, with all its admitted weaknesses, has never looked so good" (11). To the rhetorical question, 'Who wants the new program?', Armstrong concludes that "the only group supporting this new science program are civil servants in the Department of Education" (11).

It certainly seemed that way by March, 1989. Over six hundred solicited and unsolicited submissions to Alberta Education indicated the proposed changes did not have the support of many high school science teachers; most called for reconsideration of the proposed changes. Without the support of the Faculty of Science at the University of Alberta and high school teachers in Alberta, the proposed changes seemed doomed.

Matters were exacerbated by the failure of some authors working on the *Visions 1* textbook for Science 10 to capture in their writing the STS intent of the new programs. I was relieved my introductory chapter was well received, in fact the reviews of this chapter from Alberta Education were positively glowing: "Excellent effort! Author has clear idea of the science, technology, society perspectives and develops them well" (Alberta Education 1989e).

On April 3, 1989 the Government of Alberta Minister of Education, Jim Dinning, informed school boards throughout Alberta of the decision to delay the implementation of the new Science 10 program of study and changes to the other science courses. In an article appearing in the *ATA News*, DeLuna (1989c) reports Dinning felt the delay was needed to provide more opportunity for university personnel to react to draft programs, expand service offerings to help

. prepare teachers for the new courses, and give more time for the development of the *Visions 1* resource, although editors with the publishing company had not requested the extra time. Considering the political pressure on the Minister at that time, the delay seemed a wise way to stem growing controversy over the proposed changes.

But even with the announcement of the delay the tide of controversy continued to rise almost exponentially as the science education curriculum-discourse in Alberta became increasingly public. Through interviews I discovered that early in 1989 a high school science teacher and a member of the Faculty of Science at the University of Alberta separately chose to contact Ted Byfield, editor and publisher of the privately-owned news magazine, *Alberta Report*, about the lack of support for the new high school science programs (Blades 1994). The June 13, 1989 issue of the *Alberta Report* carried an article on the "Death of Science" in Alberta (23–24) that claimed university professors and science teachers in Alberta were allied in a "full-scale rebellion against Alberta Education's latest curriculum proposal" (MacDonald and Byfield 1989a, 23). Publishing selections from the Faculty of Science ad hoc Committee report, the vitriolic articles by McGeachy and Armstrong appearing in the *Alberta Science Teacher*, and quoting a University of Alberta physics professor, the *Alberta Report* article paints a strong indictment against the changes proposed by the "educrats" (23) working at Alberta Education. In an editorial appearing in the same issue, Ted Byfield (1989a) claims the controversy should be enough to motivate the Minister of Education to "block what his bureaucrats are trying to do" (44). Since the Minister is on record as being "committed to the new science curriculum" (Dinning, quoted in T. Byfield, 1989a), Byfield calls for the Government of Alberta to fire the present Minister in favor of someone willing to "consult others outside the department, not in it, to find out what kind of schools will enable Alberta to meet the competitive challenges of the 21st century" (44).

Attacks in the *Alberta Report* became even more virulent in the next issue. The cover features a full page photograph of a sullen Jim Dinning framed with the title, "Dumbing Down—That's What Experts Say Jim Dinning is doing to Alberta's High Schools" (June 19, 1989). The feature article, "'Dumbing Down' high schools," (28–34) reports on the "growing army of critics" to the proposed new science programs, even citing a rumor that the "ultimate departmental aim is to entirely eliminate physics, chemistry and biology in the secondary school in favor of a 'broader approach' through general science courses mandatory for all students" (MacDonald and Byfield 1989b, 28). The controversy surrounding the proposed changes is identified in this issue as the "universalist approach" by Alberta Education on one side, which they interpret to mean the intention that "all students are to be taught the same courses and enabled, one way or the other, to pass them" (28) and the "realistic" approach of university professors and teachers who "favor less demanding [courses] for general diploma students, but not at the expense of rigorous courses in physics, chemistry and biology for advanced diploma students, some of whom will go on to scientific careers" (28). The assertions in the *Alberta Report* articles were a frequent topic of conversation among my colleagues at Alberta Education. I remember joining my colleagues for lunch when they were in the middle of discussing Ted Byfield's blistering attack of Alberta Education that appeared in the city of Calgary's daily newspaper the *Calgary Sun* (May 28, 1989); Byfield exclaimed about "the wild stuff [that] has been going on in high school science programs" (T. Byfield 1989b, 12), advancing his recommendation the public of Alberta "cage those education monkeys!" (12).

Program managers and Program Developers at Alberta Education tried to meet media criticisms and letters critical of the proposed changes to the science programs by appeasement. Gradually the original September, 1988 Interim Draft of Science 10 became modified to include more of the traditional topics from the original Biology 10, Chemistry 10, and Physics 10 programs. For example, by May, 1989 Unit 3 (The Importance of Water) of Science 10 began to include a greater emphasis on the chemistry of water and the inclusion of topics from the previous Chemistry 10 program of study, such as atomic theory. Unit 5 of Science 10 (Scientific Evaluation of Consumer Products) was completely redesigned to focus on topics related to Newtonian physics that appeared in the previous Physics 10 program of study, such as momentum and acceleration, through examinations of how products such as motorcycle helmets meet safety standards (Alberta Education, 1989d).

These changes did little to stay the momentum of controversy over the new science programs. In the Legislative Assembly of the Government of Alberta the Minister of Education was called to answer concerns that "the Minister of Education is somehow diluting the quality of science education such that we will be graduating students who will be functionally illiterate in the sciences" (Hansard Education News 1989).[16] The exchange in the Assembly was reported in the June 26, 1989 issue of the *Alberta Report*, along with new public criticism of the changes to high school science programs by the Director of the Alberta Chamber of Resources. In this article V. Byfield (1989a) reports on the Director's concern that the changes in high school science will lead to a "severe shortage of competent engineers, geologists and scientists within 10 years, due to the "watering down" of high school courses and diversion of best students into other lines" (30). While the logic of this claim escaped me and my colleagues at Alberta Education, a similar hypothesis was made public by the Alberta Medical Association (AMA). In their *News Release* of June 27, 1989 the AMA publicly called for the Alberta Government Minister of Education to delay the implementation of Science 10 and to enhance, rather than eliminate, the previous Biology 10, Chemistry 10 and Physics 10 programs of study. The *News Release* notes that in a letter to Mr. Dinning the president of the AMA predicted that changes to the high school science curriculum will "threaten the long-term future of Medicare and the care that will be available to our patients" (Alberta Medical Association 1989, 1). This terrifying prospect would come about because, as the President explains, "without a high quality science program, Alberta students won't be qualified to train for the allied health occupations at NAIT,[17] SAIT, and the community colleges or to pursue medicine, nursing, and other professions at our universities" (1). This sensational prediction was reported in newspapers across the province and, of course, the *Alberta Report*. In early July the other major daily newspaper in Calgary, the *Calgary Herald*, reported on a letter written by the Association of Petroleum Engineers, Geologists, and Geophysicists of Alberta (APEGGA) to Alberta Education that strongly opposed the "watering down" of the high school science program (M. Byfield, 1989). In the fall of 1989, APEGGA went public with their criticism, arguing the new science programs could "damage Alberta's ability to train technical professionals" (Langford 1989, 1). At a special meeting in Calgary, members of APEGGA went on record as officially "opposing the proposed policy of the department of education to reduce the amount of time allotted to the teaching of biology, chemistry, and physics in provincial high schools" (Hellfritz 1990).

These announcements by the AMA and APEGGA touched a nerve in Alberta; many letters, editorials and articles condemning the changes began appearing in major Alberta newspapers.[18] Often these letters complain new programs 'water down' or somehow dilute science education; some letters were quite unflattering to personnel at Alberta Education:

> I feel strongly that our so called "professional" education administrators do not deserve that designation; being, that they made themselves the least-qualified, the most unenlightened and the most dangerous bunch of amateurs to be entrusted with the real improvement of educational standards. (Thomas 1989, A6)

Fuel was added to the fire of complaints with essays, speaking engagements, and interviews by Joe Freedman, a physician outspoken in his concerns about the new science programs. In his widely distributed essay intended for parents, *The Science 10 Controversy Explained*, Freedman (1989a) describes the Science 10, 20, and 30 programs as a "lower level alternative to the specialized 'academic' 10, 20, and 30 courses in Biology, Chemistry, and Physics" (2). In an interview appearing in the *Alberta Report*, Freedman admits he first alerted the AMA to the changes in science education, leading to the AMA News Release (MacDonald and Byfield 1989c, 28). In a later letter to Alberta Education, Freedman also acknowledges he pressed the AMA to ask representatives from APEGGA to denounce publicly the proposed changes (Freedman, Letter to Alberta Education, September 8, 1989).

The resistance to the proposed changes was so strong that by July the Minister of Education reached the conclusion that "the only way to move ahead was to stop and assemble a credible group" to review the high school science program.[19] On July 25, 1989 the Minister of Education announced the formation of a Minister's Advisory Committee to review the proposed changes to the science program. The purpose of this Advisory Committee, composed of representatives from Universities, Technical Colleges, professional organizations (such as APEGGA), Alberta Teachers' Association, and school districts was to provide advice of "policy and issues that affect science programs for Grades 7–12" (Ross 1989d, B3), although the actual focus of Committee meetings was the new science programs for high school.

Even as the Committee met over the late summer and early fall of 1989, controversy over the new programs only increased. During this time my colleagues at Alberta Education continued to defend the new program with enthusiasm arising from their conviction that renewal towards an STS emphasis and program structural changes were crucial to developing the scientific literacy and citizenship of students. The August 12, 1989 edition of the major daily newspaper in the Alberta city of Red Deer, the *Red Deer Advocate*, carried a full debate on the new programs, with Joe Freedman arguing the new science courses "are pulp" that contain content he describes as "pathetic" (Freedman 1989b, 5A) while the science education program manager of Alberta Education, Raja Panwar countering on the same page that the courses "are not watered-down science" but programs designed to help students "understand how the scientific principles and laws affect our lives and community every day" (Panwar 1989, 5A). This debate sparked another flood of letters to the editor of newspapers and weekly magazines complaining about the proposed changes to high school science education in Alberta. The cartoon below that appeared in an Alberta newspaper is more than tongue-in-cheek in its portrayal of public perceptions of the new science courses at that time.

Figure 3.1 Cartoon About the New Science Programs in Alberta[20]

From August, 1989 to December, 1989 further drafts of Science 10, 20, and 30 were produced, this time with "the assistance of science teachers and university professors" (Palmer 1989b); although it was clear to everyone at Alberta Education by late fall, 1989 that the new programs were in serious trouble. Compounding the development of the programs was the continuing trouble experienced by Gage Publishing in pulling together the *Visions 1* textbook for Science 10. Gage personnel complained the program of studies for Science 10 kept being modified by Alberta Education personnel, while Alberta Education personnel charged that the authors of various chapters in the new textbook did not have the ability to place into writing the STS spirit of Science 10. I was out of province during these summer months and totally unaware of the developments in the science education curriculum-discourse of Alberta. When I returned in early September, I found a very upsetting letter from Gage Publishing informing me that Alberta Education had recently rejected the introductory chapter I had written for being "too much like social studies" (personal communication, September 6, 1989). It seemed that now I, too was experiencing trouble writing to the expectations of Alberta Education personnel.

Meanwhile, the Minister's Advisory Committee had met several times to discuss the future of the proposed new science programs. At a November 24, 1989 meeting of the Minister's Advisory Committee several options for the high school science program were considered. The Committee elected to retain the structural changes to the high school program, increase the credit values of all discipline courses to 5 credits each, and completely re-examine the content of all high school science courses. In a January, 1990 Alberta Education *News Release*, the Minister of Education made the decisions of the Advisory Committee public, adding that "teachers, post-secondary institutions, and professional groups" would be involved "in the next state of development of all the new science courses" (Alberta Education 1990a, 1). To give this consultative process enough time to operate, the Minister also announced *another* one year delay in the implementation of the new science programs. The content of the original Science 10, 20, and 30 program of studies was officially dead; the Minister's announcement paved the way for a new program which he promised would give "greater focus on the scientific concepts and skills fundamental to biology, chemistry, physics, and other sciences" (Alberta Education 1990b, 2).

Structuralistic Explanations of the Evolution of Science 10, 20, and 30

Reflecting on the evolution of controversy in the development of Science 10, 20, and 30 the Deputy Minister of Education for the Alberta Government mused that some of the controversy was the result "of flawed consultation early on in the change process" (Duke, quoted in Eamon 1989, 3). The Deputy Minister's analysis is structuralistic, an approach that elaborates and extends technical-rational methods of curriculum change. Structuralism as a mode of analysis is based on the assumption that phenomena, including human interactions, display an "underlying structure, not too surprisingly, that is defined, in part, by relationships among their constitutive elements" (Cherryholmes 1988b, 16). In the technical-rational model, structuralism as analysis becomes prescription when used to define policy and practice (Cherryholmes 1987, 1988b). For example, the Deputy Minister's assertion is based on his analysis of the structure of the curriculum-discourse in science education during the years of controversy; his analysis becomes prescription when goes on to say that further consultation would likely have prevented further controversy in that curriculum-discourse.

Structuralism as method and prescription in education curriculum-discourse is an elaboration of technical-rational approaches to curriculum change: relationships between teachers, principals, students and other members of the educational community are considered as part of the so-called factors that must be considered in order to derive strategies that lead to the correct formula for curriculum change. From this highly technical-rational approach, curriculum change is a matter of dealing with enough factors to effect the change, since the "more factors supporting the implementation, the more change in practice will be accomplished" (Fullan 1982, 56–57). Structuralist perspectives to curriculum change have dominated the educational discourse on change since the mid-seventies.[21] This discourse advances theories of curriculum change which involve detailed examinations of the structure of educational systems in order to facilitate implementation of an intended change. For example, in his study on how to implement school change, *The Culture of the School and the*

Problem of Change (1982), educator Seymour Sarason argues that
change begins with the discernment of the "overt behavioral or
programmatic regularities" (4) of education systems. The prescriptive
nature of such a structuralist approach towards curriculum change
leads naturally towards a managerial view of the change process. In
his essay on school change, educator P. Murphy (1986) adopts a
structuralistic approach by suggesting that successful change occurs
when educators "manage situations so that many of the factors
associated with a specific intervention are given consideration" (17).
The technical orientation of such an approach is explicit in the
argument that curriculum change will be successful when the correct
"initiating strategies" are tied to "managing a product" (Goddard
1989, 14–15). Educator Earl Newton (1991) suggests a change
process which follows the phases of "adoption, implementation,
institutionalization or continuation" (3). Essential to this process,
argues Newton, is an understanding of the structures of schooling.

   One of the best representations of a structuralist approach to
curriculum change is presented by educator and curriculum theorist
Michael Fullan in his book, *The New Meaning of Educational Change*
(1991). In this work Fullan elaborates on the factors that should be
considered when attempting change:

> The theory of the meaning of change and the change process provides us with an
> underlying conception of what should be done. This guide to change enables us
> to locate specific factors, to observe how they work in concrete situations, and
> to explain why they function as they do, and with what consequences for school
> improvement. (Fullan 1991, 93)

How might Fullan's work help make sense of the evolution, or
perhaps devolution, of Science 10, 20, and 30 during 1988 and 1989?
Few of those involved in the science education curriculum-discourse
of Alberta during 1989 could argue with Fullan's observation that
"real change involves loss, anxiety, and struggle" (31). In addition,
Fullan reminds us that often "people do not understand the nature or
ramifications of most educational changes" (36). Given the fear and
uncertainty arising from change proposals, Fullan suggests the
initiation of change must consider several key factors (50–64). Fullan
acknowledges these factors are not presented in any particular order,
but represent a nexus of inter-connections and relationships that must

be considered if the change initiation is to be successful. First, the quality of innovation must be considered (51–53). An application of this factor to the evolution of Science 10, 20, and 30 might present questions about the extent Alberta Education personnel collaborated with members of the various Faculties of Science of Alberta's universities to ensure the quality of the new science programs. If the consultation had been broader at the beginning, perhaps the Report of the ad hoc Committee of the Faculty of Science at the University of Alberta may never have been written. Second, Fullan advocates access to information on the proposed changes and the establishment of a communication infrastructure to ensure this access (53–54). In Alberta, much of the communication of the proposed changes to secondary school science education was limited to conference presentations and selected workshops with the audience almost always teachers. Fullan's second factor suggests that by involving the media right from the beginning in supporting the intended changes Alberta Education personnel may have found the program considerably less challenged. For those with concerns, a 'hot-line' might have been established, promising an open, public forum on the direction and content of the new science programs. Third, without the support of administrative structures, assures Fullan, change "never occurs" (54). Instead of waiting for the reaction of public school boards, Alberta Education could have involved key spokespersons in these boards and Superintendents of Education in the curriculum design process, ensuring supportive stakeholders in the new programs. Fourth, Fullan acknowledges what Alberta Education personnel discovered in 1989: Community support is essential (56–58). Again, communication through the media to communities throughout Alberta may have allayed many fears and concerns about the proposed programs. During their many teacher workshops, Alberta Education personnel might have aided the cause of curriculum reform by inviting the general public to attend. Last, Fullan argues the implementation of a proposed change has a greater chance of success if the resources supporting the change are developed before the change is initiated. He notes that "just because it is a good and pressing idea, doesn't mean that the resources are available to carry it out" (64). Perhaps if the publishing company were able to develop a really exciting, dynamic textbook and a practical, innovative teachers' guide illustrating what students would be studying in the new program, opposition to the changes by teacher organizations may have turned to support. It seems reasonable, even natural that with more consideration of these factors mentioned by Fullan, and other factors suggested in structuralist approaches to curriculum change, the controversy surrounding the development and implementation might have been avoided.

This common-sense, technical understanding of curriculum change is challenged, however, by the continuing narration of the evolution of Science 10, 20 and 30; the events that follow demonstrate the barrenness of technical-rational structuralism, opening our conversation to consider other ways to understand possibilities for curriculum change in science education curriculum-discourses.

The Griffin Arises: The Reconceptualization of Science 10, 20, and 30 in the Alberta Science Education Curriculum-Discourse

It is a rare revolution that has been true to its initial vision.
—Seymour Sarason, *The Predictable Failure of Educational Reform* (1990, 8).

With the January, 1990 announcement by the Minister of Education that the entire science program would be reconsidered, Alberta Education personnel were able to start over in the development of the new programs. This time, each member of the development team would be able to consider factors they neglected during their first attempt at change in high school science education. Right from the announcement itself, Alberta Education personnel portrayed the development of the new Science 10, 20, and 30 courses, and the new science disciplines courses, as dependent on consultation with professional organizations, teachers, and the general public. The *Alberta Report* responded immediately with a photograph on the first page of a smiling Government of Alberta Minister of Education with the caption "A consensus on school science" (January 15, 1990 issue). In this issue *Alberta Report* staff writers Kubbish and Byfield (1990) describe the membership of the Minister's Advisory Committee as "something of a coup" (26) and offer praise for the ability of this committee, which they note was chaired by the Minister, to reach a consensus in "record time" (26). In an article appearing in *The Edmonton Journal*, (January 27, 1990) reporter Panzeri (1990a) observes that Education Minister Jim Dinning is now receiving "applause where he once received criticism" (A8). Panzeri also reports the Director of Curriculum of the Edmonton Public Schools was "pleased with her preliminary look" (A8). The *Letter of the Day* in the February 8, 1990 issue of the *Edmonton Journal* praised the Alberta Minister of Education for being the "first Minister in many a moon to listen, and respond, to public criticism before introducing a new curriculum."[22]

During the first months of 1990 curriculum developers at Alberta Education began the unenviable task of building the science programs anew. One colleague at Alberta Education was impressed with a proposal by the American Association for the Advancement of Science (AAAS) that student science literacy is encouraged when science education is built on major themes in science. The rationale of this premise is that "an understanding of a few thematic ideas" in science "is especially useful in thinking about how things work" (American Association for the Advancement of Science 1989, 9). These and other ideas for rejuvenating science education by the AAAS are summarized in their *Project 2061* initiative.   Drawing insights from *Project 2061*, Alberta Education personnel involved in the design of the new science programs outlined six "conceptual organizers," or themes, that provide a "useful way to bring cohesion and unify scientific concepts" (Alberta Education 1990c, 2). The six major themes in science that would be highlighted in the new science program are: change, diversity, energy, equilibrium, matter and systems. By the end of January the science development team at Alberta Education produced a tentative list of concepts and possible topics that reflect these six themes. Anxious to avoid past mistakes, the development team at Alberta Education immediately began touring the province to solicit feedback on their ideas for new science programs.

The development team soon discovered, though, that "there was not a lot of constructive comments from teachers when given the opportunity."[23] One team member found that of the "many that did respond, mostly they wanted everything in!"[24] The significance of this consultative act is considered more fully in Chapter 4; one noticeable effect was a general acceptance among teachers of the ideas proposed by the Alberta Education development team. The February 12, 1990 issue of the *ATA News*, reports the changes introduced by Alberta

Education now has the support of President of the ATA Science Council. The President of the Alberta Teachers' Association was also quoted in this issue as being "pleased with the involvement of various groups in the development of the new curriculum" (Teachers cautiously..., 1) a process the President felt "should be used as a model for other educational issues" (1).

Protest turned to praise in the media as the development of the new courses seemed to meet the approval of everyone; well, almost. Reported P. MacDonald (1990) notes in an *Alberta Report* article that the University of Alberta Faculty of Science was "pleased that professors have been promised to have more input" (32) in the design of the new programs. Kubish and Byfield (1990) report in the same publication that the President of the Alberta Medical Association found the changes to the Science program "reassuring" (26). *Edmonton Journal* reporter Panzeri notes that the Assistant Superintendent of Curriculum for Edmonton Public Schools felt the changes in the new programs present "the best chance for a turn around" in science education (1990b, B3). Panzeri reports in his article that while Science 10, 20, and 30 represent 'science for the masses', the Minister of Education has promised the new courses will be rigorous, guarantied by the addition of a mandatory diploma exam for Science 30.[25] In a later article, Panzeri (1990c) comments that the Minister, Mr. Jim Dinning, has proved "deft in a thorny portfolio" (G1, G3), praising him as a man willing to listen to the people. A good example of the perception in the media of developments in Alberta's high school science education can be found in a feature on the new programs in the Canadian daily newspaper, *The Globe and Mail*. The article notes that much of the criticism over the first round of science courses rose from how "course designers glossed over basic principles and concepts" (Lewington 1992, A4). This problem was rectified, the article claims, by the program designers going out to "get people's ideas for a completely new design" (A4). Graham Orpwood, one of the chief coordinators of the Science Council of Canada study of science education in Canada, is quoted in *The Globe and Mail* article as observing that with the newest changes to their secondary science program, "Alberta is ahead of any others in pushing ahead into new territory" (Orpwood, quoted in Lewington 1992, A4). These accolades were dampened somewhat by concerns from some educators in Alberta that the restoration of full credits for all science courses recreates a 'credit crunch' in schools that may mean some students will have to spend an extra year in high school if they enroll in courses in the fine arts (Ross 1990). One teacher was quoted as saying "I don't think science is everything" (A5), however in Alberta this would have to be considered a minority opinion at this time.

A Discussion Draft of a completely new set of Science 10, 20, and 30 programs of study was produced by Alberta Education in April, 1990. This overview of the new vision for science education introduces the goals of the new program, six organizing themes, and the expectations of attitudes, skills and knowledge for learners. The content of Science 10 is sketched out; the themes of energy, matter and change were slated to receive emphasis in this course. These themes were translated into four units which existed in only a summary form in April:

> Unit 1 focuses on the role of radiant energy from the sun in sustaining life and driving weather systems. In Unit 2 the processes by which matter and energy are exchanged between living systems and their environment are studied, and change is illustrated by the growth of living organisms. Unit 3 investigates the changes in matter and energy that occur during chemical reactions. Unit 4 examines different forms of energy and the principles that govern energy transformations. (Alberta Education 1991, 5)

Certainly a sketch of the direction and content of the new Science 10 course was a relief to Gage Publishing. Faced with the daunting task of completely rewriting their draft chapters for the *Visions 1* textbook, many authors, including myself, elected to accept payment for services to date and withdrew from the project. Gage was also reimbursed by Alberta Education for their expenses in preparing a draft document that never became published. In this sense, both Gage Publishing and Alberta Education started anew on the Science 10, 20, and 30 project during 1990. With pilot testing of Science 10 slated for the fall of 1991, each organization had almost a year and a half to prepare their respective documents.

The April, 1990 Discussion Draft of Science 10 was shared with teachers throughout the province; over 1500 response guides were sent out with 375 returned by individual teachers and 29 by groups. In addition, the science development team met with approximately seventy percent of all high school science teachers in the province.

Through this consultative process personnel at Alberta Education found that teachers generally agreed with the concepts and skills in this new Science 10 course, value knowledge as more essential than application in science education, and favor keeping the current content (i.e., themes) and sequence of the new science program (Alberta Education 1991).

At this point in the story of the evolution of Science 10, 20, and 30 a strange, almost isolated, event happened. Late in the spring of 1990 some of the personnel at Alberta Education responsible for the design of the Science 10 program met with a university professor to re-examine the Science 10 program of study. The agenda for this meeting, according to the professor, was to pursue the question, "What would a general science course, intended for academically oriented tenth graders, look like?"[26] The professor notes that this meeting became "very stimulating" due to the "number of ideas" that were shared.[27] The meeting was also productive. One seconded associate with Alberta Education recalls that "a fine curriculum" for Science 10 was developed that that day.[28] What emerged was a conceptual theme that linked together new topics and ideas in science into a "modern, contemporary course" that recaptured the original vision of the Science 10, 20, and 30 programs of study.[29]

Most of the individuals involved in planning this newest version of Science 10 were on summer holidays when this latest draft program of studies was shared with Gage Publishing. A Seconded Associate who was working at Alberta Education that summer recalls that Gage personnel were "infuriated" with "what they perceived as another change to the curriculum,"[30] since the newest version was a significant change from the April, 1990 Discussion Draft they were using. Meanwhile, the member of the university community involved in the design of the new Science 10 course was experiencing "increasing unease" as the summer wore on because this individual was not being sent "any written material in terms of the course."[31] At the end of the summer this individual was rather surprised to discover that "the basic structure" of the Science 10 course "was revised rather drastically" to being back in line with the Discussion Draft of April, 1990.[32] The version circulated in August, 1990 seemed to this member of the university community as a science program of "essentially stand alone units with only token connections" in a program that "still represents outdated materials [and] outdated concepts."[33] Seconded

Associates working on the Science 10 program that summer agree with this assessment, but claim they were unable to continue developing the Science 10 program proposed by the group that met in June, 1990. Not only were personnel with Gage Publishing upset with the latest changes, but senior Career Associates with Alberta Education also found the June draft "unacceptable" and requested those Seconded Associates available that summer to "re-work" the draft to the "specifications" of the April, 1990 draft.[34] It was the expanded version of the April, 1990 draft that was to become the final program of study for Science 10, delegating the June, 1990 draft as a mere footnote in the narrative of the evolution of Science 10.

This odd incident seems significant to me, however. I have a copy of the June, 1990 draft of Science 10 proposed by the group that met that day. In my opinion, this version of Science 10 was more dynamic and more in tune with the interests of young people than even the original 1988 version of Science 10. As we shall see in Chapter 4, I believe the development, and subsequent rejection, of this new and exciting program for Science 10 late in the evolution of Science 10 is more than just an isolated incident in the science education curriculum-discourse of Alberta.

By late August, 1990 personnel at Alberta Education were able to produce a final draft of Science 10. This draft was based on the April, 1990 draft and became, with only minor modification, the official and final program of studies for Science 10 for the province. Work then proceeded quickly to develop the final versions of the Science 20 and 30 programs. At the annual meeting of the Alberta Science Teachers' Association in the fall of 1990, Alberta Education representative Raja Panwar was careful to explain that this final version of Science 10, 20, and 30 "will achieve excellence by providing a more rigorous science education. This rigor will be achieved by helping students understand basic scientific concepts, principles, and laws and by the real-life applications of science and technology" (1991, 8). He continued by assuring his audience that "the proposed Science 10/20/30 program is designed for academic students who want a strong foundation in science. Science 10, as a compulsory course, will give students a broader understanding of the important scientific concepts in biology, chemistry, and physics" (9).

Gage Publishing had been busy, too. With a secure program of studies for Science 10 by September and a more concentrated author team, a draft outline of the *Visions 1* textbook was available by mid fall, 1990. I was briefly employed that fall to review this draft for Gage Publishing and sent them ideas and materials, some of which would come to be eventually incorporated into some of the chapters of *Visions 1* textbook for the Science 10 program. I assumed this would be my last work for Gage Publishing, but in early 1991 I agreed to become involved once again in the science education curriculum-discourse by writing the Teachers' Guide for the completed new version of *Visions 1*.

What is the Meaning of Educational Change?

Plus ça change, plus c'est la même chose.[35]
—French Proverb.

My narration of the evolution of Science 10, 20, and 30 ends with the publication of the August, 1990 program of study for Science 10. This program of study proved to be the final version, after some 13 changes, of Science 10. A postscript, however, is in order. In the months that followed drafts of Science 20 and 30 were written that met that same general approval as Science 10. I remained involved in the curriculum-discourse as an enthusiastic supporter of the new programs, partially out of friendship with my colleagues at Alberta Education and because I believe, and still believe, that integrating the 10 level specialist courses into one course developed with an STS approach was a step in the right direction. In June, 1991 Alberta Education held workshops at the University of Alberta to support teachers about to pilot the Science 10 in the new school year. In my involvement as a workshop leader I was struck by the enthusiasm for Science 10 displayed by most teachers. All of us knew the Science 10, 20, and 30 initiative was alive when in October, 1991 the Faculty of Science at the University of Alberta approved the addition of Science 30 to the category of senior secondary school science courses (such as Biology 30, Chemistry 30, and Physics 30) graduating students may use for admission to the Faculty (Faculty of Science 1991, 1). Conceived almost a decade earlier, Science 10 became a reality in the classrooms of teachers piloting this new science in September, 1991. The following year science specialist courses at the 10 level ceased to exist in Alberta; Science 10 was now in place in the secondary schools across the province of Alberta.

How are we to make sense of the genesis and evolution of Science 10, 20, and 30 in the science education curriculum-discourse in Alberta? The original vision for science education in this curriculum-discourse focused on developing an STS approach that would help all children to become critical, scientifically literate citizens. This movement towards renewal was catalyzed by the growing crisis in science education: declining student interest in science-related careers, poor enrollment and achievement in high school sciences—especially physics—and growing concerns that high school science was rooted in subjects too esoteric to a population worried about environmental degradation in the midst of increasing technological complexities in almost every area of life.

In 1990 I engaged several groups of students about to graduate from high school in long, deep discussions about their school science experience. My conversations with these seniors reveal the general disappointment students feel with the their senior high school science education (Blades 1992). I recall that Dede[36] found "all that cell stuff" she learned in Biology 10 to be "terribly irrelevant" (10), a sentiment I found universally shared by the students interviewed. Sally's comment reflects a consistent concern among students about the usefulness of their science education: "For chemistry, I don't think I'm ever in my life going to need stoichiometry or stuff like that. I don't know... I can't even think of a job where you'd use it!" (11). Every group of senior students I met with expressed concern that their science education, especially topics in chemistry and physics, did not connect to their daily lives and may prove not relevant in the future. Dick described physics as "plugging numbers into a formula" but complained that he had "no idea how half the formulas work" (11). Students would gladly trade highly quantified studies of Newtonian physics for more modern topics in physics, such as the existence of black holes and the theory of relativity. Students were able to list other topics they would like to study in high school science: the human body, environmental science, and the philosophy and history of science were a few of the topics mentioned. Many of these topics, and others identified by students during our meetings, are found in the 1988 Interim draft of Science 10. The vision that introduced this course to the public sprang, I believe, from teachers with ears open to the voices of their students, eyes open to the growing crisis in science education, and hearts hopeful they could really make a difference in this crisis with a program that would prove exciting and motivating to children.

This vision never had a chance. Over time controversy mitigated against the original draft until the program was re-worked and completely changed, appearing on the organizational skeleton of the former vision. Still, one could counter, everything turned out right in the end since the new programs have not only been 'implemented' in schools, but these programs have won approval from organizations previously antagonistic to the original programs of study for Science 10, 20, and 30. From this perspective, personnel at Alberta Education simply failed to consider the necessary factors in implementing change first time around; the success of the revised program that appeared in 1990 indicates that eventually Alberta Education was able to get it right. Through the correct consultation strategies and sensitivity to the demands of academic and other organizations, Alberta Education was able to turn protest into praise. To this structuralistic interpretation I must reply with a summary of the final draft of the Science 10 program of study which appears on the next page. I would invite you to turn to page 46 and read once again the summary of the original draft in Table 2.1, comparing it to the one that follows in Table 2.2.

Table 2.2 Science 10 Draft Course of Studies, 31 August, 1990[37]

Unit	*Topic*
1: Energy From the Sun	Energy from the Sun sustains life on Earth, weather systems are driven by solar energy, calorimetry, thermal energy, the Coriolis effect, tornadoes, hurricanes, thunderstorms, hailstorms, Chinooks, meteorologic data, hydrologic cycle, water and phase changes, moderating effects of large bodies of water.
2: Matter and Energy in Living Systems	Cell organelles, mitosis, diffusion and active transport in cells, ATP, photosynthesis (general terms), multicellularity, survey of transport, excretion and gas exchange systems in the biology of selected organisms.

3: Matter and Energy in Chemical Change	Mixtures, solutions, compounds, physical and chemical changes, classification of elements, predicting properties of elements, types of chemical changes (synthesis, replacement, etc.), naming and writing formulae for selected compounds and chemical reactions, atom, isotopes, conservation of matter, stoichiometry.
4: Energy and Change	Forms of energy, the Sun as the source of most forms of energy, units for energy (Joule), KILOWATT/hr; conservation of energy, first and second laws of thermodynamics; energy transformation of energy, Newtonian physics, one-dimensional uniform motion using graphical and mathematical techniques, Work = F x D, E= VIT, formula for KE and PE; energy conversions and efficiency, interpreting empirical data, measuring input and output of systems.

The summary found in Appendix A of this book of the topics in the previous Biology 10, Chemistry 10 and Physics 10 programs of study in Alberta confirms the fact that the final program of studies for Science 10 represents, with the possible exception of Unit 1, an amalgam of topics from Biology 10, Chemistry 10 and Physics 10. If renewal in science education means finding new ways to explore the relationships between science, technology and society in ways that are distinct from the approaches of science courses developed in the fifties and sixties; if renewal means pursuing topics and issues free from the shackles of traditional science education content, *then the attempt at change in science education in Alberta must be considered overall a failure.* The very fact University Faculties of Science applaud the new Science 10 course should raise suspicions little change has been accomplished: It was the familiarity of topics that made the new science programs so dramatically acceptable to teachers and professional organizations. Anyone steeped in a traditional view of high school science education could point to the first, 1988 draft of Science 10 and say, "Where is cell anatomy? Newtonian mechanics? Stoichiometry? We always teach those topics in the sophomore year!" The fact these topics were not present in the original Science 10 was deliberate; developers wished to present something new that might stimulate, rather than frustrate, the attitude of children towards science. Should we be surprised, then, that their efforts were greeted with such skepticism? When rigor means calculating momentum, yield of a chemical reaction or the ability to recite the steps of mitosis and meiosis, it's little wonder the original Science 10 was categorized as "diluted" science first by academics within University Faculties of Science, then through media characterization and professional organization involvement that was clearly a bandwagon effect.

This reaction was not unique to Alberta. Educator Robert Fowler (1990) reports how an attempt to change curricula in the Canadian province of British Columbia found similar resistance from teachers and academics, leading to vociferous debate through the media that eventually served to undermine the change attempt. Science educator Roger Bybee's (1992) analysis of attempts in the U.S. to change science education towards an STS perspective reveals that "little is being taught about STS in school programs" (81) and that a large gap still exists between talking about STS science education and actual cases of successful change. Certainly the newest round of reforms in response to the second crisis in science education have not enjoyed much success. British attempts to introduce STS science courses met with increasing centralized control as the new programs were labeled 'soft' by academics, leading to the expulsion in 1988 of science, technology and society from the national curriculum (Jenkins 1992; Solomon 1991, 1994). The study by Australian science educator Peter Fensham (1988a, 1993) of attempts at curriculum reform towards an STS approach in science education in the Australian state of Victoria reveals tremendous barrier to curriculum change imposed by academics, offering a reason for this resistance to curriculum change in science education at the high school level:

> The dominant academic response to the current reforms (and to those in the 1960s) is consistent with a strong sense of science education at schools as 'preparatory'. Thus, the content and knowledge of worth for the senior secondary sciences is to be determined by the knowledge and expansion of it that is now well established as the content of freshman science courses in physics, chemistry and biology... In the 1980s and 1990s freshman studies in physics and chemistry in particular have changed only slightly from the 1960s despite the major changes in these sciences as a whole in this period. The concerns of academic scientists about school science curricular [sic] are presently to *prevent* them from deviating from the smooth continuity their now traditional content provides. (Fensham 1993, 61–61, emphasis his.)

Fensham's comments suggest any attempt at curriculum reform faces the formidable obstacle of the re-generation process of tradition. If this is the case, then structuralistic analysis and prescription would, in fact, ironically serve the maintenance of the status quo. This is exactly what happened in Alberta. Criticized for not consulting enough, which is a structuralistic interpretation of why the changes were so difficult the first time around, personnel from Alberta Education then tried to appease academics and other professional organizations through consultation and the inclusion in Science 10 of science topics expected by these groups.. As traditional topics in grade ten science began to appear in the re-worked Science 10, the praise and approval of this new-yet-old science course by academics makes sense since, in effect, *nothing had changed* except the way in which these topics were organized at the Grade 10 level. And it pains me to say this, knowing a little of the heartache experienced by those who really believe, and still believe, in the importance and value of that first attempt at significant change in high school science education in Alberta.

The Barren History of Curriculum Change

Perhaps there is some consolation to those involved in the genesis and evolution of Science 10, 20, and 30 in the knowledge that despite constant effort and millions of dollars, curriculum change has proven extremely difficult in practically every area of the school curriculum. In his review of educational reform, Aiken (1989) describes the mood at the end of the sixties and seventies as a diminishing optimism in the possibility of curriculum change. He notes that during the seventies "people began to notice that the prevailing models of educational research and scholarship were producing little noteworthy change in educational practice" (202), a view supported in similar reviews by Fullan (1993), Stevenson (1973) and Wood (1990). Educator Larry Cuban's (1984) extensive review of major attempts from 1890–1980 to reform American high school practice discovered that despite major expenditures and effort, little curriculum change has actually occurred. According to Cuban, American school practice and structure has remained amazingly uniform over these decades; in fact, claims Cuban, schooling seems to be a resilient social institution which is highly impervious to attempts at change despite the almost cyclical pattern of change efforts (Cuban, 1982, 1990). Canadian education demonstrates a similar resiliency to change with almost no results after decades of attempts (Common, 1981). Seymour Sarason's latest book, *The Predictable Failure of Education Reform* (1990) poses a question that succinctly summarizes the poor record of attempts at curriculum change since World War II: Why, in the light of the fact that in the post-World War II era we have poured billions of dollars into reforming schooling, do we have little or nothing to show for it? (3). Paul Hurd (1991b), that veteran of many curriculum reform efforts in high school biology education, notes in an essay that "despite the turmoil over science education during the past decades, not much has happened" (35).

The Determined Hope of Structuralism in Educational Discourse

As I reported earlier in this chapter, structuralistic analyses and prescription in technical-rational approaches to curriculum change have dominated educational discourse since the mid-seventies. The logic of this approach leads naturally to the thought that since "changes do not inevitably lead to the predicted result, perhaps there is something wrong with the rational model" (Wise 1977, 49). Instead of examining the model itself, the failure of curriculum reform has been rationalized during the past decade as a problem of knowledge: change has *yet* to succeed because the correct techniques have not been fully articulated and then applied. To find the key to effective curriculum change, so the argument goes, more research into the structural complexities of public schooling would be needed. Thus, the majority of educational research on curriculum change during the past decade has probed deeply into the structures and dynamics of schooling in an effort to solve the riddle of curriculum change, *leaving largely unchallenged the very presuppositions of this technical-rational approach to curriculum change.*[38] The result has been the entrenchment during the past decade of structuralistic approaches in the technical-rational tradition of education. Examples of this entrenchment abound. Turney (1976) recognized that "most of our past effort at educational change has failed...because we did not realize the magnitude of the task" (233). He then elaborates some of the factors that should be considered when initiating change. Crocker (1982) argues that successful curriculum change involves solving "the problems of different perspectives and of structural components of the school setting" (35). Miller and Seller (1985) support Crocker's view, suggesting curriculum change involves a type of 'transaction' between the players in the change during the steps of development, implementation and evaluation. Leithwood (1986) suggests the "solution to the problem of improving school effectiveness using the planned change approach is essentially the task... of facilitating organizational growth" (6). This growth occurs, according to the author, through the familiar steps in the technical-rational model of curriculum review, development, and implementation. In a reflection on what he has learned about curriculum change, Fullan (1993) acknowledges that "it is one thing to have a list of factors, and another to know how these factors interact and unfold" (120). Still, Fullan betrays his structuralist stance when he continues in his article to elaborate eight lessons from the history of curriculum change that "represents dilemmas, *with corresponding lines of action*" arising from an understanding of the *"systematic reality* and dynamic complexity" (124, emphasis mine) of educational change.

Rethinking Curriculum Change

Technical-rational approaches to curriculum change, even with the elaboration of structuralism, will likely continue to prove barren in helping us find hope and possibilities for curriculum change. This prophesy is more than an extrapolation of the dismal history of attempts at curriculum change; the very presuppositions of the technical-rational act undermine the value of technical-rational approaches. Three assumptions in the genesis and evolution of Science 10, 20, and 30 illustrate this irony:

1. Assumption of expertise: The original intention of people involved in the design of Science 10, 20, and 30 was to produce a course of study that would engage all students in thoughtful study of the nature of science and the relationships between science, technology, and society (Alberta Education, 1989b). Over time the curriculum-discourse included the voices of academics and professional organizations. Representatives from these groups claimed the right to also determine the direction and content of the new programs, shifting expertise from the original design team to the public forum. The consequence was an "academic influence" (Fensham, 1993) in the curriculum-discourse that catalyzed a shift towards emphasizing the expertise of non-education specialists in science education curriculum reform.

2. *Assumption of curriculum:* As was noted earlier in this chapter, the original vision for science education renewal in Alberta came to eventually focus on issues of the practical expression of ideas. In this natural progression definition of the word 'curriculum' moved from vision to materials. As early as January, 1989 'the curriculum' in the science education curriculum-discourse referred to the draft program of studies and developing *Visions 1* textbook. For example, when Freedman (1989a) refers to the "new science curriculum for public schools" (1) he immediately refers to programs of studies; this type of referential is constant among all the members of the science education curriculum-discourse at that time. The perception of curriculum as a document and materials to be used assumes curriculum is something developed external to the classroom then implemented, with the aid of teachers, into lessons. The focus on documents-as-curriculum shifted the science education curriculum-discourse at the time towards a view of curriculum change as a technical-rational problem.

3. *Assumption of method:* In this chapter we have seen how curriculum change in Alberta is approached as a task accomplished through the familiar steps of the technical-rational model: Assessment, design and development, implementation, and evaluation. As this approach began to prove unfaithful during controversy in the design and development stage of Science 10, people clung even more to a technical-rational model by elaborating the factors to consider when the design and development was attempted once more. The results of this trust in a technical-rational approach proved to be misplaced, however; the design and development of a new high school science program in Alberta turned out to be little more than a reorganization of traditional science topics.

You will recall from our conversation in Chapter 1 that these three assumptions are the same ones that were foundational to science education reform in the sixties (see pages 18–20). This is not surprising; in each wave of reform *the same technical-rational model of curriculum change dominated the curriculum-discourse.* Neither should the failure of significant change in Alberta surprise us, for that has been the demonstrated legacy of the technical-rational approach.

Some change in science education during the sixties was evident; new programs designed during that era *did* appear in some schools in various interpretations, a few no doubt close to what the people designing the new programs intended. We need to remember, though, that this is no longer the fifties and sixties. The hope and promises of modernity during those decades were unfulfilled; as theologian and philosopher Os Guiness (1979) observes in his critique of Western humanism, "rationalism and optimistic humanism have thus turned out badly, and so has the entire Western culture" (35). In the midst of growing ecological emergency, exponential growth of technological knowledge, and failure of science and technology to solve our social ills, we in the West have become sullen (Borgmann 1992), unsure of what we should know or what we should do. In this crisis of modernity, we are faced in education with a model of curriculum change founded on the very modern premise that change is possible through a scientific analysis of the factors needed to ensure the change. The case of the genesis and evolution of Science 10, 20, and 30 in Alberta illustrates the irony of our situation: a new science program was designed to meet the crisis of modernity through a process that is fundamentally modernistic! Given this entrapment in our conversation on the evolution of Science 10, we might agree with long-time science educator Paul Hurd (1991b) that

> breaking out of the intellectual strait-jacket and nostalgia that characterize traditional science courses will not be easy. We must begin from scratch. Little will be gained by simply revising and updating old subject matter, tinkering with the instructional system, modifying assessment techniques, or reorganizing institutions. (35)

But how can we begin from scratch? If technical-rational ways fail to help find hope and possibilities for curriculum change, how else can curriculum change be understood? Is it possible to break free from the entrapment of technical ways of thinking? At a time when the need for change in science education is critical, where does hope for change exist?

It was these questions that occupied my thinking during the summer of 1989. As the controversy in Alberta over the proposed science programs swelled I spent a few days camping with my family. Once again destiny intervened in my life, this time through the people camping next to us. As we visited, I shared my interest in curriculum change, experiences in Alberta, and the questions I was pondering. "Have you read Foucault?" they asked. I admitted I knew only of the French physicist, Jean Foucault; was this who they meant? They laughed, and told me to pick up some of the works by Michel Foucault, the French philosopher. I told them I would. Later during the summer I found a collection of Foucault's essays (the philosopher, not the physicist), *The Foucault Reader* (Rabinow, 1984a). I found the words by this man quoted on page six of the book riveting. "It seems to me," expounds Foucault, "that

> the real political task in a society such as ours is to criticize the working of institutions which appear to be both neutral and independent; to criticize them in such a manner that the political violence which has always exercised itself obscurely through them will be unmasked, so that one can fight them. (Foucault, quoted in Rabinow 1984b, 6)

As I returned in the fall of 1989 to my studies at the University, employment with Alberta Education, and work as an author of the introductory chapter to *Visions 1* I found these words by Foucault kept returning. The controversy over the new science programs and subsequent failure of significant change seemed like an act of violence towards everyone involved. But how can we fight such acts? I began to expand my reading of this philosopher, discovering to my delight inspiration and instruction. By November that year I began to have a sense that somehow the ideas of Foucault "will be essential" (Journal entry, November 1, 1989) in the task of addressing questions about the possibilities of curriculum change. As noted earlier, my main interest, however, was an essay on technology by the German philosopher Heidegger. One passage in particular offered a profound insight (Heidegger 1977):

> The essence of technology lies in enframing (*Das Ge-stell*). Its holding sway belongs within destining. Since destining at any given time starts man [sic] on a way of revealing, man [sic], thus underway, is continually approaching the brink of the possibility of pursuing and pushing forward nothing but is revealed in

ordering, and of deriving all his [sic] standards on this basis. Through this the other possibility is blocked. (307)

In this passage Heidegger suggests technological orientations are not just the destiny of the modern era, but are active, a 'destining' that reveals nothing since all standards are based on technological thinking. The major point of Heidegger's essay is that technological approaches and thinking enframe (*Ge-stell*) our destiny and thus limit possibilities. Commenting on Heidegger's notion of *Ge-stell*, philosopher David Levin suggests in his wonderful book, *The Opening of Vision* (1988) that we are born "with eyes opened by enchantment" (58), but 'growing up' is actually a process of "progressive closure of the dimensionality of Being" (59) which is our modern, technological destiny. Levin argues the result of this destiny is a restriction of vision: in modern expressions of the Great Conversation we live, claims Levin, with a "certain 'normal' blindness" (60) to possibilities. If Heidegger's view of modern technological thinking is correct, then technical-rational approaches to curriculum change are hopelessly enframed and enframing, limiting possibilities for change. Seen this way, curriculum change involves somehow breaking free from the enframing nature of well established, technological approaches to curriculum change; what I metaphorically call in an earlier work finding a "5th corner" of a new frame of seeing (Blades 1990). But how do we find this opening of vision, this new way to think about and look at change in ways not thought or seen before? My reading during 1990 led the way: To address this fundamental question about curriculum change, we need to include the words of the French philosopher Michel Foucault in our conversation.

Chapter 3

Foucault's Invitation to Research Power

Introduction: Beyond Modernity in a Curriculum-Discourse

When I was a high school teacher I sponsored an annual overnight camping trip to a mountain range. Standing on the peak of a mountain is a singular experience: one feels a sense of exhilaration and oneness with the world spread before you. During one particular trip my group decided to hike down to a small lake nestled in the mountain range. We reached the lake easily enough, but during the climb back mists rolled in. In the reduced visibility I somehow became separated from the main group. Still, after so many trips to this area I had become so familiar with the surroundings and landmarks that I felt confident I could find my way back to the group, even in the mist. I continued to climb. After awhile the mist cleared somewhat, and I found myself on a small ledge completely opposite from where I should be. Even worse, below was a sheer drop of perhaps 500 meters directly into the lake. In terror, I realized there was no way out! I clung to the wall, wondering what to do.

My situation is a metaphor of our modern age. Modern expressions of the Great Conversation center on a belief in the "steady progress of reason and freedom" (Fraser and Nicholson 1990, 22) through the twin techniques of prediction and control. But the promise of modernity to "liberate humankind from ignorance and irrationality" (Rosenau 1992, 5) has become increasingly suspect in the light of world events this century. In her synopsis of post-modernism, sociologist Pauline Rosenau notes that "world wars, the rise of Nazism, concentration camps (in both East and West), genocide, world-wide depression, Hiroshima, Vietnam, Cambodia, the Persian Gulf, and a widening gap between the rich and the poor makes any belief in the idea of progress or faith in the future questionable" (5). As the twentieth century comes to a close we "no longer have the confidence to invest belief in the foundational myths of inevitable human rationality or social progress" (Mercer 1990, 49). The Great

Conversation has begun to hesitate with voices on the margins that speak of hopelessness and despair. Humankind has climbed onto a ledge, and as the mists clear we know we are trouble but there seems to be no clear direction which way to go.

Education has, since the late sixties, continued to climb the metaphorical mountain confident in technical-rational approaches to curriculum change. Despite the growing mists of doubt about the actual success of the technical-rational model, educational discourse has clung to the promises of modernity, investing hope that eventually a solution to curriculum change would appear. Part of the Great Conversation, educational discourse is also located on a ledge high above a great fall. In this precarious position, many in education discourse continue to grasp prediction and control as if "it were the sole alternative to sullen silence" (Borgmann 1990, 2). But Heidegger (1977) reminds us that prediction and control are rooted in technological thinking which, through destining, has placed humankind in danger.

Flat against the mountain, high up on a ledge I had a real sense of the word danger! I began to yell for help. After a few moments a member of my group heard me and began to give me directions out of my predicament. I had to trust her advice since I could not see where I was going. But she could see the way clearly, and her voice was able to guide me to safety.

So it is in our modern condition. In the last half of this century many philosophers have sought a way out of the destining of modernity. Their project has been to move beyond the modern, to find 'post-modern' responses to the danger of technological destining. Their example responds to our call for help in curriculum change, a direction that may guide education discourse off the precipice of modernism. A post-modern project in curriculum change, however, is disquieting and unfamiliar: we are asked to abandon beliefs fundamental to the Great Conversation, such as the idea of a rational and autonomous human subject, belief in the ability of any meta-discourse to represent the truth of first-order discourses, and any notion that a single right practice exists (Lyotard 1984; Madison 1988; Vattimo 1988). Clearly, a post-modern project will not enable us to propose a general theory of curriculum change! Instead, the move towards post-modernism begins with an "archeology of modernity" (Huyssen 1990, 260) that in a curriculum-discourse requires the deconstruction of the very enframing *(Ge-stell)* that presently binds possibilities for change. This deconstruction effectively turns a curriculum-discourse on itself by questioning what the curriculum-discourse does to limit possibilities for change and, in the process, hopefully opens new possibilities. This is a difficult task, but we are not alone. There are voices calling across the mountain to help us: One of these voices comes from the French philosopher Michel Foucault.

Re-Searching Power

In all events a *will to power* is operating.
—Friedrich Nietzsche, *On the Genealogy of Morals* (1967, 78, emphasis his).

Researching Possibilities for Curriculum Change

During the summer of 1989, right at the height of controversy in Alberta over the proposed changes to senior high school science education, I was teaching an undergraduate summer course in science education in a different province. As you recall from Chapter 2, while camping with my family before reaching the province I met two students who recommended I read the works of Michel Foucault (1926–1984).[1] Teaching that summer allowed me some time for reading so I decided to take the advice of the two students and purchased the *Foucault Reader* (Foucault 1984a), a selection of Foucault's essays and excerpts from some of his books. I immediately was captured by this work. Paul Rabinow comments in the introduction to this reader that Foucault believes we are engaged in political struggles all the time (Rabinow 1984a, 6). The point of these struggles, claims Foucault, is "to alter power relations" (Foucault, quoted in Rabinow, 5). That made complete sense to me. The power Alberta Education held in the science education curriculum-discourse seemed to me to be usurped by the power of the University of Alberta Faculty of Science. If this power could be altered or controlled, then perhaps curriculum change would have proceeded more smoothly.

I soon discovered, however, that Foucault means something quite different than my structuralistic view of power. In his essay *Truth and Power* appearing in the *Foucault Reader*, Foucault (1984b) describes power as something "exercised—concretely and in detail—with its specificity, its techniques and tactics" (57) in what he calls 'relations'. Later in this essay Foucault cites an example of what he means by power: In European feudal societies, power functioned through "signs of loyalty to feudal lords, rituals, ceremonies, and so forth, and levies in the form of taxes, pillage, hunting, war, etc." (66). Foucault then claims that in the seventeenth and eighteenth centuries institutions devoted to the study of population demographics, public health, and safety were born. Foucault claims the rise of interest in the most minute detail about individuals, expressed in concerns about the housing, fertility and longevity of the masses, re-presents a new form of power that "begins to exercise itself through social production and social service. It becomes a matter of obtaining productive service from individuals in their concrete lives" (66). Instead of power functioning to modify outward behavior, as it once did in feudal times, during the seventeenth and eighteenth centuries power literally became incorporated in the sense that "power had to be able to gain access to the bodies of individuals, to their acts, attitudes, and modes of everyday behavior" (66–67). Foucault continues, "hence the significance of methods like school discipline, which succeeded in making children's bodies the object of highly complex systems of manipulation and conditioning" (67). And, Foucault maintains, it is these "implicit systems in which we find ourselves prisoners" in our modern era (Foucault 1989a, 71). I found Foucault's essay on power very upsetting. Was Foucault suggesting that in my role as high school teacher I had been part of a complex nexus of manipulation and conditioning that is the functional expression of power in a system? Was power something that defines how I thought and acted in my everyday life? I was to spend a good part of my summer contemplating the implications of this thought.

Sometimes in a life a junction of events serves to completely turn around thinking. When I returned in the fall to my studies at the University and my position with Alberta Education, I found out the new programs were in jeopardy and the textbook chapter I had written for Science 10 rejected for being *too* STS in orientation! One of my university courses that fall explored what was for me the timely topic of curriculum change. Each member of our class was asked to give a presentation of possibilities for change in their subject interest area. Frankly, given the history of Science 10, 20, and 30 I had become skeptical *any* possibility for real change in science education existed.

As I set out to plan my presentation, it occurred to me that in all my thinking about curriculum change, I had never really defined change itself. What *is* change? While pondering this question someone very close to me shared how they had converted from one religion to another. Certainly their conversion was accompanied with a change in life; I decided exploring the conversion act might reveal insights on change. I found the word "conversion" literally means to completely turn around, to face a totally new direction, revealing a new horizon of possibilities. But how could this turning happen in curriculum-discourse? Heidegger's words returned to me: "the essence of technology lies in enframing. Its holding sway belongs within destining" (Heidegger 1977, 307). Heidegger continues to suggest this enframing (*Ge-stell*) blocks any other possibility. Heidegger's observation suggests any curriculum-discourse enframed by technical thinking will experience a destining that blocks possibility for change. If this is true, then change in a curriculum-discourse would involve some way of breaking free from this destining, to completely turn around and find a new direction. Clearly change involves more than tinkering with an existing system, change is much, much more difficult: it is an effort to break from the systems in which we are trapped.

Exactly at the time this occurred to me I was continuing my study of Foucault's concept of power, widening the scope of my reading to include interviews with Foucault and commentaries on Foucault's works and ideas. To the question, "How do you uncover today's discourse?" (Foucault 1989a, 63) Foucault replied that he tries to show "those systems which are still ours today and within which we are trapped. It is a question, basically, of presenting a critique of our time" (64). These systems are able to exist within the social body through a multiplicity of force relations which Foucault calls *power*. A crack in the frame of technicality appeared in my thinking: I began to believe dis-covering the procedures of power in a curriculum-discourse might expose possibilities for escaping the technicism that has driven curriculum-discourse for decades. I was able to complete my presentation for my class on change, which I entitled, *Possibilities for Change in Science Education*. A journal entry captures how I felt when I realized change is possible: "I'm excited! I believe I'm on to something with Foucault. A research proposal is forming, but there is much to do. I must read Foucault carefully" (Journal entry, October

30, 1989). I also note in that entry that increasingly I was finding my work at Alberta Education "a hindrance" to my studies. On December 13, 1989 I resigned from Alberta Education. Ironically, the last validation I was working on was a review of the doomed 1989 Science 10, 20, and 30 programs. This report, like the original programs themselves, was destined to be never finished.

What is the Purpose of Curriculum Research?

Research literally means 'to search again'. Doing research, then, implies that a search has already taken place and that another search is needed. What is research in education? With the texts of the science education curriculum-discourse in Alberta, I originally searched for an understanding of the genesis and evolution of Science 10, 20, and 30. This search exposed the fruitless quest of technical-rational approaches to curriculum change, leading to the prediction that structuralism in modern interpretations of the technical-rational model of curriculum change will also prove barren. As is often the case in a search to understand, new questions emerge. The questions I faced were simply, "Now what? Is curriculum change possible?" It was my reading of Foucault that encouraged me to believe this question might be addressed. As the Minister of Education announced in early 1990 a complete rewriting of the high school science programs, I was at the University of Alberta, pondering *how* to re-search power in the science education curriculum-discourse of Alberta.

Before I could proceed, I had to address the same question everyone contemplating educational research, or any research for that matter, must face: "Why bother? What is the purpose of this research act?" I could not hope to develop a new model of curriculum change; the moment research becomes analysis that leads to prescription one succumbs to the modernistic destining of technical-rational structuralism! How could my research develop a meaningful interpretation of events in the evolution of Science 10, 20, and 30 without falling into what political scientist and educational philosopher Cleo Cherryholmes calls the "structural and discursive determinism" (1985, 62) of technicality? If my interpretation of the procedures of power in a curriculum-discourse does not point to any particular model of curriculum change, then what is the point of researching the evolution of Science 10, 20, and 30?

In my case, I came to believe the value of my research lies in how this act *can initiate a conversation of critique*. I remember one sunny afternoon during my first year teaching I happened to have a rare free period, so I decided to sit on the front steps of our school. After only a few minutes, the principal of our school joined me. Sitting together, this principal charged me to always remember that I am a teacher first, a subject specialist second. "You don't teach science," the principal continued, "you teach children." I was startled; I had never thought of teaching in these terms, defining myself as a biology teacher until that afternoon. I began to ponder what it means to teach children, initiating what educational researchers call an on-going "interpretive inquiry" (Jacknicke and Rowell 1987; Soltis 1984) of critique that was to affect my whole orientation to teaching, even to the present. Through constant critique on my life-as-teacher, my thinking about teaching changed from a subject focus to a focus on the child. Foucault defines critique as "seeing what kinds of self-evidences, liberties, acquired and non-reflective modes of thought, the practices we accept rest on" (Foucault 1982, 33); a dis-covering of the way we think and act. As I found out that afternoon conversing with the principal of our school, "the moment one begins to be unable, any longer, to think things as one usually thinks them, transformation becomes simultaneously very urgent, very difficult, and altogether possible" (34). Therein lies hope and possibility: *Our hope is that critique of the enframing nature of technical thinking in a science education curriculum-discourse itself is transformational, revealing possibilities for change in the curriculum-discourse.* From this perspective, research is not a smooth process leading to a product that can be presented, but an on-going invitation to critique, an opportunity to crack open the destining of technicality. Since I was part of the science education curriculum-discourse in Alberta, my re-search of procedures of power in the evolution of Science 10, 20, and 30 is reflexive, an act that introduces into a science education curriculum-discourse a conversation of critique on how this discourse prevents change, with the hope that conversations of critique might discover possibilities for change.

Such research in education is a messy, personal business. Clear steps will not be obvious and no product forthcoming. I can not tell someone how to begin or proceed, neither do I recommend anyone follow in the footsteps I have taken, even if I could retrace them with perfect clarity. What I can do, however, is share with you my research journey and, in the next chapter, the procedures of power I discovered. It is precisely in this sharing that research becomes even more personal. In the Introduction of this book I have described the reading of the text before you as a conversation. It is so in that my sharing enters your thoughts and, should you return to this text once again in thought or reading, a true conversation emerges in the new meanings, ideas, and departures you find. Now, I suggested in the introduction to Chapter 2 the text of this book is also part of the science education curriculum-discourse in Alberta. If your reading is conversational, you have also become part of this curriculum-discourse; we are in this together! Building a conversation of critique in the science education curriculum-discourse now becomes a joint task between you and I. The text that follows, then, extends an invitation for you to take an active part in curriculum change by joining me in a research project that begins a conversation of critique.

Foucault's Rethinking of Power

Our conversation continues with a question:

> What possibilities for curriculum change are revealed by re-searching the procedures of power in the evolution of Science 10, 20, and 30 in Alberta?

Let us continue our conversation preserving an openness to this question by avoiding forming opinions or conclusions too rapidly (Carson 1986). Instead, several new questions emerge from the question I have just posed:

> What are 'procedures of power?'
> Is it possible to re-search these procedures of power?
> If so, how might this research proceed?

These three questions were only vaguely expressed in my thinking when I met in January, 1990 with one of my Alberta Education colleagues for advice in my researching the evolution of Science 10, 20 and 30. It was a wonderful, rich meeting. This colleague was able to confirm my account of the major events in the genesis and evolution of Science 10, 20, and 30 and suggested some further documents I should review plus a list of the people I would want to speak to in my research. I record in my journal entry that evening this colleague was, "very willing to answer any questions or even tell me what I should ask different individuals" (Journal Entry, January 19, 1990). I came away from this meeting confident that "now my research details can be worked out" (same entry).

During our meeting my colleague strongly recommended I continue to gather texts from the science education curriculum-discourse since the evolution of the new programs was anything but over. I agreed, and over the next few years I was a regular visitor back at Alberta Education, collecting newspaper clippings, reading reports and surveys, interviewing those involved in the evolution of Science 10, 20, and 30 and generally gathering every trace of the evolution of these programs I could find.

At the same time, I entered into a conversation with Foucault's writings on the word 'power'. Being back on campus allowed me to spend more time discussing my studies with fellow students. On a coffee break one day a friend asked me what Foucault means by power. I admitted it was easier to say what Foucault doesn't mean. When he speaks of power Foucault does not refer to "a group of institutions and mechanisms that ensure the subservience of the citizens of a given state" (Foucault 1990, 92). To Foucault, power does not mean a "general system of dominance exerted by one group over another" (92). Correspondingly, Foucault does not adopt a Marxist view that power exists as a type of capital that can be held, exchanged, traded, or lost. Foucauldian scholars Hubert L. Dreyfus and Paul Rabinow (1982) observe that Foucault never considers power a "commodity, a position, a prize or a plot" (185). Power is not even necessarily a repressive force; indeed, claims Foucault, power "doesn't always weigh on us as a force that says no, but that it traverses and produces things, it induces pleasure, forms knowledge, produces discourse" (Foucault 1980, 119). In fact, according to Foucault power does not exist at all in the substantive sense.

Let us return to my friend's question. What does Foucault mean by power? Foucault provides a post-modern response by avoiding any suggestion of a theory of power in his many works and interviews. Foucault consistently avoids the question, "What does power mean?" by addressing a different question, "What does power do?" philosopher Gilles Deleuze (1988) describes Foucault's view of power as Nietzschean; indeed Foucault's project was very influenced by Nietzsche's *The Genealogy of Morals* (1887).[2] In this work Nietzsche calls us to question traditional interpretations of history advancing instead that behind all events "a will to power is operating" (Nietzsche 1967, 79). Nietzsche elaborates with an example: "one also imagined that punishment was devised for punishing. But purposes and utilities are only *signs* that a will to power has become master of something less powerful and imposed upon it the character of a function" (77, emphasis his). Foucault (1979) explores this hypothesis in his book, *Discipline and Punish* (1975). In this work Foucault discovers "the system of thought, the form of rationality, which since the end of the eighteenth century has underlain the idea that the prison is in sum the best means, one of the most efficient and rational, to punish factions in a society" (Foucault 1989c, 280). This system of thought, one of the many which define our modern era, is "established, consolidated, and implemented through the production, accumulation, circulations and functioning of a discourse" (Foucault 1980, 93). This discourse exists and functions through relations Foucault calls power. After nearly two hundred pages describing in often gruesome detail the genealogy of discipline and punishment techniques Foucault (1979) urges us in *Discipline and Punish* to

> cease once and for all to describe the effects of power in negative terms: it 'excludes', it 'represses', it 'censors', it 'abstracts', it 'masks', it 'conceals'. In fact, power produces; it produces reality; it produces domains of objects and rituals of truth. The individual and the knowledge gained of him belong to this production. (194)

Individuals, claims Foucault, are the "vehicles of power, not its point of application" (Foucault 1980, 98). Thus, the individual is not vis-à-vis power, they are the prime effects of power. Dreyfus and Rabinow (1982) explain this further:

> Power is a general matrix of force relations at a given time, in a given society. In the prison, both the guardians and the prisoners are located within the same specific operations of discipline and surveillance, within the concrete restrictions of the prison's architecture. (186)

In other words, neither the prisoners nor their guardians possess power, rather each group acts and thinks in ways defined by the system of force relations within which they are trapped. It is this active, continuous, forceful, anonymous entrapment and definition of being that is power. And parallels of these force relations exist within systems everywhere: in hospitals, military, religious organizations and, of course, schools, universities, and government Ministries of Education.

Foucault's view of power is comforting and discomforting at once. I am comforted to realize that the power of the status quo in science education curriculum-discourse is not held by a location or person. Applying this concept to the events surrounding the evolution of the Science 10, 20, and 30 programs means that blame becomes pointless in the failure of change; there was no conscious conspiracy toward maintaining the status quo, no group or individual *had* power over the events that led to the demise of the original program and subsequent devolution of the new program towards an amalgam of what existed before. *The events themselves were expressions of power.* But from this realization springs the discomforting thought that we are all trapped in a curriculum-discourse, destined to fail at change before we start by the technicality of our systems of thought and action. It is precisely the formation and functioning of this destining and how we might fight against it, that is, how change is possible in the established order of things, that is Foucault's project.

The Influence of Foucault's Project

Given Foucault's unusual and provocative perspective on power it is not surprising Foucault's project has entered sociological discourse, although it seems the writings of Foucault defy easy categorization. Foucault's work has been described in sociological literature as structuralist, post-structuralist, irrationalist, relativist, anarchist, nihilist, neo-eclectic, phenomenological, empiricist, and even neo-positivist! Foucault deplored attempts to categorize his work, beginning one of his books with the request that readers "do not ask who I am and do not ask me to remain the same" (Foucault 1972, 17). When asked to describe his work, Foucault was characteristically vague:

> My own work? As you know, it's very limited. Very schematically, it consists of trying to discover in the history of science and of human knowledge (*des connaissance et du savoir humain*) something that would be like its unconscious. (Foucault 1989d, 39.)

Dreyfus and Rabinow argue classifying Foucault's work will remain elusive since Foucault presents a "sustained and largely successful effort to develop a new method" (xii) of research in the human sciences.[3] This new, Foucauldian method has been adapted widely to research in such diverse areas as social origins of pornography, implications of feminism to change in social order, the sociology of work, the discourse of development in the Third World, English literary criticism, and sociological studies of culture. Even a cursory glance through the *Social Sciences Citation Index*[4] reveals that Foucault's works have been and continue to be cited and contested extensively in the humanities and social sciences.

Foucault in Education Discourse

References to Foucault in educational research are becoming increasingly popular, although still somewhat limited. In most cases, Foucault is associated with the use of the word 'power' in the research, although the conceptualization of power may bear little in common with what Foucault means by this word. Aside from such cursory references, there exists a growing number of studies in education inspired by Foucault's work and style of inquiry. For example, Da Silva's (1988) study of inner city schools in a Brazilian city develops from a Foucault's perspective on the dynamic of power and knowledge. Luke, Castell, and Luke (1983) demonstrate in their work how Foucault's notion of power can lead to critical questions about the role and authority of textbooks in schools. Continuing on this line of inquiry and drawing extensively from Foucault's insights into the relationship of power and knowledge, Cherryholmes (1988a) develops the very Foucauldian argument that textbooks are a type of discourse which results from "severe forms of restraint" (8) such as provincial guidelines, avoidance of controversy, and the expectation and desires of the teachers. This restraint, argues Cherryholmes, is part of an educational discursive practice which shapes the discourse of a textbook through the visible and hidden effects of power; as we shall see in the next chapter, there is evidence to support Cherryholmes' argument.

Even though the explorations of Foucault's insights to educational research are very limited, educator James Marshall (1989) feels that Foucault "has much to offer education" (101). With his tongue firmly in his cheek, Marshall feels that even if Foucault's work proves to be wrong, it is "right enough to be disturbing" (101). In an introduction to a collection of essays which examine and reflect on the implications of Foucault's thinking to education research,[5] educator Stephen Ball (1990) suggests a Foucauldian analysis of discursive practice in education presents real hope in unmasking "the politics that underlie some of the apparent neutrality of educational reform" (7). Cherryholmes (1987) supports this position, arguing that the insights of Foucault apply to understanding curriculum change. Cherryholmes observes that the search in educational discourse to find a fixed theory which can, once and for all, "tell us what curriculum is and authoritatively tell us what to do when it comes to developing, implementing, and evaluating curriculum" (309) is misplaced. Foucault teaches us, suggests Cherryholmes, that our discourse about education should turn from "talking primarily about taxonomies of objects, systems of disciplines, and learning objectives" (310) towards a discourse about "the kind of society and schools we want knowing full well that they constitute each other" (310).

The few existing Foucauldian studies of curriculum change efforts are diverse in topic and presentation, but all focus on Foucault's conceptualization of power. Freedman and Popkewitz (1988), for example, examine the relationship between a discourse of curriculum change and power in their study of the development of art education from 1860 to 1920. In his investigation of curriculum reform in Canada, Curtis (1988) noticed a tendency of reforms, especially initiatives generated by local schools, to be increasingly controlled and frustrated through the centralization of reform administration. The inevitable surveillance and control of the reform by a centralized agency functioned to limit the involvement of teachers and students in the reform. Drawing on the insights of Foucault's work, Curtis claims this functioning is the effect of power in attempts at curriculum reform. As we shall see in Chapter 4, this same type of delimitation by a centralized agency affected the possibility of change in the science education curriculum-discourse in Alberta.

Foucault's insights helped Bjerg and Silberbrandt (1980) understand the increasing bureaucratization and final demise of an attempt at curriculum reform at a Danish university. Not only were the effects of power in enframing and limiting possibilities evident in this attempt at curriculum change, but Foucault's concept of how truth interacts with power was also clear. The development of a public truth that the reform project was out of control eventually led to the steady invasion of administrative restrictions which re-introduced the limits of dominating curriculum meta-discourses. The result was the predictable demise of the reform. Bjerg and Siberbrandt come to the conclusion in their study that "social change is not brought about as the result of transformation of academic institutions. The problem is part of a total social context of power structures" (260). Drawing from the work of Foucault, they situate hope for curriculum change in a openness to possibilities which comes from a greater understanding of role of power in discursive practice.

In the previous chapter I argued that educational discourse in Alberta is enframed by technicality, offering little hope to those voices calling for change in science education. To this dilemma Foucault presents an agenda of hope through his invitation by example to re-search procedures of power in a curriculum-discourse. Our conversation continues by exploring *how* these procedures of power might be discovered.

The Archaeology of Power in a Curriculum-Discourse

> How shall you rise beyond your days and nights unless you break the chains which you at the dawn of your understanding have fastened around your noon hour?
> —Kahlil Gibran, *The Prophet* (1977, 42–43).

Collecting Documents

During the spring of 1990 I continued to gather texts from the evolution of Science 10, 20, and 30 while at the same time continuing my effort to make sense of Foucault's concept of power. I actually was engaged in two processes at once: every text I collected extended my original search to understand the evolution of Science 10, 20, and 30 while, at the same time, I re-searched these texts to discover how power operated in the science education curriculum-discourse. This was not a tidy process! Minutes of a meeting, an article in a newspaper, or some other document that came my way would typically stimulate new questions in my re-search, requiring further documents. The word 'document' is defined widely; any textual material related to Science 10, 20 and 30 was collected, such as newspaper articles,

Alberta Education publications, drafts of textbook chapters, news bulletins by professional organizations, and the like. Every document I collected was studied, then grouped into one of five categories:

1. Documents generated from communications with Gage Publishing and Alberta Education.
2. Articles and other publications (e.g., cartoons) in the newspapers of Alberta, Canada, and the *Alberta Report.*
3. Publications from professional interest groups such as the Alberta Medical Association, Association of Professional Engineers, Geologists and Geophysicists in Alberta, and universities in Alberta.
4. Documents from the Alberta Teachers' Association and affiliated member groups, such as the Edmonton Regional Science Council.
5. Publications from Alberta Education related to the science education curriculum-discourse, including all drafts of the Science 10, 20, and 30 Programs of Study.

These documents were then used to prepare the events matrix chart described in Chapter 2 (page 58). Developing this chart was a dynamic process that continued as long as documents were collected. I was continually moving items from one category to another (and sometimes within categories), adjusting the chronology of events and noting significant movements in the curriculum-discourse while at the same time trying to understand what effects of power were revealed by the developing chart.

By March, 1990 I found the events matrix chart developing well, but my research faltering. I note rather sadly in my journal: "My research seems to be getting nowhere. The job seems so massive" (Journal entry, March 8, 1990). Mere hints, if that, of nature of power in the curriculum-discourse seemed to emerge from the developing events matrix chart. After several months of exploring Foucault's idea of power I assumed an understanding of how power operates in a curriculum-discourse, what I was beginning to call the 'procedures of power', would become self-evident as I gathered documents. Instead, what did emerge in quantity from my original search to understand the evolution of Science 10, 20, and 30 were questions! For example, how did the phrase 'watered down science' first enter the curriculum-discourse? I had reports of consultation with teachers by Alberta Education personnel, but what did this consultative process do? Several accusations and insinuations pervaded the science education curriculum-discourse. How did these affect the lives of those involved in the discourse, in turn affecting the discourse itself? By late spring I realized my research of the evolution of Science 10, 20, and 30 would need to delve deeper into the impressions, memories and experiences of events of which documents constitute a mere shadow: I would need to interview people involved in the discourse.

Archaeology as a Trachealizing Act

Exactly *how* the procedures of power could be known through the study of documents and interviewing was certainly less than clear. Overwhelmed by the sheer amount of documents available and possible number of people involved in the discourse, my research bogged down. I shared my growing frustration with a professor at the University. He listened patiently, then posed a simple, direct question: How did Foucault go about researching?

Intrigued, I immediately began to study Foucault's research approach. Foucault describes his strategy for discourse analysis as the "archaeology of knowledge" (Foucault 1972, 1989e). After my experience the previous spring, I readily agreed with Foucault that discovering procedures of power in a discourse is indeed an archaeological task! Characteristically, Foucault means more than exhaustive research and painstaking reconstruction of texts when he refers to his research as archaeological.

First, Foucault admits he is not searching for the foundations of knowledge in a discourse, nor relations in a discourse that are "secret, hidden, more silent or deeper than the consciousness of men [sic]" (Foucault 1989e, 46). Foucault is not interested in a hermeneutic analysis of discourse.[6] To understand discourse-practice Foucault inverts the traditional approach of hermeneutics to understanding meaning-giving through an analysis of discourse-products (e.g., texts, symbols, spoken words). Foucault suggests this search for meaning in the products of a discourse could go on forever and thus will always remain elusive; instead, argues Foucault, we should examine how discourse is *used*, by revealing the *practice* of discourse in the social order:

> I'm not looking underneath discourse for the thought of men [sic], but try to grasp discourse in its manifest existence, *as a practice* that obeys certain rules— of formation, existence, co-existence—and systems of functioning. It is this

practice, in its consistency and almost in its materiality, that I describe. (46, emphasis mine.)

Foucault's archaeological research does "not treat discourse as *document*, as a sign of something else," (Foucault 1972, 138, emphasis his) but instead is concerned with discourse "as a *monument*" (139, emphasis his) in social practice. Foucault deftly side-steps the hermeneutic question, What does discourse *mean*? by asking, What does discourse *do?*, followed closely by the political question, How else could it *be?*

Second, Foucault refuses to separate knowledge from power. Foucault agrees with social-critical theorists[7] such as Habermas (1982) that knowledge is always tied to human interests but Foucault finds departure from social-critical theory by arguing there is no distinction between knowledge, human interests and power. For example, Foucault demonstrates that the rise of interest by the Bourgeoisie in the incarceration and rehabilitation of prisoners in eighteenth and nineteenth century France was not primarily an interest in the phenomenon of delinquency, but a discourse of power based on the production of truth, justified as the acquisition of knowledge. After all, points out Foucault (1980):

> the bourgeoisie could not care less about delinquent, about punishment and rehabilitation, which have little economic importance, but it is concerned about the complex of mechanisms with which delinquency is controlled, pursued, punished, reformed, etc. (102)

In other words, what the discourse on delinquency in the eighteenth and nineteenth century, and the accompanying medical discourse on madness, *did* allow was more access and surveillance of the common people by the bourgeoisie. This access was legitimized as knowledge needed to search for, study, and rehabilitate the madman and delinquent. Foucault suggests we adopt an attitude of suspicion towards the discourse on madness and delinquency in nineteenth century France; the search during that time to cure madness and solve delinquency may be less altruistic than it seems.

Third, Foucault's archaeology of power/knowledge is a type of deconstruction that 'trachealizes'[8] discourse. The word 'deconstruction' has various meanings, but generally refer to the act of questioning "prevalent philosophies, ideas, assumptions, and constructs regarding current social, political, and economic practices" (Buck and Osborne 1990, 178). Philosopher G. B. Madison (1990) describes deconstruction as "essentially a critique" in post-modernism (110), represented in the works of Foucault and the contemporary French philosopher Derrida, which involves an "attack on the very notion of the subject and of lived experience as the ultimate source of meaning" (92).[9] While Foucault and Derrida have a "similarity of critical focus" (95) they operate from very different strategies and agendas. To Derrida, deconstruction is *le jeu* (the game), an approach which recognizes there are "only differences" (Derrida 1982, 11) in discourse, since "every concept is inscribed in a chain or in a system which it refers to the other, to other concepts, by means of a systematic play of differences" (11). This deconstruction as a play of differences cannot speak from a position, and thus, according to Madison, it speaks from nowhere, "leads us nowhere, and this is precisely why it is nihilistic" (110).

Foucault adopts a different approach. The purpose of his deconstruction is to reveal possibilities of freedom from the systems in which we are entrapped while avoiding any presumption of a meta-discourse. From this post-modern stance, deconstruction is "more of an approach to understanding human discourse and behavior than a particular method of analysis" (Buck and Osborne 1990, 179). Foucault's approach in his deconstructive archaeology of knowledge is to *trachealize* a discourse: metaphorically Foucault wrestles with the discourse with the intention of exposing the weakness of the discourse for all to see. This deliberate, aggressive research act attempts to show that "things are not as obvious as we might believe, doing it in such a way that what we accept without saying no longer goes without saying" (Foucault 1982, 34). And so we come to the heart of Foucault's project: As the procedures of power/knowledge in a discourse are dis-covered it is no longer possible to think as one thought and freedom becomes possible. The current Dalai Lama of Tibet (Tenzin Gyatso 1990) defines freedom as "the right to determine our own destiny as individuals" (270). If, as Foucault suggests, our very thoughts and acts are destined by power, then only when power is wrestled with, deconstructed, laid bare, and exposed for what it is and what it does in lives can one begin to "think differently than one already knows" (Gillan 1987, 153). When this happens, destiny opens and we can become free. What is Foucault's project? I return to the very first statement by Foucault I read:

> It seems to me the real political task in a society such as ours is to criticize the working of institutions which appear to be both neutral and independent; to criticize them in such a manner that the political violence which has always exercised itself obscurely through them will be unmasked, so that one can fight them. (Foucault, quoted in Rabinow 1984b, 6)

The object of this warfare is individual freedom. The implications of this warfare and possible locations where this struggle might take place in science education curriculum-discourse are the central themes of Chapter 5.

The Dynamics of Interviewing

It is clearly inappropriate post-modernly to attempt to replicate Foucault's archaeological methods, since this would amount to structuralistic adaptations of Foucault's work. Instead, Buck and Osborne (1990) suggest a Foucauldian deconstruction in educational research can occur with some "aspects of Foucault's style" (179) by using "strategies similar to those which Foucault used on his own deconstructions" (179). Foucault's style is simple. When asked how he chooses which historical documents to use in his own research, Foucault (1989f) replied, "I will respond by saying that in fact there must not be any privileged choice. One must be able to read everything" (3). Foucault's thoroughness in research inspired me to gather every written trace of the evolution of Science 10, 20, and 30 I could find, but my archaeological research had access to a type of text Foucault did not generally use: the living memories of individuals involved in a curriculum-discourse.

Journal entries and notes from early January, 1991 on my research approach to interviews demonstrates the power of the technical-rational model. At that time I considered interviewing as process where procedures of power in a curriculum-discourse would become evident through a linear, rational inquiry process that involved a set of definite steps:

1. Drawing up a set of interview questions based on Foucault's work.
2. Gathering answers to these questions through interviews.

3. Using these answers, along with the documents I gathered, to discover procedures of power in a curriculum-discourse.

My thinking indicates a fundamental belief in progress through rational technique, in my case questioning and interview strategies. Even as I was working at deconstructing technical-rational approaches to curriculum change, my interview strategies were based on technical-rational presuppositions! This fall into technicality was an easy act, arising from many years of participation in educational discourses which are dominated by technical thinking. The ability of this thinking to pervade my own, even as I sought to work against it is a good example of what Foucault calls power. This power encouraged me to split theory and practice in my thinking: my theoretical understanding of the dynamics of a curriculum-discourse, even my theoretical understanding of the need to deconstruct this discourse, was not related to my research practice! This condition did not last long, however. Two events during the first weeks of the new year were to help me break my technical approach to interview research, setting in motion conversations that were to reveal procedures of power in the evolution of Science 10, 20, and 30.

Rethinking Interviewing. In early January, 1991 I had the opportunity to share my research proposal ideas with other students. To prepare for this event, I attempted to portray my research to date in some graphical form. What developed was a messy series of double arrows, lines, and circles. Two lessons emerged from this attempt: First, I found educational research an untidy endeavor, not at all amenable to easy flow charts or technical-rational logic! Second, a graphic representation of progress sometimes leads to insights. In my case, I quickly realized I was experiencing a modern enframing *(Ge-stell)*. My research questions were initially developed through engaging in a type of conversation between Foucault's works and the documents I gathered, but when procedures of power in the science education did not immediately become clear in this conversation, I thought of *using* the procedures of power presented in Foucault's works to formulate my interview questions. Until I prepared a graphic of this act, I did not realize that using Foucault this way was precisely modernistic: I had assumed power in every discourse functions through the same set of procedures. So, in essence I was heading in the direction of establishing a meta-discourse on power supported by research, a thoroughly modern, technical action! If I were to remain open to my original research questions (page 98) I would have to reconsider my interview approach.

In their classic reference on qualitative research, *Qualitative Data Analysis,* educational research theorists Matthew Miles and Michael Huberman (1984a) recommend interviewing as one way to clarify trends and relationships that appear tepid or fuzzy (226–227). Their advice prompted me to consider interviewing as the introduction of a new set of texts in my search to understand the evolution of Science 10, 20, and 30 and then research these texts, along with other texts I had gathered, to discover procedures of power in science education curriculum-discourse. This meant interviewing would need to proceed through two steps. The first step would involve a chance for people involved in the curriculum discourse to, in the words of qualitative research experts Michael Connelly and Jean Clandinin, "tell stories of those lives" (1990, 2). I would collect these stories and, in conversation with Foucault's works, re-search for the procedures of power emerging from the stories and documents I gathered.

Connelly and Clandinin (1990) recommend an interview procedure where meetings are "conducted between the researcher and participant, transcripts are made, the meetings are made available for further discussion, and they become part of the on-going narrative inquiry" (5). In her work on sociological research Louise Kidder (1981) suggests the first requisite for beginning this conversational process is an effort by the researcher "to create a friendly atmosphere and to put the respondents at ease" (179). I decided meeting respondents at a location and time suitable to them might help create an open, inviting situation. To help our conversation begin, I drew up the following general questions:

1. How would you describe your involvement in the genesis and/or evolution of Science 10, 20, and 30?
2. The evolution of Science 10, 20, and 30 has progressed over a number of years. Which stages can you identify in this evolution?
3. Which events (political, social, economic) do you feel played major roles in the genesis and evolution of Science 10, 20, and 30? How were the events involved in the genesis and evolution of Science 10, 20, and 30?

Even before I began conversations with people involved in the science education curriculum-discourse I realized the questions asked during this initial meeting could vary from this general set depending on the individual. Any specific questions I intended to ask during conversations arose from questions I had gathered from my reading of the documents arising from the Science 10, 20, and 30 program initiatives. For example, documents suggest the Minister of Education formed an Advisory Committee to deal with controversy over changes to the high school science program in Alberta, but was the formation of this committee some sort of political strategy? I decided I would ask the Minister of Education during our first conversation together.

In spring, 1991 I prepared a preliminary list of individuals to contact about beginning re-search conversations on the genesis and evolution of Science 10, 20, and 30. Documents were helpful in identifying some of the most public figures in the curriculum-discourse, but my years as a participant-observer with Alberta Education taught me that behind a document or newspaper clipping is often some hidden story. For example, I had written entire sections of an Alberta Education publication on thinking skill development even though the publication does not report my involvement. This is fairly common in government; many people contribute to a document that might list only one author or none. Authors 'behind the document' may have stories that shed light on the procedures of power in a curriculum-discourse. I asked some of my colleagues at Alberta Education to suggest people I would want to talk to, and with their advice and what I gleaned from documents I added to my original list of potential candidates to interview, eventually forming a list that included employees of Alberta Education, academics, secondary school science teachers and other members of the educational community in Alberta, and members of the publishing community involved in the Alberta science education curriculum-discourse.

Establishing Validity. Conversations began October, 1991. To help these conversations become research I audiotaped our first meeting, transcribed the tape recording, and then use this transcription, along with the events matrix chart, to discover procedures of power in a curriculum-discourse. But how could I ensure the procedures of power I identified would be a reliable perception of the curriculum-discourse? Educational researcher Neil Johnson (1987) reminds us that "perceptions shape human attitudes and behavior; their impact is persuasive and unavoidable. They provide bases for understanding reality-objects, events, and the people with whom we interact—and our responses to them" (206). I decided to ensure the reliability of my perceptions of power in the curriculum-discourse by allowing my conversations with those I interviewed to continue over several meetings, focusing on the procedures of power I identified after our first meetings.

Establishing and then validating the procedures of power I discovered involved several steps. First, I met with each person individually. At these meetings individuals were asked to share their perceptions of the evolution of Science 10, 20, and 30 by responding to the three general questions listed above. In every case, interviews deviated from these general questions as individuals amplified certain points or shared particular stories. Most initial meetings were one to two hours in length, although a few were longer. Every conversation was audiotaped; before the meeting each individual was asked for permission to audiotape our meeting and permission was granted in each case. I then prepared a literal transcription from the tape and listened to the recording once again to correct errors in transcription.

The next step involved a deconstruction of the transcription using summary notes I made from studies of Foucault's works. The purpose of this deconstruction was to discover procedures of power in the curriculum-discourse; an outline of the questions I used appears below:

1. How might this system of curriculum-discourse present an effective system of exclusion?
2. How is division and rejection used in the discourse?
3. How was discourse institutionalized?
4. What major narratives exist (as truth statements?) What is the functioning of these narratives? How were truths maintained in this discourse?
5. In a specific type of discourse on science curriculum, what is the most immediate, most local power relations at work?
   A. What forms of knowledge/power exist?
   B. How does the transmission of knowledge play a role in power?
   C. How does power exist as a matrices of transformations—shifting, mutable, and plastic?

The deconstruction of each interview using these questions led me to discover a set of procedures of power that operated in the curriculum-discourse. Sometimes these procedures were similar to those Foucault articulates, such as 'the production of truth', but new procedures Foucault does not articulate also became apparent as I interpreted each interview in conversation with Foucault's works. Each interpretation was typed and then given to the person interviewed for review and validation. Some did not wish a second meeting, trusting me to interpret our conversation fairly. Others requested we continue our conversation via notes written on interpretations of our conversation I sent. I met with the majority of individuals a second, and occasionally a third time to discuss the interpretation. These successive meetings with individuals were also recorded, and the transcriptions used to validate the original interpretations which were then corrected and sent back to the individual. If needed, a new meeting took place but most of the individuals elected to send me corrected copies of the latest interpretation. Eventually agreement on interpretations were established and I searched the interpretations for similarities in the procedures of power identified. I describe in my journal the interpretation process as "lengthy but really fun" (Journal entry, November 24, 1991) after completing the first one. This opinion was to change as weeks became months while I worked at the other interpretations!

While working on my first round of interpretations, however, I came to face an ethical issue that threatened to stop my research completely.

Ethical Considerations. My journal entry in early November, 1991 records that "my work on interpretations has encountered a real snag" (Journal entry, November 6, 1991). I note the issue "marries ethics and validity into something personal and difficult. This is not a problem I could have anticipated" (same entry). The concern expressed in this journal entry began with my first interpretation of a conversation with an employee of Alberta Education. As I read the transcript of our meeting and reflected on the works of Foucault I discovered a very clear portrait of the procedures of power in the evolution of Science 10, 20, and 30. Some of the procedures were similar to observations on power by Foucault, others I believe to be unique to the science education curriculum-discourse in Alberta at that time. As I note earlier, to validate my interpretation I was planning to share the procedures I identified with my colleagues, together revising the interpretation through further conversation until we reached agreement. I note in my journal the dilemma I faced validating my research interpretations:

> There are *people* here. These people are more than acquaintances. The friendship I've experienced allows unique entry into the discourse at many levels—but trust is part of this entry. My interpretation reveals a whole set of ideas, thoughts, rituals, methods which implicitly are at work [in the discourse], how will [names deleted] feel? These impressions are mine and not valid unless confirmed by those who are, in fact, part of the discourse! But by giving my interpretation I'm also exposing the discourse to what it is—I'm deliberately trying to open a crack in the frame and, in the process, invite others to push on it. (Same entry, emphasis in text.)

In Chapter 2, I mentioned that Alberta Education as corporate individual does not exist, in the sense that one can not speak of Alberta Education doing anything; it's the people working within an institution called Alberta Education who act. Speaking of an anonymous Alberta Education diffuses the fact that behind events and documents are the lives of individuals, many my friends and colleagues. This is, of course, a dilemma in participant-observation research since, as modern physics has taught us, "an observer cannot observe without altering what he [sic] sees" (Zukav 1979, 92). Through involvement as a participant in the science education curriculum-discourse I could not help but affect the events I was researching and the lives I touched, perhaps in positive ways, perhaps not. This thought paralyzed my research but galvanized by thinking: Do I have the right to continue my research conversations, knowing they may well initiate conversations of critique in the lives of the people I engage in conversation?

I sought advice on this issue. Over a long coffee break one day with a professor in our department I explored the implications of the ethical issues I faced. In our meeting this professor helped me identify two questions I would need to address before I could continue with my research. The first concerned my list of potential people for research conversations. The professor asked why my name wasn't on this list. I had to admit, it was a good question. I was involved directly in the Science 10, 20, and 30 curriculum-discourse as a writer of the introductory chapter of the textbook to accompany the new Science

10 course, author of sections of the Teacher's Resource Manual for Science 10, critical reviewer of the developing *Visions 1* textbook, and author of the *Visions 1 Teachers' Guide*. How could I be left out? Yet, it did seem odd, to say the least, to interview myself! Popkewitz (1988) argues that understanding our roles in curriculum-discourse is essential to understanding how power enframes curriculum-discourses:

> While we are immersed in our personal histories, our practices are not simply the products of our intent and will. We take part in the routines of daily life, we use language that is socially constructed to make camaraderie with others possible, and we develop affiliations with the roles and institutions that give form to our identities. We speak not only as ourselves but, as Foucault reminds us, as part of discourses of power as the social complexities and subtleties of intellectual life are inter-related with institutions. That which is seemingly normal and natural about our participation in the world are the very acts about which we need to become curious and critical. (379–380)

Educator and curriculum theorist Madeleine Grumet (1981) suggests keeping an autobiographical journal has tremendous potential to yield deep, critical insights into curriculum experiences. Subsequent reflection, or 'reconceptualization' of these insights requires the writer to be an "active interpreter of his [sic] past" (144). Fortunately, I had been keeping an autobiographical journal for several years and I decided to use my entries to 'self-interview' my involvement in the Science 10, 20, and 30 curriculum-discourse. Any inquiry into human events produces a discourse which Foucault (1988) reminds us, "can no way be dissociated from the exercise of power" (106). Foucault suggests this presents less of a problem and more of an opportunity to discover how power, truth, and knowledge circulate in our own lives. The process of discovery may not be very pleasant, however. For example, I have shared in this chapter through my journal entries how I came to realize that I also was enframed by technicality during my involvement in the evolution of Science 10, 20, and 30.

The second question posed by the professor that afternoon was more difficult: What is the responsibility of the researcher in education? My immediate reaction was to emphasize the responsibility of the researcher to ensure the search for freedom in the research act does not directly harm those willing to be involved in the research. In my case, many of the individuals I wished to engage in conversation were still employed at Alberta Education. To have their confidence and honesty in conversation meant I would need to present the procedures of power I identified without necessarily referring to the individuals interviewed. The location and institutional role of the individual is important, however, to understanding how power functions in a curriculum-discourse. To protect these individuals from possible harm I decided to use general titles, such as 'Seconded Associate with Alberta Education' or 'Member of the Publishing Community' in my interpretations. Care was taken to not reveal any particular individual idiosyncrasies that might also reveal the identity of individual.

The responsibility of the researcher involves more than protecting the identify of those involved in the research act. The professor's question forced me to consider *who I am* in the research act. This act, *my act*, of researching is, after all, performed by an experienced teacher and researcher. I can not avoid the fact I am also an intellectual engaged in research (Giroux 1985). After my meeting with the professor I returned to *Truth and Power*, the very first essay I read by Foucault (1980). In this essay Foucault suggests in society the intellectual "is not the 'bearer of universal values'. Rather, it's the person occupying a specific position—but whose specificity is linked, in a society such as ours, to the general functioning of an apparatus of truth" (132). By 'truth' Foucault refers to those elements in discursive practice that make power possible. We are subjected, claims Foucault, to "the production of truth through power" (93). Cherryholmes (1985) paraphrases Foucault's notion of 'truth' the following way:

> If what can be stated is regulated by discursive rules and practices, what can be true or false is so regulated. The existence of constraints on what can be uttered and, thus, on what can be true is one mechanism by which power and truth interweave. (52; see also Foucault 1980, 131.)

Since intellectuals are specifically linked to institutions intimately involved in the production of truth, Foucault (1980) suggests "it is necessary to think of the political problems of intellectuals not in terms of 'science' and 'ideology' but in terms of 'truth' and 'power'" (132). Precisely because intellectuals operate and struggle "at the general level" of what Foucault calls the "régime of truth which is so essential to the structure and functioning of our society" (132) hope for change exists in that intellectuals can ascertain "the possibility of constituting a new politics of truth" (133). If, as I have suggested earlier, freedom means being able to break from the destining of enframing, and if this enframing is made possible through the dynamic nexus of truth, knowledge and power, then intellectuals not only may play a role in deconstructing truth in discourse, intellectuals *must* be involved in a critical, post-modern, deconstructive research if change is to happen. The implications of this belief will be explored further in Chapter 5.

I thought of all the students I once taught, and all the students I was influencing by teaching their teachers. The world these children inherit desperately needs the skills, attitudes, and understanding these children could develop through new science curricula. In this great need, change is blocked by a tradition in the curriculum-discourse of technical thinking mediated by truth, knowledge and power. I suddenly came to realize my research presented a great opportunity: *through my re-search interpretations I had the opportunity to introduce into the on-going science education curriculum-discourse conversations of critique.* As an intellectual engaged in research, to have stopped at this point would have been unethical and irresponsible to my role and position as a scholar and my calling as teacher in the human activity we call education. I decided to press on with my research, sharing my interpretations with people willing to enter into conversations with me about the evolution of Science 10, 20, and 30 and the procedures of power that enabled the dynamic, conserving status quo.

An End and a Beginning

By late spring, 1992 I had directly engaged in extensive interviews with many of people involved in the genesis and evolution of Science 10, 20, and 30, continued my studies of Foucault's works, and reviewed the journal entries I had made since coming to study at the University of Alberta. Researchers Egon Guba and Yvonne Lincoln (1982) suggest "when various bits of evidence all tend in one direction, that direction assumes far greater credibility" (107). What I discovered when I compared interpretations of interviews and examined documents was the consistent appearance of eight procedures of power and two characteristics of power.

I originally set out three years earlier to try and understand the development of Science 10, 20, and 30 in Alberta. Over time, I became involved in a project seeking to discover the procedures of power that function to prevent curriculum change. This research journey demonstrates we can not separate ourselves from our research act; research is not a straightforward process or a series of steps towards a goal identified before beginning. Research, in my experience, is an exploration into unknown territory, a 'searching again' motivated by hope and possibility of freedom from the destining of technicality. My research journey was conducted primarily through a conversational approach that allowed interpretations to emerge through continual dialogue with Foucault through his work, stories of those involved in the science education curriculum-discourse, documents I gathered re-presented in an events matrix chart, and my own story in the text of my journal entries.

And so we come to the end of my narrative, but to the beginning of hope in our conversation. That summer I left Alberta and my life as a student to become an Assistant Professor of Curriculum Studies at a university in a different province. I first came to the University in Alberta interested in philosophy, became captured by the problem of curriculum change and was enriched—and, as we shall see, changed—through my many experiences. I also was able to discover how power prevented curriculum change in the senior high school science education program in Alberta. Foucault (1984a) prophesied that once the procedures of power in a discourse were discovered, one could find ways to fight the frames that bind us. Sadly, Foucault died before being able to fully explore the practical implications for action arising from his archeological projects. We have the opportunity, however, to continue aspects of Foucault's project of hope and freedom in an education discourse, beginning in Chapter 4 with the discovery of the procedures of power in the evolution of Science 10, 20, and 30 in the science education curriculum-discourse of Alberta.

Chapter 4

Procedures of Power in a Science Education Curriculum-Discourse

Introduction: Wrestling an Angel

Let us continue our discourse on curriculum change with a midrash from the life of the ancient Biblical figure Jacob. A midrash provides, usually through the creation of allegorical narrative, "interpretations of particular words, letters, and modes of writing" (Jacobs 1984, 22) of a discourse, usually Biblical, that lead to certain insights and lessons for living. In our case, an unusual event in the life of Jacob leads to a midrash that provides a metaphor that can take our discussion on the procedures of power in the science education curriculum-discourse in Alberta—and curriculum change in general—a step further.

First, a context for this midrash. Jacob is the grandson of Abraham (ca. 2000 BCE),[1] the Biblical founder of the Jewish people. According to the Bible, God promises Abraham the land of Canaan, present-day Israel, as an inheritance. Patrilinear inheritance was traditional Middle East practice, thus Abraham's grandson Esau inherited the same promise from God. Jacob, Esau's twin, was born moments after his brother. When the twins became young men, Esau, famished from hunting, sold his birth-right to Jacob for some of Jacob's food. Later Esau came to regret this rash act, vowing to kill his brother in order to regain the birth-right. Hearing of his brother's threat, Jacob fled to the East to work for his uncle. Twenty years pass and, according to the Biblical account, God instructs Jacob to move with his wives and children to the land promised to Abraham. Just before crossing the stream that bordered this promised land, Jacob sends messengers asking forgiveness from his brother Esau living just south of the stream. Jacob's messengers return with news: "Your bother Esau is coming to meet you, and four hundred men with him" (Creation House 1973, *New American Standard Bible* (NASB): Genesis 32:6). Jacob was terrified, forced to decide if he should cross the stream, possibly risking his life and the life of his family at the hand of Esau's force the next day, or turn back to the security of his former life. He spends the night in crisis.

It is the odd events of this night that we shall consider. The passage reads:

> Then Jacob was left alone, and a man wrestled with him until daybreak. And when he saw that he had not prevailed against him, he touched the socket of his thigh; so the socket of Jacob's thigh was dislocated while he wrestled with him. Then he said, "Let me go, for the dawn is breaking." But he said, "I will not let you go unless you bless me." So he said to him, "What is your name?" And he said, "Jacob." And he said, "Your name shall no longer be called Jacob, but Israel; for you have striven with God and with men and have prevailed." (Creation House, 49–50: Genesis 32: 24–28)

The man Jacob wrestled with is traditionally interpreted as an angel (Kline 1970) sent by God; Jacob's prowess in wrestling this heavenly messenger led to the blessing of Jacob's name becoming Israel. But this makes little sense. First, Jacob's adversary is called in Hebrew, *'ish*,[2] which refers to a man and not necessarily an angel at all. Second, even if the opponent were angelic, how could Jacob, a mere mortal, actually be winning the match so that, in a sense, the angel has to cheat by supernaturally dislocating Jacob's thigh? Third, how is being named Israel, literally, "wrestles with God," any sort of blessing?

But suppose the man Jacob wrestles was *himself?* A closer look at the Hebrew text explains this midrash for us, shining new light on the passage: In torment, Jacob spends the night alone wrestling with the decision to go ahead and seize the blessing, with associated dangers, or to return to what once was. During this time of intense struggle, Jacob was not able "to prevail," which can also mean, "to understand, or comprehend." For most of the night, Jacob's wrestling did not lead him to find direction. At this dark point in Jacob's life his thigh was "touched." The word for "thigh" can also refer to an innermost place of our being, "touched" more correctly rendered, "struck." In the dark still, Jacob had to strike into his innermost being to find his way. Then, as the sun appeared, the man Jacob's wrestles calls out, "Let me go," or more correctly, "Let me be free." Jacob knows this freedom is possible and he is unwilling to move until a blessing comes to him. What is the blessing? *Change.* Jacob realizes change is possible, but it is not enough to work on the surface: one must wrestle alone in a deep, difficult struggle that may be painful. As the dawn breaks, Jacob faces a question: "What is your name?" The word "name" can also mean "essence"; thus a critical question anyone must face contemplating change emerges from our midrash: "What is your essence?" Jacob can no longer be Jacob; he has chosen to wrestle in his life and in this struggle Jacob becomes a new person. He is no longer Jacob but Israel. The dawn breaks as Jacob limps over to his promised land to claim his inheritance, in some pain from his change but able to face his fear of Esau; Jacob is free.[3] This freedom of change is not easy, but the account of Jacob and the angel teaches us it is possible. But in order for change to be possible we first must wrestle.

Allegory and Post-modern Dis-covering

> It is our business not to supply reality but to invent allusions to the
> conceivable which cannot be presented.
> —Jean-François Leotard, *The Post-Modern Condition* (1984, 81).

Paradox and Possibilities in Post-modern Writing

Many facets of human experience are not easily explained, depicted or presented through printed words. For example, while I know from my experience how I feel when a group understands for the first time an important concept I am teaching, I have trouble writing out precisely what this feeling is. There are elements of joy, to be sure, certainly satisfaction, often surprise, always delight; but these adjectives fail to capture the moment, they are but shadows of something else. I call this inability to exactly capture ideas the poverty of words. The paradox and possibilities of this poverty becomes apparent in the attempt to write text post-modernly.

What does it mean to write post-modernly? To understand the paradox and possibilities of post-modern communication, we first must explore briefly the purpose of text in modernity. One of the central goals of modernity is the achievement through rational inquiry of "a basic, fundamental knowledge" (Madison 1990, x) of an existent world external to self. This research agenda rests on the positive presupposition that this basic, fundamental knowledge *can* be obtained, concomitant with the belief that clear, representative communication of this knowledge is possible, and that this knowledge can be used to further human progress.[4] In modernity writing is thus a technical act involving careful delimitation and definition of terms towards achieving a sense of closure of meaning between the text and the reader. The ultimate goal, then, of communication in modernity is absolute flawless communication between the author and reader via the representation of the world through text. The dream of the modern philosopher, explains Boyne (1990) is a universal language for humankind which would be

> a perfect reflection of the real world. The utter perfection of such a language would be marked by its utter transparency. It would in no way obscure or distort the world which it represented. (91)

This quest for perfect, objective communication is a hallmark of our modern era. While such a task may initially seem futile or even naïve, the belief that "I know what you mean" is more than cliché in modern communication, whether speech or text: We often live out daily the modern assumption that when reading a text or hearing someone speak *we fundamentally are receiving a reasonable version of what the author means and how the world is*. Thus, text is assumed in modernity to be objective in the transfer of meaning.

But is an objective access to meaning through text possible? In the latter part of this century philosophers such as Barthes, Blanchot, Foucault, Gadamer, and Heidegger, to name a few, have challenged the modernist presupposition of a rational representation of meaning. Perhaps the most virulent and consistent attacks on modernistic views of communication have come from the French philosopher Jacques Derrida. Philosopher John Caputo (1987) captures the essence of Derrida's argument well:

> whatever unities of meanings are constituted in natural languages, whatever normalized form experience assumes, whatever institutionalization our practices receive, all are alike vulnerable, alterable, contingent. They have not fallen from the sky; they are structurally, eidetically[5] vulnerable, however much they have tended to gain acceptance. (144)

To argue that communication is an event that is contingent, particular, open and vulnerable to interpretation is to move from modern towards post-modern thinking. I will not attempt to define post-modern, as

Huyssen reminds us, "the term *postmodernism* itself should guard us against such an approach" (236, emphasis hers). Instead, I will use this word as a "breaking away" (236) from modernity within modernity, an attempt to distance discourse from the metaphysical privilege of theoretical thinking (Gruber 1989). From a post-modern perspective, the notion of an objective meaning represented by any text is an "ultimately unacceptable fantasy" (Boyne, 91) with an underlying sinister element. For the notion of objective meaning-making and transfer leads inexorably to the terror of totalizing narratives of the world, or 'metanarratives', that define what may be spoken and how this speaking is to be understood.[6] It is these metanarratives, suggests Foucault, which serve "normalize individuals through increasingly rational means, by turning them into meaningful subjects and docile objects" (Foucault, quoted in Dreyfus and Rabinow 1982, xxvii). So, although somewhat an oversimplification of the post-modern point, Foucault and others argue the modernistic belief in objectivity in communication and realism in representation of the world through text provides opportunity, ultimately, for the objectification of human life, a modern destining of technicality which Heidegger (1977) declared is fundamentally *dangerous*.

Yet we live with each other. And, in the case of our particular discourse, for the sake of our children and the future the need for change in the curriculum-discourse of science education compels us to continue to find post-modern ways to communicate. But can this communicating be meaningful if the words I choose are divested from objective meaning? More to the point of the discourse of this book: If I have discovered what I call 'procedures of power' in a particular curriculum-discourse, and if I believe it important to realize how these procedures operated to secure the status quo and thus prevent change, how can I present these procedures in a way that opens, not closes meaning, in a way that does not present a metanarrative of curriculum change? Can an author speak post-modernly through written words?

This speaking might begin with a break from the tradition of modernism through the rejection of "conventional, academic styles of discourse" (Rosenau 1992, 7) often dependent on rational argumentation and increasing focus to secure meaning. Instead, authors attempting to write post-modernly might employ "audacious and provocative forms of delivery, vital and intriguing elements of genre or style and presentation" (7). To find interruption in the act of reading, parts of words may be surrounded by parentheses, sudden and unexpected use of punctuation and/or breaks in text may appear, graphic arrangements and clever imagery could be used to give the text a sense of performance, rather than objectivity. This variety in presentation is designed to "shock, startle, and unsettle the complacent social science reader" (7) with the intention to "instigate the new and unaccustomed activity of post-modern reading" (7). This reading takes meaning from statement to question, demanding the reader "face up to the difference and difficulty which enter into what we think and do and hope for" (Caputo 1987). In other words, from a post-modern perspective meaning exists in a multiplicity—*as meanings*—between the space formed as questions emerge between the author's presentation and the reader's reading. Text becomes more than words on a page, but an *invitation* to consider what it means to live through constant, never-ending negotiation, revisiting, and reflection on what the author has given to the reader. Thus the post-modern author, according to Lyotard (1984), assumes

> the position of a philosopher: the text he [sic] writes, the works he produces are not in principle governed by preestablished rules, and they cannot be judged according to a determining judgment, by applying familiar categories to the text or to the work. (81)

The purpose of this writing is to invite radical thinking, to provoke and interrupt the reader so that they may discover the difficulty of life in distance from the comforting and dangerous definitions of modernity.

Clearly this writing is a type of ethical practice, for in committing words to a page the post-modern author calls the reader, like Jacob in the introduction of this Chapter, to wrestle an angel, in this case the presented text, with the conviction that in wrestling comes the blessing of change. Post-modern writing is not an exercise in relativism nor is meaning-making anarchistic. It is the exact opposite: a practice that realizes Being is defined, delimited, and determined by modernity and seeks to find, through text, those who will join with the author in breaking what Heidegger calls *Ge-stell*. Writing, then, can be more than mere placment of words on a page; writing can also be seen as a struggle for freedom, reading an engagement in the partnership of this struggle where meaning(s) exist somewhere in-between. The result of this writing is an active, critical, continual conversation that searches and questions, finds and loses; a conversation that is a quest for freedom from the discourses which define who may speak—and what may be said.

Allegory and Metaphor in Post-modern Writing

If post-modern writing is an ethical act to open possibilities for freedom from the destining of modernity, then the author has an obligation to not make the presentation *so* strange or (not)familiar that the reader becomes bored or unable to make any sense of the text. As Caputo (1987) succinctly reminds us in his book, *Radical Hermeneutics*, "the point is to make life difficult, not impossible" (7). Thus the post-modern writer has a paradoxical obligation to the reader: to write in such a way that meaning stays open, but also clearly enough that meaning remains possible. Playing (with)in the text may, for some, allow this opening; for others the presentation may simply be silly. I believe two literary devices enable the task of post-modern writing by opening the familiar: metaphors and narrative allegories.

"Metaphors," notes Jerome Bump (1985) in his delightful essay, *Metaphor, Creativity and Technical Writing*, "enable us to make new connections and see things in a new way" (447). The creation of metaphors opens possibility by prompting questions that further a discourse. For example, the introductions to Chapter 3 and 4 use metaphors to open up questions in our discourse-through-this-book. The introduction to Chapter 3 might prompt the questions such as: How is our modern situation similar to being lost on a precipice in the mountains? Is there significance to using mountains in the metaphor? What might mists depict? Do the voices that helped me find a way off the precipice suggest where hope may lie in our modern situation? In this chapter the introduction uses a metaphorical style called a midrash. Again questions arise: What might the Angel in this metaphor represent in a curriculum-discourse? What acts might wrestling represent? And, foreshadowing Chapter 5: How is becoming a new person related to curriculum change?

But sustaining a metaphor past a few pages can be difficult, although I have demonstrated elsewhere (Blades 1995) how a metaphor can be used to suggest possibilities for change in curriculum-discourse. In my effort to disclose the procedures of power I discovered in a curriculum-discourse I turn in this chapter to a literary method that allows a longer presentation in text while retaining openness: the allegory. Allegories are a method of presentation in which an idea, person or event stands for itself and/or something else. Derived from the Greek *'allegorein'*, which means to speak as to imply something else, allegories have provided throughout time a way for authors to introduce critique to discourse while avoiding premature closure of meaning. The exploits of Don Quixote, discoveries of Gulliver, Christian's journey as a pilgrim or the obsession of Ahab to find the Great Whale are but a few of the masterful allegories used by authors to present to the public an invitation to discuss something else. For example, while Orwell's *Animal Farm* (1945) can be read as a child-like story of animals taking over a farm, readers quickly see this work is also an allegory of something else.

Given the richness of and potential of allegories to open conversation, it is perhaps surprising allegories are rare in education writings about curriculum change. Perhaps the dangers of using allegories have encouraged a cautious stance to the use of allegory in understanding curriculum. After all, the point of the allegory may be missed entirely, or perhaps the readers might read into the allegory representations of people, actions, and events the author did not intend—But, wait! These concerns are modernistic. The post-modern author is not responsible for meaning, only for initiating conversations of critique. The reader must consider the extent the destining of modernity influences their response to the presentation of text. Allegories help the author say something else, immediately allowing questioning to surface, rather than closing conversation. For example, I could have chosen for Chapter 4 of this book to present by list and subsequent elaboration the procedures of power I discovered through the research approach outlined in Chapter 3. Certainly such listing is easier than the struggle to develop a post-modern way to write. But a more academic or traditional presentation could be easily appropriated by a modernistic reader as a list of the factors to be considered to ensure a curriculum change proceeds as planned. This appropriation flows from the assumption the procedures I name are generic to other curriculum-discourses, thus (in)forming structuralistic metanarratives about curriculum change. In this way, the destining restriction of possibilities for curriculum change I discover might be served by my presentation of procedures of power in a curriculum-discourse! The only way out of this modern encircling is to find a post-modern way of sharing these procedures, a path of interruption and (hopefully) surprise; a pathway that leads to thinking and questions of critique, not closure and meta-theorizing.

Entering into this type of writing requires me to wrestle as I write, to struggle to find a way to allow openness and stimulate questions as I share the procedures of power I have found. Why bother? I agree with Lyotard (1984) that for too long "we have paid a high enough price for the nostalgia of the whole and the one, for the reconciliation of the concept and the sensible, of the transparent and the communicable experience (81). He continues by calling for the direct challenge to the activity of *Ge-stell*: "let us wage a war on totality; let us be witnesses to the unpresentable; let us activate the differences and save the honor of the name" (82).

To engage in this most post-modern agenda I present the procedures of power I discovered operating in a curriculum-discourse through an allegory of a Quest. The purpose of presenting what I have discovered in allegorical form is to extend an invitation to journey together as we wrestle with an angel that has for too long limited the freedom to change by defining who may speak and what may be said in a curriculum-discourse. To engage in this wrestling, I revisit through an allegorical story-telling the evolution of Science 10, 20, and 30 in Alberta. This visitation is a repetition (Kierkegaard 1983) where our conversation is "recollected forward" (131) through allegorical telling; that is; we recollect the events in the evolution of the Science 10, 20, and 30 programs so that we can move to laying bare the procedures of power at work in the science education curriculum-discourse of Alberta. In this movement, allegorical presentation becomes part of the trachealization of a discourse, a discovering of *Ge-stell* and, hopefully, a revelation of possibilities for change. The allegory that follows of a Quest within a Kingdom is thus an invitation to enter into a conversation of critique, a challenge, in the words of philosopher Maxine Greene, to "surpass the given and look at things as if they could be otherwise" (1988, 3).

The Quest

The Kingdom was the envy of the entire world, or so we believed. For decades past living memory the Servants of the King worked with characteristic zeal and dedication to transform this realm into a modern, efficient machine. No resource was left to chance; no tree left unmarked for processing, no stone unturned; every idea was exploited for material gain. Through technological innovation these Servants helped build public confidence in the King's doctrine of *Prosperity Through Progress*. All citizens had homes, places in society, and expectations of possibilities for their children. The future seemed secure and safe as Servants continued on their relentless course to discern "the knowledge of all causes, and secret motions of things; and the enlarging of human empire, to the effecting of all things possible" (Bacon 1942, 288). We continued to live confident in the King's ability and the collective wisdom of the Servants to solve any problem that might threaten the realm. But then children began to disappear.

No one knows why or where they go. At first, symptoms such as "the decline of literacy, the lack of scientific understanding, the deplorable state of physical fitness, [and] the cancerous growth of the video industry," (Borgmann 1992, 10) seemed to implicate some disease affected the minds of our children. From these initial symptoms the condition became worse as children began to wander in a state of numbness the well-designed streets of the Kingdom. Content with the music of their Fathers, the affected children continued to drift until they became, by almost imperceptible degrees, invisible. I should add not all the children in our Kingdom were affected by the strange malady, making an understanding of this bizarre phenomenon difficult. Some children were able to grow up and thus find a meaningful location in the structure of the Kingdom. But distressing numbers of our children became afflicted by the new, strange condition and, before they could find their place in the Kingdom, these children disappeared.

The situation had reached the point of crisis. Now completely dependent on the vast infrastructure composed of the often inexplicable and intricate scientific workings of the myriad of Servants, the Kingdom—indeed, the very power of the King—was being increasingly challenged by the attrition of aging Servants! As children continued to disappear it became clear somewhere in the hierarchy of the Kingdom that if this trend were to continue there would be less children available to apply for a career as Servants to the King, or even to take their rightful place as citizens in the Kingdom. Some Scholars even argued publicly that at present rates, *all* the children in the Kingdom might disappear in only a few generations. While the general public did not generally believe in these gloomy predictions, still grumblings of concern could be heard in the taverns, town halls, and public meeting places. Some citizens for the very first time boldly suggested the King's power was limited, or even that the King did not know everything important to know. Everyone agreed something had to be done to stop children from disappearing.

Rumors are the King himself consulted with the finest, brightest Servants about the strange malady, but these Servants were not able to explain the phenomenon, much less propose a cure. For a few decades Servants encouraged the initial training of children in Servanthood. The results, despite massive investments of funds and personnel were dismal; in fact, their efforts led to an increase in the rate at which children disappeared! The Priests[7] of the King's Cathedral, responsible to ensure children become active, willing members of the Kingdom through formal instruction, searched their ancient books on childhood phenomena. No reference to the disappearance of children could be found. Government officials met and deliberated, sometimes directly involving the Priests teaching children the basics of Servanthood. Through these meetings it became clear no solution to the disappearance of children could be found among previous tactics or strategies. A few Cathedral officials and Scholars in the Kingdom dared to suggest the resources of the Kingdom were not enough to solve the problem of disappearing children. After much discussion, the Cathedral executive was persuaded to organize a small team of experts charged with the task of traveling outside the Kingdom to see if a cure for the disappearance of the children might exist in another realm. And so the Quest for The Answer to the problem of disappearing children began.

The Kingdom had been so successful dealing with problems that pathways to other kingdoms seemed to exist in mostly ancient legends or the speculation of philosophers. Cathedral officials had maps that led from the center of the Kingdom but the maps were surprisingly vague at the margins, at least to those who now wanted to travel to this area and beyond. Still, the few Cathedral officials who initiated the Quest believed with firm conviction those on the Quest would be able to find the edge of the Kingdom and answers to the problem of disappearing children in the lands beyond.

I was late joining the group that actually set out on the Quest, delayed by my apprenticeship as a Scholar. I knew a team from the Cathedral had formed to begin the Quest and I was aware they had reached the first fork in the King's Highway that led away from the center of the Kingdom. My expertise as a Priest and experience with the Servanthood, together with my knowledge of the extensive and often bewildering roadways in the central part of the Kingdom, led to an invitation to join in the Quest. Like many of the Priesthood, I was deeply concerned over the disappearance of children in our Kingdom and gladly accepted the chance to play a role in the success of the Quest.

Before departing I thought it might be wise to take some items with me. I estimated the journey to another kingdom would be fairly straightforward, so I packed lightly. Aside from the usual traveling necessities and a small tent, I also brought three scholarly books, a notebook to keep a journal of my travels on the Quest, and a general map of the Kingdom. I left my home on a bright, sunny day and immediately set out on the main road that led away from the center of the Kingdom.

After a few days I found the group that had embarked on the Quest sitting at the junction where the King's Highway forks. The group was smaller than I expected, composed mostly of a few Career Associates from the Cathedral executive and a handful of Priests seconded to the Quest. This friendly, cooperative and highly talented group greeted me with enthusiasm and invited me to consider the maps they had brought with them for this part of the journey. I admitted the maps were next to useless, not even indicating the fork in the pathway they had just encountered. Prior to my arrival I discovered a major map-making company was supposed to play a key role in the Quest. I was approached by the company to help in the production of a map that would be useful to those on the Quest. Oddly, then, I found myself participating in the Quest and trying to help produce a map for the journey at the same time. To make the challenge even more difficult, no one involved in the Quest knew the exact route out of the

Kingdom, although everyone agreed that working together we would find it.[8]

When I arrived I immediately recognized where the group was located. The fork to the right was called the Great Loop. In a gentle arc this roadway directed travelers back to the city in the center of the Kingdom via a scenic route along the shores of the Great Lake just outside the central city. The map I brought with me indicated the group must travel along the left fork in the road if they are to leave the Kingdom. I was a little nervous showing my map to the group since the traditional route, and indeed the road more often traveled, lay to the right. However, when I showed them my map the group from the Cathedral "loved it and seemed relieved to see it finally on track with what they wanted" (Journal entry, March 25, 1989). I note later in the same journal entry, "it feels good to have helped and to be involved in introducing a curriculum I believe is an important first step towards a science education orientation which is progressive and a better reflection of the way science is being reconceptualized in the world." I joined the party and walked with them along the left fork in the pathway, confident we were traveling on the correct direction towards The Answer.

Procedures of Power in a Curriculum-Discourse

> Power is not an institution, and not a structure; neither is it a certain strength we are endowed with; it is the name that one attributes to a complex strategical situation in a particular society.
> —Michel Foucault, *The History of Sexuality, Volume 1* (1990, 93).

We had not traveled far along the left fork when I saw someone standing by the side of the path. It was Michel Foucault. I recognized him from a picture on one of his books. No one else in the party paid any attention to him and simply walked by, but I knew from his writings that this Scholar had spent time in the Lonely Mountains at the edge of the Kingdom. These mountains totally enclose the Kingdom and our team would have to eventually find a trail through the mountains to travel to a new kingdom. Surely Foucault would know the pathway that led to new realms, or at least we could benefit from his mountaineering experience. I stayed to visit, intending to catch up to the team later. In Chapter 3 I described how the visit became longer than I anticipated at first and how this philosopher came to travel with me on my journey in the Quest. Thinking back, this rather chance meeting became quite significant as I began to make sense of events during the Quest through conversations with Foucault. This sense-making is, of course, my own and possibly someone else would discover a different set of procedures of power that affected the direction and success of the Quest.

The previous chapter explains how, in conversation with Foucault, I discovered procedures of power that defined the progress of the Quest. This trachealization of a curriculum-discourse revealed two general strategies of power: First, procedures determined who could speak in the curriculum-discourse, defining who was able to take part in the Quest. Second, procedures determined what could be said in the curriculum-discourse, defining the route of the Quest. As we shall see, these strategies, possible through particular procedures of power, formed a dynamic system of inclusion and exclusion destined to play a decisive role in the success of the Quest.

Destining Who Can Speak in a Curriculum-Discourse

The Modification and Legitimization of Hierarchies

Foucault and I struggled to catch up to the others on the Quest, now a considerable distance away. As we journeyed toward the team, Foucault asked me the purpose of this journey. I replied that we are traveling out of the Kingdom to find The Answer to the problem of disappearing children. But, I confessed, to our knowledge no one has actually made such a journey successfully. I turned to Foucault and asked, "You've been in the mountains at the edge of the Kingdom. Is there other realm beyond?" I thought I heard him reply that there was, but I could not hear him clearly for the noise behind us.

It was a small, but loud, group of Priests. They had heard of the Quest and were attempting to catch up to the original Quest team now just visible on the horizon ahead. They ran right past Foucault and me. We hurried on to join the team, arriving to intense arguing between the team from the Cathedral and the Priests. One Priest claimed the Quest was a "trivial" way to deal with the problem of disappearing children (McGeachy 1989, 3). A leader of the group of Priests pointed out that, in the opinion of a certain group of Priests who met to consider the potential success of the Quest, the maps the team were using were hopelessly inadequate. The leader insisted that more map-making was needed before the group ventured further.[9] Another Priest was calling loudly for the team to abandon the Quest altogether (Armstrong 1989). Clearly these Priests were upset with the team. As I listened to the concerns of the Priests I realized that despite working within the Cathedral organization, these particular Priests embraced a separate identity from the Cathedral because of their work with children. This defining gave the Priests the freedom to express their conviction that the team had made a wrong decision by taking the left fork in the King's Highway, thus challenging the authority of the existing hierarchy in the Cathedral organization.

The arguments quickly became personal. Team members suggested Priests had lost confidence in the rightness of the Cathedral executive who were, after all, there to serve the Priesthood and the children in the Kingdom. The Priests countered that only they, closest to the children in the daily activities of the Cathedral, know what is best for the children. Each Priest then tried to impress upon the team the importance of taking the road to the Village that lay ahead, convinced this route would best lead to The Answer. The team members, convinced they were already on the correct route, declared they would not take the right turn ahead that led to the Village. Tension mounted and for a moment neither group spoke. Finally, the team turned and continued on the journey. The Priests returned to their cities, but not before shouting their intention to force the Cathedral organization to change completely the direction of the Quest.

We continued the Quest in relative silence for the next few days. As we walked, the map-making company strove to produce innovative maps to help guide the team. We had to consult these maps often, choosing to remain on the left fork of the King's Highway even though this route was traditionally only used in the movement of workers and machinery to and from the industrialized western regions of the Kingdom. Still, our map-makers assured us this route would lead us out of the Kingdom. After only a few days one of the members of the group saw in the distance the very peaks of the Lonely Mountains, a certain sign we were moving steadily away from the center of the Kingdom. As our view of the mountains increased, so too our optimism that we would reach the borders of the Kingdom within a week. Foucault, however, continued to be in a somewhat somber mood, souring a little the hope I felt at this part of the journey.

Bureaucratization. We had just passed the junction to the Village, when a foul wind began to blow from the western regions of the Kingdom. While we knew the King's factories lay directly to the west, few citizens, unless employed directly by the factories, ever saw the factories, much less smelled the polluted air created by the furnaces that ran constantly. The stench was, at times, unbearable and sometimes we found we could only breathe if we walked backwards, facing the center of the Kingdom. Still, the team was resolute and no one talked about turning back. Our maps indicated that every step on this part of the King's Highway brought us closer to the river on the northern plains that, according to legend, marked the boundary between the beginning of the Lonely Mountains and the end of the King's realm.

After only a few days we were met at a turn in the road by a large group of officials from the Cathedral. One of the Cathedral executives told us that a problem in the Quest had developed. Apparently some of the Priests involved in the challenge to the team early in the journey contacted key members of the Servanthood to share concerns about the direction of the Quest. These Servants then contacted commanders in the King's army. Sadly, in our Kingdom there is no great love between Military and Cathedral organizations, although both institutions serve King and Kingdom well. Military commanders seized the opportunity to complain openly about the Quest in village squares and marketplaces throughout the Kingdom. Understandably, the executive of the Cathedral was concerned about this latest development and decided to "invest a lot more resources towards development" of the Quest.[10] These resources included increased funding and involvement of Cathedral personnel in the development of the Quest so that the Cathedral organization could ensure the team continued to travel in the right direction.

The result of this investment was increasing involvement of Cathedral executives in the movement of the team. In some cases, notes one team member, senior Career Associates with the Cathedral "became directly involved" in dictating the route of the team.[11] Another team member complained that as conflict about the Quest became more public, "more and more managers were put in charge of the new programs, complicating what had to be done."[12] This bureaucratization led to logistic problems in map-making and planning the route for the Cathedral team as "so many different levels in the bureaucracy between [names deleted] and the program managers have to be gone through."[13]

Increasing bureaucratic organization of the Quest also served to reassure everyone in the Kingdom that the Cathedral was fully in control of the direction of the Quest. All new maps had to now be approved by the Cathedral executive who collectively decided to not allow further travel by the team unless it was "well thought out, well resourced, and ready to go."[14] Over this part of the journey Cathedral officials began to accompany the original team members, informed by runners that continually brought messages to the team from the Cathedral executive.

A message came a few days later that the team was to take the first possible right turn. Those traveling with the original team found the turn a kilometer up the road: a path that led into the King's forest. Original team members complained about the order, pointing out their success so far in finding a way out of the Kingdom; also the team had traveled beyond the King's factories in the west, and the air was now much more clear. The turn towards the forest was only a narrow path, hardly a road leading out of the Kingdom. Using runners, the turn in direction was confirmed by the growing bureaucracy of managers, directors, and consultants at the Cathedral involved in the Quest, thus "making the voices of the [names deleted] somewhat more quiet" in future discussions about the direction of the Quest.[15]

Silence. As we turned to enter the forest we paused to look one last time at the mountains, now clearly in view at the horizon of the Kingdom. Some of the original team members shared my concern the path we were on would lead us right back to the center of the Kingdom, although with our new companions everyone felt uneasy questioning the wisdom of the Cathedral. A few of the original members of the team quietly asked one of the runners to deliver a letter to some Scholars. This letter informed the Scholars of the situation and asked for support in helping the team return to the previous route. The team members were convinced these Scholars would help since "they have some knowledge that is unique to their line of work that the teaching force and general public could benefit from."[16]

The Scholars considered the maps and communications sent from the team, and returned a message stating the sentiment that they felt "it would not be appropriate"[17] to defend the original direction of the team at this time. At the campfire that evening I could feel the disappointment of the team. As we commiserated, one team member hypothesized that perhaps the Scholars did not want to seem to side against the Servanthood now that the Quest was beginning to develop a poor public image.[18] But it was more than this. In a later communication, a Scholar explained that among their kind "there was a lot of concern" the map produced during the Quest was "not as good as it could be or should be."[19] The Scholars, while generally in favor of the idea of the Quest clearly held reservations about the way the journey was headed.

The following morning the pathway led us deeper into the forest. Previous to this turn the mountains had been visible, but now we were surrounded by a seemingly endless sea of trees. Each tree carried a small sign indicating its fate; Servants had been here before us. The day was beautiful and warm and I cheerfully began a conversation with Foucault as we joined the others in the Quest. I asked him why the Scholars seemed to be unwilling to help us in the Quest. To this question Foucault characteristically asked another: Could silence be "part of the strategies that underlie and permeate discourse?" (Foucault 1990, 27). I was not sure, so I asked my companion if silence could be considered another form of speaking. Before he could respond to this idea, a messenger arrived.

It was bad news. The military had announced in every part of the Kingdom that an influential group of Servants had just withdrawn their support of the Quest. I thought this inconsequential since it seemed to me this support was never there in the first place, but other team members were devastated. Even worse, in a scathing public announcement these Servants even went so far as to publicly question the wisdom of the Cathedral executive to initiate the Quest in the first place. At this point it certainly seemed that the Cathedral was "clearly losing the public relations battle."[20]

The messenger gave me a note. A Scholar had written to me, explaining that the rejection of the Quest by these Servants represented a "very powerful signal" to the Cathedral that the

Servanthood, and some of the Scholars, "did not like what was going on."[21] I shared the note with Foucault. Certainly the silence of the community of Scholars at this critical time in the Quest supported the notice of rejection by the Servants. This silence effectively gave support to a shift in the hierarchy of authority for the Quest away from the Cathedral towards the Servants in the Kingdom. Military assistance helped legitimate this new hierarchical arrangement with the general public. I looked at Foucault, smiled, and said, "There are many ways to speak, are there not? Perhaps silence is one of them." He nodded, but then turned to me and asked why, if I was so concerned about the change in direction of the Quest, I did not return with the messenger and complain to the Military about the actions of the Servants.

Me? The question was unkind! I mean, I believed in the Quest as much as anyone in the team, but I was only along to help prepare maps, to observe how the Quest was going and to record this story. At any rate, why would the Military listen to *me*, a mere apprentice to Scholarship? I turned to Foucault and asked, "Why me?" He replied that even an apprentice Scholar "can operate and struggle at the general level of that régime of truth which is so essential to the structure and functioning of our society" (Foucault 1980, 132). I had no idea what he meant and was offended by the answer. Later I wrote in my journal that my conversations with Foucault are causing "a lot of conflict" (Journal entry, April 2, 1991) as I was beginning to realize that I too am "part of the apparatus" of silence (same entry). For the first time in my journey, I regretted bringing Foucault along. It would not be the last.

Active Marginalization
Everyone on the Quest knew there would be challenges, but we were not prepared for how our days in the forest seemed to stretch out until every hour felt like a day and every minute an hour. Still we traveled on. Days passed, relieved only by the occasional representative from the map-making company. Even these interruptions proved to be more a source of irritation as the maps shown us were increasingly vague. Even worse, delays in the arrival of maps forced the company to stop and camp, sometimes for days, before proceeding. A constant light drizzle and cloudy skies only added to our ill humor.

When a representative came wondering if we had any ideas on how future maps should look, some team members vented their frustration, accusing the company of not caring about the Quest at all. The representative acknowledged the business interests of the company, but added that, once involved, everyone in the company had come to believe in the Quest for the sake of "the teachers, and for the kids."[22] It was odd, but during the increase of criticism and hardship during the Quest team members and I had forgotten the original reason we left on the Quest. We began concerned about children in the Kingdom, but events had destined us to think more about the concerns of the Priests and Servants in the Kingdom until, as one team member put it, "the voices of students were completely pushed to the margins."[23]

Voices Without a Voice. Perhaps it was a return to thinking about the disappearing children that led me to begin to see and then hear phantoms in the forest. The next day I thought I saw someone, a child perhaps, standing between the trees. When I turned to look again, the apparition was gone. All day long figures seemed to be just out of the range of actual vision. I tried looking straight ahead, but then suddenly I would catch—what was it? There! Again, perhaps a glimpse, then the phantom disappeared. I was not frightened by these visions, but distracted. My colleagues, however, seemed to not notice these ghostly appearances at all.

We reached a small stream. It was a pleasant site, and the waters of the stream were cool, clear, and unpolluted—a rarity in the Kingdom these days. We all agreed this stream must be a tributary of the Great River which, travelers say, flows beside the Last Road encircling the Kingdom. We drank freely from the waters, and took a much needed rest. But I could not sleep. As I lay in the grass, I kept hearing the unmistakable sound of children speaking. I sat up, but all I could see were phantoms in the trees. I concentrated my whole being on listening. Then I heard gentle voices, speaking quietly but clearly and with accord, telling me that we should take the next path out of the forest. No one else seemed to be listening to these voices, although team members did comment on the haunting melodies of wind in the trees and the comforting sound of the water falling over the stones lining the stream. Perhaps that was all I was hearing. I turned to Foucault; he was listening intently. "What do you hear?" I asked. He replied that he heard the voices of those "excluded while being transmitted a knowledge traditional in nature, obsolete, 'academic' and not directly tied to the needs and problems of today" (Foucault 1989a, 65). "But they have something to tell us," I added, and I shared with Foucault how these voices shared with me a way to get out of the forest and back towards the mountains.

These voices without a voice, as I came to think of the phantom words in the forest, were correct in their prediction. After leaving the stream we came to a small junction. One path headed north while the path we were on curved just up ahead. I suggested that the north trail would be the path children might want us to take (Blades 1992a, 1995). But among the team the "concept that student voices might be an integral part of a curriculum-discourse never seemed to be considered."[24] Unwilling to risk controversy again, the majority of members elected to follow the directive from the Cathedral executive and not deviate from the trail they were on. I was told not to worry, since there must be many ways out of the Kingdom. I was not at all certain of this, but conceded the decision to move on might work out. We continued on our way, leaving behind the pathway north.

Personal Invasion. Very quickly the path in the forest widened and began to arc towards the south. I dreaded this movement, for according to my maps we were heading directly back towards the center of the Kingdom. I did admit, though, to a feeling of relief as the sky cleared and the pathway became a small road. The team began to make excellent time, hiking with determination that soon the mountains would appear once again on the horizon.

The road ended abruptly at a large circular clearing in the forest. We knew from popular description we had arrived at King's Clearing. Here nearby villagers met for games, fellowship, and to discuss how to implement policies of the King. A welcoming place, to be sure, but we all knew the large highway at the opposite end of the Clearing led directly south to the Great Loop and on to the Central City in the Kingdom. Clouds began to cover the sky and discouragement settled on the group as we slowly realized our journey in the forest had directed us away from our original objective.

To add to the grief of the team, messengers arrived almost every hour that day with updates on the controversy surrounding the Quest. Far from dying down, as we all had come to hope, resistance to the

Quest was spreading throughout the Kingdom. Military commanders had worked with some of the Servanthood to spread the message that the Quest was somehow contributing to the problem of disappearing children! This latest gossip was disheartening to everyone connected with the Quest. That evening military commanders even began to send their own messengers to the team in the clearing. These newest messengers told of how the entire Cathedral organization was quickly losing support for the Quest. That night it began to rain.

The weather became worse the next day. Everyone became cold and wet, our misery heightened by the constant and sometimes unbelievable messages about the controversy surrounding the Quest. We were shocked when the King's physicians and engineers publicly denounced the Quest. Dire warnings of bridges collapsing or widespread failure of health care in the Kingdom were predicted should the Quest continue. Citizens, understandably concerned if misinformed, became increasingly critical of the Cathedral organization, and the Chief Executive himself. There were even reports of the Military hanging throughout the Kingdom posters making fun of the Quest. It was if the entire Kingdom had turned against the Quest. Team leaders sent a message to the Cathedral asking for directions. The Chief Executive of the Cathedral sent word back that he had formed a committee with representatives from the many interest groups critical of the Quest. The purpose of this committee, claims the Chief Executive, "was to move critics into the zone of consultation" to "ensure the programs move ahead."[25] Until this committee made its final recommendations concerning the Quest, we were told to simply stay where we were. The Cathedral sent us waterproof tents and told us to make camp.

Although hard to believe, a southerly wind began to accompany the rain, making it very difficult to even set up tents in the clearing. Team leaders ensured everyone else had a warm, dry tent to enter before finally working on their own tents. These leaders were becoming very soaked and I worried for their health. By some cruel twist of events, these leaders had also become the direct targets, often in a personal and pungent way, for criticism by Priests and citizens about the Quest. One of the team leaders shared with me how some messages involved "personal assaults on his professionalism" as a Priest.[26] A team member later recalled how these messages "placed tremendous pressures" on this leader's family.[27] Waiting in the Clearing during the intense criticism of the Quest was "an awful time" according to a team leader.[28] This leader agreed with my observations that the Quest was now invading our personal lives, to the extent that criticisms challenged the "very essence of who we are and who we are becoming."[29] This personal invasion led to a type of "paralysis"[30] as the discourse about the Quest turned increasingly negative. It was if a force was pushing the voices of the team to the margins, while allowing other voices to dominate the agenda of the Quest. For the first time, members of the Quest, including the community of map-makers, began to have doubts the Quest would ever succeed. One member of the map-making community recalls during this time lying "awake at night," often from a sense of "burnt out" over the endeavor.[31] But what did we expect, really? As this map-maker observed, all of us on the Quest were but a "handful of pioneers who were trying to change something by doing something new."[32] Perhaps the odds were against us from the start of the Quest.

The Voice of Critics. That night a message came that the Chief Executive's committee might save the Quest after all. The rain let up a little so we lit a bonfire and began to feel hopeful. Out of the dark came two figures towards our encampment, a Priest and a village doctor. We recognized the Priest immediately. He had been a leader of the group that first met us on the King's Highway. The doctor we knew by reputation as a severe critic of the Quest and instrumental in raising public awareness and criticism of the Quest. Neither men were invited to sit by the fire.

The Priest spoke first. He had traveled from the southern city in the Kingdom to meet directly with the team on the Quest. He expressed concerns that the direction of the Quest was "flawed in several ways."[33] According to the Priest's recollection of this meeting, team members were unwilling to "admit it's all wrong" because "people have made a reputation with the new programs."[34] I observed that everyone around the campfire did not acknowledge the concerns of this Priest, choosing to ignore him totally. Yet the concerns this Priest shared that evening were not about the Quest itself, but the direction the team was traveling. For example, the Priest had examined the maps prepared for the Quest carefully and from his experience with children this Priest had come to believe one entire part of the map was completely useless. But the Priest was not invited to sit by the fire and discuss these concerns, but dismissed with a curt "we'll take this under advisement" by the team.[35] The Priest left in disgust and I walked with him across the clearing. I asked him if he was all right. "I'm not argumentative at all," he told me, "this whole thing has taken a helluva [sic] toll out of me."[36] I was struck how even some of the voices critical of the Quest were seemingly pushed to the margins of our curriculum-discourse, this time by the team on the Quest. I asked the Priest if he intended to keep his concerns forthcoming. He turned to me and told me that, for the sake of the children he would continue to speak, for "it has to be done."[37] He left and vanished into the night.

The doctor was faring somewhat better. He had been invited to share his concerns, but by the time I returned to the campfire I saw that in addition to team members and the doctor, a host of Military messengers were also gathered around the campfire. These messengers were charged by their commanders to run back to cities and villages, reporting on the latest developments in the saga of the Quest. The doctor began the argument with a statement that the force of public and non-Cathedral professional opinion was against the present direction of the Quest. A team leader suggested that had not these criticisms developed in the first place, the team probably would be in another kingdom by now, ready to return with The Answer to the problem of disappearing children. The doctor countered the present maps of the Quest are "illogically fragmented mishmash" (Freedman, quoted in T. Byfield 1989a, 44) that are useless in finding any way out of the Kingdom. He told us that without meaningful input from the Servanthood, any further attempt at a Quest is "fundamentally flawed" (Freedman 1989a, 5). The team leader countered that the Quest is not designed to serve only the Servanthood, but to solve the problem of disappearing children in the Kingdom. At any rate, only the Servants in the central city rejected the Quest, Servants in the southern city seemed to be generally supportive. In a reassuring voice, the leader reiterated that he and the entire team were committed to finding the best possible route to the next kingdom. But the doctor voiced his doubt the Cathedral "even knows what that is" (Freedman, quoted in V. Byfield 1989b, 44). This final comment sent messengers running throughout the kingdom and ended the argument; the doctor was ignored.

The doctor left that evening convinced more than ever his concerns were valid and important and I had the unmistakable feeling we would hear more from this physician. What struck me about the conversation around the campfire was how the team members and the doctor were not really arguing about the same thing. The team interpreted the doctor to be challenging the idea of the Quest, when this doctor seemed to be voicing his concern for the direction of the Quest. Earlier in the argument the doctor had stated that, in his opinion, no one questioned having a Quest (Freedman 1989a, 4), but there were valid criticisms about where this Quest was headed. A few years later, an executive in the Cathedral organization told me that it was unfortunate this doctor was "not responded to properly."[38] When I asked him what he meant, he replied that had the Cathedral "moved totally towards what he wanted we would be much farther ahead" in the goal of the Quest.[39] This executive recalls that while the doctor did present some rational and important points but, because the doctor was cast as an antagonist to the Quest, these points were not considered thoroughly by the Cathedral organization. This was unfortunate, notes the executive, since the voice of this doctor could have provided a " a very strong support" for the Quest if given the chance.[40] But again another voice of critique in the drama surrounding the Quest was pushed to the margins and eventually the ideas of this physician, some very legitimate, were left out of the discourse at that time.

The Strategy of Consultation

Weeks passed and the rains slowed somewhat, but even on the days when it was not raining the sky stayed cloudy. In hushed whispers between tents team members began to predict the end of the Quest. Then messengers came to me, sent by the map-making company. The Cathedral executive had decided to terminate my services as map-maker. I was deeply hurt, doubly because I would have preferred executives talk to me first. Now *my* voice was being marginalized and I did not like this one bit. Upon reflection, however, I realized this cancellation gave me the chance to resume my studies towards becoming a Scholar. I wrote in my journal that the entire team seems to be fighting a force determined to prevent the Quest. I wondered about this force: "How can we fight it? Perhaps with critical reflection—something dormant in the lives of children and absent in the development of the new programs" (Journal entry, November 18, 1989).

A new year dawned, and with it notice that the team was to move out of the clearing. I was very happy for the team members, but the news was a mixed blessing. While the Quest out of the Kingdom would officially continue, the team was ordered to use only well marked, traditional routes. This meant leaving the Clearing by the south road. Still, heartened to be moving again, team members quickly broke camp and set out with renewed vigor. The team was resolute, determined to find a way out of the Kingdom even using traditional roadways. Walking briskly, the team was able to cover distance well and in a few hours came to a major crossroads.

Signs indicated which way to travel. The road to the right, Village Way, was a well-used road that led, presumably, to some village in the Kingdom. Straight ahead was a double lane highway that led due south to the famous Great Loop that ran around Great Lake at the center of the Kingdom. The road to the left, with the odd name of Theme Way, was obviously little used. As the team considered their options, one team leader noticed a map lying by the signposts. Examining the map, the leader could not believe his good fortune. Written in some foreign script, the map suggested traveling the left road would take travelers eventually to the Mountains. The team decided to travel along this road.

Before venturing out, a strategy session was called. There was general agreement the announcement by the Chief Executive of the Cathedral that the Cathedral would reconsider the direction, but not the mandate, of the Quest gave the team the "clean slate" they needed to continue.[41] To deal with any future resistance by the Priesthood, team members planned "quite a long period of consultation" with Priests using questionnaires and meetings.[42] In addition, team leaders decided to dispatch members of the team to every city, village, farm and factory to secure support of the public and Priests for this new turn in the direction of the Quest. Borrowing from tactics used by the Servanthood, the Military was asked to help support the new direction.

A month later the team reassembled a few kilometers down Theme Way. I was given permission to accompany the group as an apprentice Scholar. At the time I was not at all sure my studies related to the journey of the team, but I was quite glad to remain in contact with members of the team, many who had become personal friends. Foucault, now a constant companion during my time apprenticing for Scholarship, also accompanied me during this part of the journey.

I met up with the team and immediately asked how the consultative process fared. A team member shared with me it was a learning experience: "That taught me that a lot of people didn't bother, of those groups who said they were interested."[43] When groups so critical of the previous direction of the Quest were asked for possible directions of the Quest, this member found that "of the many that did respond, mostly they wanted everything!"[44] The team member wondered, "so where does that leave you? Maybe the important thing is to provide the opportunity."[45] Another team member readily agreed with this assessment of the process of consultation.

Apparently the Priests that met with this member of the team were not able to give many constructive comments about the future direction of the Quest.[46] While some Priests still remained suspicious about the intentions of the team members, every team member I spoke with felt that at least consultation had dealt effectively with potential resistance by the Priesthood, paving the way for the Quest to continue. A team leader explained that conflict during the early part of the Quest caused "an unwinding" that led to "complete loss of control" of the journey by Cathedral executives.[47] The leader explained that the team decided to change tactics, giving the appearance of listening to the voices of the Priests so that the Quest could continue without interruption.[48] I added that "in this way control is retained through collaboration."[49] The leader agreed, but noted that initially consultation was designed to find "a vision everyone could buy into."[50] This leader discovered though, like other team members, that when asked the Priesthood proposed every possible direction for the Quest. This lack of clear direction from the Priests led the team leaders to believe the Cathedral team had essentially a "carte blanche to make the decisions" on which direction to continue the Quest.[51]

As my interviews continued it became increasingly clear that the team had been sincerely interested in the opinion of the Priests and Servants, but also that consultation was used as a strategy of political maneuvering to affirm a direction for the Quest already chosen by the Cathedral executive and Quest team leadership.[52] "As a procedure of power," a Servant told me later, "a ritual of compromise" was used to make the Cathedral organization "look good" while ensuring the accepted direction is "what they wanted all along."[53] While an organized conspiracy did not seem to exist, at least on a conscious level, nevertheless consultation ensured the Quest would proceed under the control of the Cathedral. Thus, the hierarchy of authority for the Quest shifted back to the Cathedral through the procedure of consultation.

But not entirely. Ironically, consultation also opened the possibility for a conservative response. The Chief Executive of the Cathedral expressed his concern that consultation also allowed conservative critics to demand the team take more traditional routes on the Quest, possibly frustrating efforts to find a way out of the Kingdom.[54] Consultation also proved costly. One executive in the Cathedral organization recalls that during the consultation period "we were desperately concerned about the delay"[55] since children were still disappearing at an alarming rate.

Foucault had listened in while I completed my interviews. As we walked with the team down Theme Way on this newest turn in the Quest I asked Foucault if consultation and marginalization might be procedures used by the Cathedral to regain power over the direction of the Quest. Foucault reminded me that power is not to be "taken as a right, which one is able to possess like a commodity, and which one can in consequence transfer or alienate" (Foucault 1980, 88).

"So you do not hold a Marxist view of power as commodity?" I asked. Foucault shook his head and then tried to turn our conversation to the post-modern with his reply that when thinking about power we must avoid any "theoretical coronation of the whole" (88).

But I was not convinced to abandon a theory of power yet. "Well, then, perhaps power," I proposed, "is more like a battle for control, a type of warfare by one organization over another." But if this were so then how would you explain bureaucratization of an organization during the battle for control, I wondered. The procedure of bureaucratization was a problem in understanding power as a struggle for control but what about the active marginalization of those critical of the Quest? Then Foucault pointed out that students, although not actively critical of the Quest, were still marginal to the discourse of the Quest. His comment reminded me that some of the people I interviewed expressed the opinion that had the organization listened instead of marginalized voices antagonistic to the original direction of the Quest, we all might be traveling in the mountains, or beyond, by now. Foucault (1990) explained that while "there is no power that is exercised without a series of aims and objectives" this does not mean that power "results from the choice or decision of an individual subject" (95). Foucault explained that when trying to understand power we should

> not look for the headquarters that presides over its rationality; neither the caste which governs, nor the groups which control the state apparatus, nor those who make the most important economic decisions. (95)

"But," I argued, "if our understanding of power does not begin with questions about how power is held or which groups rule over power, what might we ask about how power operates?" Foucault smiled. I was thinking about the Quest when Foucault asked me:

> What were the most immediate, the most local power relations at work? How did they make possible these kinds of discourses, and conversely, how were these discourses used to support power relations? How was the action of these power relations modified by their very exercises, entailing a strengthening of some terms and a weakening of others, with effects of resistance and counterinvestments, so that there has never existed one type of subjugation, given once for all? (97)

I made some comment that this viewpoint was little help if the term 'power relations' was not defined. But Foucault was not going to allow our conversation to end.

He explained that these force relations are the "immediate effects of the divisions, inequalities, and disequilibriums which occur" in discourse-practices (Foucault 1990, 94).

"So," I cautiously summarized, "then power acts through procedures..."

"Strategies," interrupted Foucault (92).

"Or strategies," I continued, irritated at the interruption, "and these procedures are not power but effects of power. So, then what *is* power?"

I thought he was simply avoiding the question when he responded that there exists one further question to always ask about power: "How were these power relations linked to one another according to the logic of a great strategy?" (97)

"Some strategy!" I declared. "The Servants did not stop the Quest and the Cathedral executive has the Quest going in a different direction!" Foucault reminded me the journey was not yet over, and our conversation ended as we walked in the quiet of contemplation that seems to accompany a beautiful road on a warm afternoon just before sunset.

Destining What Can be Said in a Curriculum-Discourse

The team made excellent time on Theme Way and hope was restored that the Quest would reach a new kingdom soon. No doubt their good progress was due to the excellent weather during this part of the trip. Aside from the occasional shower and cool night, migrating birds and warm days announced the arrival of spring. Traveling success was also due to the excellent maps the map-making company was able to prepare now that the Cathedral had finally decided which way the team would travel. I was contacted by the map-makers to act as map interpreter for this part of the journey and I happily agreed to be once again involved in the Quest. I note in my journal that "things seem more contented, secure, able" (Journal entry, July 23, 1990) at this point.

The Production of Knowledge

They were destined to remain so. The road we were on was heading due east and this direction, so the legends say, should take us to the Last Road of the Kingdom. Unfortunately, the maps used by the team at this time did not indicate how the road we were on links up to the Last Road, but everyone was confident that a direct route out of the Kingdom lay just ahead.

Past a small junction that led south to a village, traffic became heavy. It was odd, really, how citizens who had earlier condemned the Quest now greeted us and spoke of their support for this new direction the team had taken. Even the members of the Military we met on the road greeted us, everyone claiming to be a fan of the Chief Executive. We all noticed the difference in the mood of the Kingdom, wondering at the change.

Most of the team members thought the change in attitude was due to the newest production of documents to support this part of the Quest. Certainly the map-making company believed they played a decisive role in the recent acceptance of the team's new direction. Indicating exactly the road ahead, the newest maps pointed to traditional routes that led the team away from the center of the kingdom. I had asked a representative from the map-making company why the newest maps seemed to be helping. This particular representative recalls that during the earlier controversy team members "were not sure what they wanted" in a map, supposing only that they would "know it when they saw it."[56] This inability to articulate what kind of map the team wanted led, according to the map-maker, to an "endless loop" of drafts and revisions to the original map.[57] After the Chief Executive's Committee declared the Quest would continue, but along more traditional routes, the map-makers decided they would "take a more active role"[58] in the production of maps for the journey. By being more aggressive, map-makers found they "were able to change the curriculum"[59] of the Quest, shifting authority for the direction of the team towards the map-makers. This shift was demonstrated by the willingness of the Cathedral organization to even "change the Program of Studies" of the Quest so that it "goes with the text"[60] of the maps.

Team members, however, held a different perception of reasons for the acceptance of the current direction of the Quest. I mentioned to a team leader that an executive with the Cathedral shared with me how the decision to travel Theme Way out of the Kingdom enabled the Servants, the most outspoken of critics, to see the "bigger issues" surrounding the Quest.[61] According to this executive, these Servants, at least the ones located in the central city of the Kingdom, were more interested in saving children for the Servanthood than finding a cure for all the children in the Kingdom.[62] This "fundamentally different perception about the nature" of the Quest between the Cathedral and Servanthood was part of the reason the Servanthood attacked the original direction of the Quest. The team member agreed with this assessment by the executive, noting that the decision to travel along Theme Way "helped to make the program more solid by recovering the respected solid ground"[63] of travel in the Kingdom. A different team member added that finding this solid ground meant adopting more traditional routes of travel in the Kingdom than the original route the team had taken. I asked my traveling companions if the inclusion of these traditional routes represented appeasement of the demands for tradition made by the Servanthood. A team leader jumped into the conversation at this point, enthusiastically describing the choice of roads as an "anchor" which "captured the spirit" of the Quest.[64] But what did this mean? No one answered, so I continued to walk with them in silence.

Later that evening Foucault and I made one of our frequent trips back to the central city via the many roads heading south from Theme Way. While there I asked an executive with the Cathedral how they had come to view this latest route of the team. The executive bluntly described the new direction of the team as "the approach we had to take" to enable the Quest to continue.[65]

"Then," I inquired, "does this mean the journey along Theme Way is more submission to tradition and less an effort to find a way out of the Kingdom?"

The executive thought for a moment and replied the decision to use more traditional roads was "a strategy" to find "the path of least resistance" for the Quest.[66] I then asked if the map-makers were thus forced to choose only the most traditional routes when preparing their maps for the team. The executive replied, "Absolutely, but it was directed to them [the map-makers] that way by us."[67]

Traveling north to rejoin the team, I thought about the decision to use Theme Way. Had the team chosen the road to the Village after leaving King's Clearing, possibly they would have found the King's Highway once again and perhaps a more direct way out of the Kingdom. No one I met knew with certainty where Theme Way led. It seemed to me that while team members truly believed the decision to travel Theme Way was made by the Cathedral organization, now in control of the Quest once again, the desire to not rile the Servanthood any further played a major role in the decision to take this route. What was going on? I put the question to my traveling companion Foucault.

In characteristic fashion, Foucault asked me a question about how the decision to embark on Theme Way became public. I told him that documents, specifically a vision statement and program by the Cathedral organization, were given to as many Priests and Servants in the Kingdom as possible. Foucault reminded me that maps are also documents produced to support the new direction of the team on the Quest. Foucault then asked me *how* these documents were produced. To this rhetorical question, Foucault provided an answer: Through " a regular manner by a discursive practice" (Foucault 1972, 182). He then explained that this production of documents is an expression of knowledge (*savoir*) in a discourse.

"By knowledge," I inquired, "do you mean the knowledge of something, like how to make a map or choose a road?"

Foucault shook his head. He replied that knowledge is "that of which one can speak in a discursive practice" (Foucault 1972, 182).

"So, then the choice of roads was in some way defined by the knowledge of which way to travel in the Quest..." I mused out loud. I recorded in my journal at this time that an idea, "so tenuous" began to form from my conversations with Foucault. I turned to Foucault, with the dawning realization of what my companion was suggesting. "Do you mean we are trapped in some kind of system that produces what may be known by what may be said?" It seemed incredible.

Foucault responded with an example, again avoiding a direct answer to my question. He began by asking why I left the team briefly for a visit to the central city. My journal of that visit notes I was "preparing for a thinking skills workshop" I was asked by the Cathedral executive to give to Priests due to be involved in implementing the recommendations of the team upon successful completion of the Quest (Journal entry, April 12, 1991). Foucault asked how the planning for the workshop went. I told him that I had developed a "linear, focused, and practical 'how to' session on developing thinking skills" (same entry). Foucault wondered out loud how this presentation promoted thinking. "In the participants?" I asked, but I could see his point. I had planned a session on thinking that, ironically, was thoughtless! Yet I believed in the importance of developing thoughtful thinking. I note in my journal, "I'm playing to a frame here, [I'm] a willing agent of the very forces I'm fighting!!!" (same entry). Indeed, Foucault suggested I had fallen into the entrapment of thinking about thinking in technical ways, not with any sense of critique. Even more to the point earlier, however, was Foucault's observation that my planning is exactly what one would expect. He asked me what materials I used in preparing the workshop. I admitted all my materials were from books on thinking that presented a very technical view of thinking. Foucault then drove the point home that this knowledge would not have existed without the technicality that permeates the discourse of the Priesthood. I saw his point, concluding that "the framing of technical approaches is seductive—even more as I contribute to it" (same entry). On the remainder of our trip back to the team I thought of how else I might organize the workshop to help participants really begin to think about thinking in non-technical ways. It was very, very difficult. I note later that, "Foucault is right, to really think, now *that's* work" (Same entry, later in the day, emphasis in the text).

Foucault's view "there is no knowledge without a particular discursive practice and any discursive practice may be defined by the knowledge that it forms" (Foucault 1972, 183) became more clear to me when I returned to join my friends on Theme Way. As we walked I asked if they thought knowledge had a territorial effect, defining the direction of the Quest. Every team member agreed this was the case, at least with the Quest. They told me that during the early planning for the Quest a decision was made by The Cathedral executive to reduce funds, which are represented by credits in our Kingdom, for the Quest so that more credits could be used to strengthen other initiatives that might also help prevent the disappearance of children. But, the team member told me, Priests invested in the Quest "used their influence" to declare this shift in credits by the Cathedral a "watering down" of the Quest.[68] This 'credit crunch', as it came to be known in the Cathedral, led to an increase in the involvement of Servants, Priests, other professionals, and the public in the controversy which, the team member reminded me, "changed things considerably."[69] Another team member explained the perception that developed among the Servants and public at this time was that the "real" Quest was being "taken over" or "punished" by this credit crunch, leading to the conclusion by some Servants and Priests the entire Quest was "watered down."[70]

A team leader suggested the 'credit crunch' came to define what was important in the Kingdom.[71] The dominance of issues surrounding this credit crunch was noticeable throughout the entire journey; interest in other ways to help prevent children from disappearing waned as controversy over the financing of the Quest dominated public discourse. I turned to Foucault. "So," I observed, "funding came to dominate the discourse and this led to..." A team member jumped into the conversation, informing me that already at King's Clearing everyone on the team knew that in order for the Quest to continue, credits for the Quest would have to be restored. When this happened with the announcement by the Chief Executive of the Cathedral, the team realized they would now have "more freedom to develop" the direction of the Quest "in line with our vision."[72]

"But," I pointed out to the team member, "this vision included a partial return to orthodox ways of travel and less credits for other, potentially important ways to solve the riddle of disappearing children." I glanced at the horizon, so far away, and remembered an executive in the Cathedral organization predicted the restoration of credits to the Quest would be the beginning of a "reneging" of the original vision of the Quest.[73] As I turned back towards the team I caught a glance from Foucault. Later that night I wrote in my journal that "patterns are emerging" about the Quest (Journal entry, May 14, 1991), but what these patterns suggested I found very disturbing.

Production of Truth

After several more days of travel along the scenic Theme Way the road suddenly split into two roads. Each of the new roads at the intersection was still called Theme Way, separated only by the addition of the direction the branches led. Judging by the wear in the roadway, Southwest Theme Way led back towards the center of the kingdom. We decided to take the Northeast fork.

Litter along the road confirmed the King's engineers had not visited this branch of the Kingdom's roads for some time. This was strangely reassuring and we traveled in renewed hopes that soon we would find the Last Road and a subsequent way out of the Kingdom. A day later our expectations were not disappointed as the very peaks of the Lonely mountains appeared once again above large hills on the horizon. A sense of joy pervaded the team and everyone—well, I can't vouch for Foucault—but everyone else began to feel success for the Quest was in reach.

Our happiness was spoiled by the disgusting litter left by those who went before us. This litter also contained a selection of highly sarcastic posters from the time controversy surrounded the Quest.[74] Although faded, the posters dampened the mood of the team as they recalled the seemingly endless days in the Forest and the Clearing. A team member stopped to pick up some of the posters; we gathered around. I spoke first, telling team members the Chief Executive told me once that posters depicting the Quest as "Mickey Mouse" or "watered down" had "undermined the credibility" of the original Quest.[75] This Executive explained that these criticisms were amplified through military campaign, with the assistance of Servants and critics from the Priesthood, to the point of becoming truths about the Quest among the general public. The problem with the production of these 'public truths' about the Quest, claims the Chief Executive, is that they became so overbearing that "had we gone ahead and tried to push the programs through the fighting might have placed the entire initiative in jeopardy."[76]

Team members agreed with this assessment by the Chief Executive of the Cathedral. Someone shared how the word 'rigor' came to haunt people involved in planning and traveling the Quest. To Servants, a rigorous Quest follows strictly defined roadways along traditional routes. The team member explained that this approach has yet to find a way out of the Kingdom. The Cathedral executive supported a more open choice of pathways as the Quest progressed; what they termed finding "well-rounded' routes for the Quest. But this approach soon was labeled as lacking rigor by Servants of the central city in the Kingdom. Since Servants seem to hold more esteem in the public eye, the portrayal of the routes taken by the team on the Quest as less rigorous soon produced the public truth that the Cathedral was somehow diluting the Quest. Combined with the belief that credit cuts undermined an already weakened Quest, a sort of public panic emerged. It was all quite depressing, since these public truths seem to arise from miscommunication and misperceptions about the Quest. "For example," I chimed in, "the team *did* set out on a well-marked, clear, *rigorous* road—one of the most frequented roadways in the Kingdom." I wanted to add that a representative from the map-making company felt the *present* direction of the team along theme Way was more compromise that rigor,[77] but I decided against it.

Public truths surrounding the Quest even permeated the Cathedral organization. Team members noted with some distaste how some members of the organization suggested restoring the original credit support for the Quest would "power up" the Quest.[78] According to one team leader, the desire of the Cathedral executive to make the choice of routes appear more rigorous to critics led the Cathedral organization to order the team to turn off the road and into the forest. This invasion into the ranks of those who believed in the Quest the most demonstrates how effective a public truth can be in defining what can be said in a discourse. A team member told me that during the controversy some members of the Servanthood were invited to look over the maps team members were developing. This team member told me that once a public truth is in place, however, *"it defines what people see and say."*[79] The member experienced this first hand as the Servant handed back the map with the comment that the team was not considering the roads ahead. Yet the next page of the map *did* indicate the roads ahead, the Servant simply missed it somehow. The Servant subsequently informed the military that the Cathedral team does not even have maps indicating where they were headed, supporting the public truth that the Quest lacked rigorous planning. Foucault then mentioned quietly that this demonstrates how truths in a discourse, far from being outside power, are more the "regular effects of power" (Foucault 1984b, 73). I turned to him as he explained that

> each society has its regimes of truth, its "general politics" of truth: that is, the types of discourse which it accepts and makes function as true; the mechanisms and instances which enable each one to distinguish true and false statements, the means by which each is sanctioned; the techniques and procedures accorded value in the acquisition of truth; the status of those who are charged with saying what counts as true. (73)

"So why," I asked, "given the prestige of Servants in the Kingdom, were we so surprised the Servants had the most power in producing truth in the debates over the direction of the Quest?"

Foucault could hardly hide his disappointment. He said gently, "truth *is* already power" (75, emphasis mine). I thought about this for a long time. Later that night I couldn't sleep. I record in my journal that what Foucault said that day "hit a raw nerve with me" (Journal entry, October 23, 1991). In the same entry I observe that if truth is power, then discourse must be "regulated by rituals demonstrated by exclusion and definitions" (same entry). Suddenly I understood what Foucault meant by power, knowledge, and truth: a discursive, dynamic system that "defines what I can say and be, and in turn which I define and defend" (Journal entry, October 25, 1991). So, I'm a willing and active prisoner in some sort of giant discourse? This was a profoundly unpleasant thought and once again I wished I hadn't brought Foucault with me! Life was so much easier before my conversations with him. But I was destined to realize the importance of Foucault's insights in the days ahead.

Characteristics of Power in a Curriculum Discourse

> In the end, we are judged, condemned, classified, determined in our undertakings, destined to a certain mode of living or dying, as a function of the true discourses which are the bearers of the specific effects of power.
> —Michel Foucault, *Power/Knowledge* (1980, 94).

Only three days after my last journey entry the team reached an unusual bend in the northeast branch of Trail Way. The road seemed to make a giant curve to the right, apparently heading due south alongside the great hills now obscuring our view of the eastern arms of the Lonely Mountains. Branching off this bend in the road was a narrow dirt path leading directly into the hills. We decided to break for lunch before deciding which direction to take. The lovely warmth of the midday sun and excellent food conspired with the weariness that comes from many days of travel; soon everyone was fast asleep.

A noise along the road behind woke me. Everyone else was sleeping, including Foucault. I was glad to see him sleeping, for his intense nature (Eribon 1991; Miller 1993) had worn him completely out and lately I worried for his health. The noise behind us was a messenger, dressed in official clothes of the Cathedral. I walked up to him as quietly as possible, gesturing for silence all the while so everyone else could continue to enjoy a much needed rest. The messenger understood, and handed me a note.

It was for me. Someone in the Cathedral executive was ill and I was offered the opportunity to formally join the organization. Excellent benefits and security accompanied the offer. I would have to delay or abandon my Scholarly studies, of course, and, if interested, should report to the Cathedral in the central city immediately. A friend in the Cathedral organization had signed the offer, so I knew it was genuine.

I lay in the warm grass and thought about life in the central city. An important role in the Cathedral organization... it *was* tempting. I recorded that offer was a "a real chance to make a difference" (Journal entry, October 28, 1991). Then I thought, "or was it? What freedom would I *really* have? Perhaps there *could* be an opportunity to make a difference—but ultimately what would the plan and action and policies *actually* be?" (same entry, emphasis in text). Suddenly, I was "struck by the reality of it all, the *apparatus* exists and the process is, to some extent, inevitable" (Journal entry, October 29, emphasis in the text). I looked over at Foucault, still sleeping. "Foucault makes a lot of sense now," I wrote in my journal, "but in his ideas something terrible emerges—something almost organic, alive, an ecology of discourse. It's creepy to see how powerful the system is and how it can suck people in" (same entry). Even though deeply honored, I decided to say no to the offer to work for the Cathedral executive. As I laid back down in tall, cool grass I remember thinking that my conversations with Foucault are starting to be "all jars and shocks, leaving disquiet and discomfort in its wake. I no longer feel comfortable" (Journal entry, November 8, 1991). It took a long time to fall back asleep.

I woke up in the middle of the night to stars everywhere. As far as I could tell in the silvery moonlight, everyone was gone! I yelled out, and felt a wave of relief as I heard Foucault laugh. I could see him by the side of the road at the bend. "Where is everyone?" I asked. He wasn't sure himself, presumably the rest of the team had traveled down the main road and only just now were realizing we were still here. "Or perhaps they thought I had gone back to the city," I suggested. My companion admitted this also was a possibility. We decided to wait until morning, then travel further down the road to rejoin the others.

The Adaptability of Power

We had just cleared up from our morning meal when we heard the sound of a small group of people coming from the trail leading into the hills. The group was running and, after a few minutes, we recognized the group as some of the team members and a Scholar. They met us excited and somewhat out of breath. They exclaimed that they had found a new route that promised to lead out of the Kingdom, pointing with enthusiasm to the narrow path off the road. I thought I heard someone say the path led directly to the Last Road when another team member wondered out loud where everyone had gone.

I did not know, surmising the team had stayed together. We all sat down while events of the evening were shared. Apparently, after I had just fallen asleep, a well known Scholar had dropped by and joined some of the team members who wanted to scout the trail. The group members shared how the trail provided an easy access through the hills, leading to the beginning of a major highway. Every group member was certain this was the Last Road of the Kingdom, since beyond the road lay the unmistakable outline of the Lonely Mountains. The Scholar declared the side trip was "very stimulating" for the "number of ideas" the route presented.[80] This Scholar explained the pathway, while obviously little used, nevertheless presented a "modern, very contemporary" route. One of the group members immediately agreed the path seemed to travel in the direction the Team wished to go.[81] Everyone I traveled with that day were most excited to finally discover a pathway that "re-captured the vision" of the Quest:[82] Finding a cure to the problem of disappearing children by traveling outside the Kingdom. I still have a copy of the rough map this small group had made of their trip down the trail. Although sketchy, the map clearly indicates what could only be the beginnings of the Last Road and thus, according to legend, a way out of the Kingdom.

The scouting group had expected the rest of the team would wait for their report; apparently they did not. We discussed the situation and came to the conclusion the rest of the team must have decided to continue along Northeast Theme Way, probably camping only a short distance away from us. We decided to send a messenger to run ahead with the map so the rest of the team ahead could turn back and join us. Finally, our journey out of the Kingdom seemed at hand; soon we would be traveling the Last Road of the Kingdom!

Three days passed and still the messenger did not return. This delay led to an "increasing unease" as we were "not contacted at all"[83] about the map the group had made. The next day the group decided they had waited long enough and traveled down the road to find the missing messenger and the rest of the team. It was two full days later that the messenger returned to us. Apparently the rest of the team had traveled farther down Northeast Theme Way than we had expected. The messenger also handed us back the map we had sent.

Lines were scribbled all over the map, but the message was clear enough: "the basic structure of the course" sketched out had been revised "rather drastically"[84] towards declaring Northeast Theme Way the *only* way out of the Kingdom. But with the discovery of a direct route to the Last Road, a return to traveling along Northeast Theme Way seemed to these scouts like the team was "still representing outdated material [and] outdated concepts"[85] for finding a way out of the Kingdom. Angered with this apparent set-back, the group traveled quickly down the road to rejoin their colleagues.

It took another four days to eventually find the rest of the team. There was immediate understanding for the frustration felt by the group that had scouted the pathway through the hills. It took some time to piece together what had transpired over the days since the team had split up. Apparently the rest of the team had decided to travel only a few days down Northeast Theme Way to see if the bend in the road continued to travel along the hills. After a few days they found Northeast Theme Way turned into a new road that gently led west, away from the hills. They camped that night at this point, receiving the map by the scouting group the following morning. As excited as we had been, this part of the team were just about to turn back to joining the scouts when a messenger arrived from the west. The Cathedral executive wanted a progress report and one of the team members thought it wise to give the new map to the messenger so the Cathedral executive might examine the intention of the team to change direction towards the path. The messenger returned from the Cathedral only a day later with the news that the change in direction was considered "unacceptable."[86] The team was instructed to "re-work" the map "to the satisfaction and specifications"[87] of the executive, that is, to reconsider a more traditional route that would be more in line with what people critical of the Quest might expect. The team felt they had no choice but to prepare a map that became "something very different"[88] from what the scouting party envisioned. One team member explained that when presented with the map, someone in the Cathedral organization had "reined in" the team from the "tangent" they had almost chosen.[89]

We were so close to traveling beyond the hills. I was still angry over the last-minute intrusion by the Cathedral executive, but team members took the directive in stride, still confident the road they traveled would eventually lead out of the Kingdom. I did not share their optimism for two reasons. First, the messenger needed only two days to complete a round trip to the central city of the Kingdom, suggesting the team was closer to the center of the Kingdom than they realized. And second, the map I was drafting of our journey indicated the team had really traveled in a giant circle, confirming my first point. It was as if every opportunity to move out of the Kingdom was thwarted by some event or well-meaning directive that forced the team back towards the center of the Kingdom. This last incident demonstrated how effective this pull towards the center was. Foucault agreed with my observation that there seemed to be an "omnipresence of power" (Foucault 1990, 94) at work, always pulling the team towards traditional routes. My companion told me that his research reveals that this power is "produced from one moment to the next, at every point, or rather in every relation from one point to another" (93). He emphasized that this power is mobile and adaptable to situations, since power "comes from everywhere" (93). It is "the overall effect that emerges from these mobilities" (93) that Foucault calls power. In the case of the Quest, power operated through mobile procedures to effectively turn the team constantly back towards the center of the Kingdom. I was beginning to believe this team was destined to never complete the Quest.

The Great Anonymous

But this was their destiny, not mine. I decided to travel back and seek out the Last Road along the pathway the scouts had discovered. I bid my comrades farewell, wishing them success with enthusiasm, but not much hope. I began with them as part of the team, saw members come and go, shared in their trials and invested in their hopes. But the time had come for me to travel along a different route. During the past two years I became convinced a route out of the Kingdom must exist and together with Foucault I was determined to find it. I knew I would miss my friends from the Cathedral, but it was time to go.

I decided the path discovered earlier by some members of the group might offer the fastest way out of the hills and in only a few days Foucault and I reached the junction of Northeast Theme Way and the path leading into the hills. I found the path clearly marked and we made excellent time. In only a few hours we reached the summit of the trail where a commanding view of the plains below greeted us. I could see the trail did lead to what appeared to be the start of a major road heading northwest. Even more thrilling, we could make out the majestic peaks of the Lonely Mountains far in the distance. Encouraged by the view, we reached the end of this trail by nightfall.

The trail through the hills proved to be a pass that led directly to the start of a well constructed road. At this end of the road there was almost no sign that travelers had been here before us, but the road was in excellent condition so presumably the King's engineers did frequent the area. We traveled the only way the road led, northwest towards the Mountains.

It is amazing how something in the distance seems closer than it really is, at least that is how the Mountains seemed to me. Days became weeks as we traveled, yet the mountains still seemed a considerable distance away. I know I was poor company, often walking for hours without speaking to Foucault. When I wondered out loud if taking this road was such a great idea, Foucault caught my attention with a statement that was to occupy our conversation for days. He simply stated that there was no King.

To this absurdity I immediately pointed out that in order for a Kingdom to exist, there has to be, by definition, a King. Foucault asked me why this had to be so, adding that just because a Kingdom existed and ran well does not at all require a King at all. I thought this was purely silly, and told Foucault so. But my companion was not so easily put off this topic; our conversation continued for many days. My argument for the existence of the King focused on the need for centralized control in the Kingdom. I presented my case carefully, suggesting the Kingdom would quickly fall into anarchy should there not be a King.

Foucault, of course, did not agree. He suggested the King could disappear, yet everyone was so used to acting as if their King existed that life in the Kingdom would simply continue as it always had. To make this point, Foucault asked me about the history of membership in the team that left on the Quest. I recalled a map-maker told me the constant migration of people in and out of the team on the Quest made developing a map difficult. The map-maker thought some continuity in team personnel "would have helped" the role of map-makers in the Quest.[90] A Scholar claimed the continual change in map-makers during the Quest delayed establishing the sense of community needed to produce high quality, useful maps.[91] Yet one executive with the Cathedral told me the changes in team membership proved to be "significant" in assisting the Quest to continue,[92] especially during the controversy. The map-making company did seem to be able to produce the maps needed for the team to continue; in fact they claimed that the newest set of map-makers they assembled were better than previous writers. In each case, movement of people in and out of the Quest was seen as improvement in the personnel associated with the Quest. But this contradicts the view that continuity of personnel is important in a project the magnitude of the Quest. It didn't make sense and I couldn't see how this contradiction related to the existence of the King.

We came upon a stone bridge arched over a small stream. I had been so totally engrossed in my conversation with Foucault that I hadn't noticed the landscape change. To the north the Lonely Mountains were plainly visible, rising with majesty from the northern plains. The stream before us appeared to cross this plain, likely originating at the foot of some glacier in the mountains. At the bridge the stream split into two, one branch heading along the roadway on the right, another turning sharply to head towards the forest we could see in the distance on our left. It was a beautiful, cloudless day and the bridge seemed almost magical with the sound of the water rushing beneath us. We paused in our journey to admire the view of the forest. I closed my eyes, basking in the peace of the moment.

I glanced ahead of us and saw for the first time a small trail leading to our road from the forest. A wave of shock came over me as I realized exactly where we were. The forest was none other than the King's Forest, and the stream the very one the team and I passed in the forest. The memory of the haunting sounds of the voices of children came to me as I realized that the trail these voices told us to take did lead directly to the road I was now traveling. I looked at the direction ahead. There could be no doubt, the signs were unmistakable: legends spoke of a road beside a river at the outer reaches of the Kingdom, a road that would lead to a trail out of the Kingdom. Foucault and I were traveling on the legendary Last Road.

I was anxious to continue traveling as quickly as possible, but my companion was not. Perhaps the sunshine was too warm or the bridge too idyllic, at any rate Foucault suggested we have lunch at this beautiful site before continuing. I reluctantly agreed. The memory of the voices of children seemed to affect Foucault as well. We talked about the Cathedral, which Foucault described as part of the "highly complex systems of manipulation and conditioning" of the bodies of children (Foucault 1980, 125). These systems could only exist through "access to the bodies of individuals, to their acts, attitudes and modes of everyday behavior" (125). I agreed, but reminded Foucault it was hardly a great insight that the Cathedral controlled the lives of children. But Foucault was not at all finished. He asked me if I thought the Kingdom worked through "the productive service from individuals in their concrete lives" (125). Again, I conceded this was the case. Foucault asked if I thought this service was the result of some oppressive force. I replied this was not likely, since most of the people I knew enjoyed their service to the King; being forced to serve would likely lead to revolution, I added. Foucault agreed with my analysis; he continued on his line of reasoning by then asking *how* the service of the people in the Kingdom is coordinated. I surmised some type of surveillance system might exist, perhaps through the military, although I could not provide any evidence for such a system. Foucault continued to propose that with such a system one "must be able to simultaneously both to increase the subjected forces and to improve the force and efficacy of that which subjects them" (104).

"But," I observed, "this means a King must exist!"

Unless this system involved "a tightly knit grid of material coercions rather than the physical existence of a sovereign" (104), countered Foucault.

"Is this nexus of relations, concretely expressed in the lives of individuals, what you mean by 'power?'" I asked.

Foucault replied it is, adding that this type of power

> is in every aspect the antithesis of that mechanism of power which the theory of sovereignty described or sought to describe. The latter is linked to a form of power that is exercised over the Earth and its products, much more than over human bodies as their operations... It enables power to be founded in the physical existence of the sovereign, but not in continuous and permanent systems of surveillance. (104–105)

And these systems of surveillance are possible, Foucault suggested, through "procedures which allowed the effects of power to circulate in a manner at once continuous, uninterrupted, adapted and 'individualized' throughout the entire social body" (119).

Unnerved, I replied, "Are you suggesting, Foucault, that instead of power located with the King, that power is now expressed in the day to day lives of the citizens of the Kingdom?" I thought of the Quest and turned white. "Then," I continued with dawning realization, "it did not matter *who* migrated in and out of the Quest, procedures of power were at force to prevent the team from ever leaving the Kingdom." And if this was the case, I thought, then one *would* expect interpretations of the effects of movement of people in and out of the Quest to be contradictory since the lack of success of the team could be blamed on either lack of continuity of personnel or not enough changes in personnel when necessary. Either way, though, it did not matter to the final result. As I pondered these things, I felt as if some idea, some important insight lay just out of reach. Later that evening I wrote in my journal that "I feel as a small child, groping for a light switch in a dark, unfamiliar room" (Journal entry, November 10, 1991).

The following day we made excellent time, traveling now due west along the Last Road. The road was mostly deserted, the few travelers we did meet were Scholars and Scholars-in-Training. Still troubled by Foucault's ideas of power, I wondered aloud if, in the final analysis, Foucault might not be criticized for "seeing power everywhere, and, in the final analysis, of reducing everything to power?" (Foucault 1988, 104). Foucault did admit that this was "an important question" (104). While he "refrained from seeing power everywhere," (105) he confessed that one of his research interests was discovering how the "procedures for training and exercising power over individuals" were "extended, generalized, and improved" (105) from the eighteenth century onwards. These procedures, Foucault explained, are "often quite explicit at the restricted level where they are inscribed" (Foucault 1990, 95). He reviewed the procedures we had encountered with the team: bureaucratization, silence, marginalization, consultation, and the production of knowledge and truth. While the logic of these procedures may be perfectly clear, "it is often the case that no one is there to have invented them: an implicit characteristic of the great anonymous" (95).

"Thus the reason you believe there is no King, right?" I added. He smiled, relieved I think to see I was beginning to understood what he was saying. I continued, "If these procedures of power are adaptable and anonymous, then all of us are part of these systems of power, including you, Foucault."

My companion agreed, recognizing that in the trachealization of procedures of power "the disease he seeks to cure is part of an epidemic which has also affected him" (Dreyfus and Rabinow 1983, 202).

One group reported seeing the glow of a great city or some evidence of industrialization from the southern regions of the inland sea. Another group found a small collection of huts built by people who called themselves pioneers. I was personally amazed these people could speak the same language as everyone in the team (something I worried about, remember?) and inquiries soon revealed that the children of these pioneers were not disappearing. Everyone is certain hope for finding a cure for our disappearing children exists with these people.

In the hope you find what you are looking for,

T.M.

I looked and behind the letter was another, more recent letter:

A few weeks later
David—

Odd news. Some of our team traveled the region from the southern part of the great sea to the glow, only to discover the light was caused by the central city of our Kingdom! We now know we did not travel outside the Kingdom after all. I know how much you wanted to find a way out and believed that is where hope for our children might be found, but perhaps you are looking too far afield.

We have discovered an entire region of the Kingdom hitherto virtually unknown. The people here are happy, if poor, and seem oblivious to the benefits offered as citizens of the Kingdom. In many ways, the entire region is a completely underdeveloped wilderness. Even more exciting to us is the fact that the disappearance of children is unknown here. Perhaps some medicinal cure or mineral in the ground protects these children, we are not sure. The King's physicians will be here shortly to examine the children themselves and we expect engineers and Servants to follow. The pioneers here will surely be glad to have the health of their children and the development of the region entrusted to skilled experts.

While we did not find a way out of the Kingdom, everyone here is quite happy with what we have discovered. Executives from the Cathedral came to see us yesterday. An executive told us that we should be proud of what we accomplished, since "there are some things you can't do, there's a limit to acceptable change."[93] Another executive put it this way: "It may not be the kind of changes we would like, and it may not be as far along as we wanted to go, but something has happened."[94] We all sense our team has managed "a step" that will prove to be evolutionary in finding a cure to the problem[95] of disappearing children.

Now David, I realize the danger in a small amount of movement is that "you may be getting anywhere,"[96] but we are convinced that our Quest will not prove in vain. Like the Chief Executive of the Cathedral says, at least in our exploration of this new territory we can "see possibilities and then have the chance to try out new ideas."[97] We think those possibilities are here and so our Quest is, after such a long (and sometimes painful!) journey, finally over.

All the best,

T.M.

I put the letters in the envelope and looked towards the western horizon. The smoke that hangs over this region had lifted somewhat and I could see clearly the deforestation of the western hills, the great factories of the Kingdom and the shores of Long Lake, rumored to be the most polluted waters in the land. Behind me the bridge led to a pathway leading directly to the Lonely Mountains. I turned to Foucault and told him of the contents of the letter. "Do you realize where they are?" I asked rhetorically. "They traveled for over two years to end up almost directly in the center of the Kingdom!" I exclaimed in despair. Foucault nodded with understanding, but said nothing. "the Quest is over," I said with bitterness in my voice. "And somehow," I continued, "I know the cure for the disappearing children won't be found in the eastern regions of this Kingdom." I followed the path of the river below me, watching how its course turned in a great arc towards the industrial regions. Then an idea occurred to me. "If a King does not exist," I told Foucault, "then power is a system that preserves the status quo." He looked at me, but did not speak. Encouraged, I continued, "But *must it always be so? Will power always pull us back to the center?*" I turned and faced the Lonely Mountains, so beautiful and now so close. I did not know if the trip outside the Kingdom was possible, but I knew I had to try. I turned to Foucault and said with conviction, "Let's go."

Is Change in a Curriculum-Discourse Possible?

True enlightenment is to really know, really feel, your ontological dilemma.
—Morris Berman, *Coming to our Senses* (1989, 310).

The mountains were much closer that we could have guessed from the bridge and we crossed the northern plain quickly. The trees were blackened and in some cases dead from the pollution of the factories, spoiling our view but not our determination. Eventually the trail led to a series of small hills directly beneath the shadows of the Lonely Mountains. Then the trail began to lead at a sharp incline.

The mountain air was cool and refreshing, but I could hardly get enough as I struggled to breathe during the ascent. The trail, fortunately, was well marked, but I could tell that my travels had not prepared me for the physical exertion required. We had to stop often. All around us was silent and I had the distinct impression the mountains were watching us. The trail soon became nothing more than a series of cairns set every few hundred meters. A few times we missed these rocky markers and had to go back and try again. Finally the trail became more level as we hiked directly into the mountains. We caught our breath and, encouraged by more level territory, began to hike with great energy along a rocky ledge that seemed to be a pass through the mountain range. Foucault estimated that at our present speed we should be through the mountains before nightfall. Then it started to snow.

Snowfall is a present danger any time of the year in the mountains. Soon everything was white and our trail less obvious. We were in danger of losing our way totally when I caught the light of a mountain chalet. The temperature was falling and our choices very limited. We made our way to the chalet.

A warm welcome and meal awaited us. The family that owned the chalet were poor, but used to helping strangers in trouble in the mountains. They had anticipated someone might be dropping by and prepared a little extra of their Friday night meal. While we ate and exchanged news, two beautiful children shyly peeked in from another room. I asked about the children. Our hosts told us these were the last children in the mountains, all the others had slowly disappeared. I was amazed children were disappearing even in the margins of the

Kingdom, but our hosts told us the plague was especially severe in these regions. I caught the peeking eye of one child, who returned my smile. They're both old enough to be studying at the Cathedral, I thought. I looked into the faces of our generous hosts. They were frightened for their children, but gravely concerned for all the children in the Kingdom. I could not help but share the mission my companion and I had chosen. The family was greatly interested in our travels and troubles. When I finally came to the end of the tale, our hosts told us the route we had chosen would not take us to the other side of the mountains. They told us their children knew the way out and that the children would lead us.

Thankfully the snow abated and in a few hours we left the warmth of the chalet, led by the two children. I was reluctant to leave the hospitality of the family, but my rest there gave me the courage to continue. Our guides were sure-footed and we had some trouble keeping up. After a few curves and turns which I thought I'd never remember, we suddenly came to a beautiful forest with a well marked trail descending out of the mountains. Our helpers accepted our gratitude and cheerfully returned to their home waiting deep in the mountains, waving as they left.

At the Edge of Modernity

We had not traveled very far before we realized the trees were bursting with tiny sparrows following us. In our Kingdom there is a legend that before becoming a Priest you must live as a sparrow first. I remember thinking that if this were true, our Kingdom would have many Priests soon! The little birds provided cheerful company for us and we could not help but laugh as they frantically made their way from tree to tree. The forest was very much like the King's Forest we had encountered so many months ago, except the wilderness more pristine with no evidence of markers placed by the King's Servants. This absence was a sure sign we had reached the furthest regions of the Kingdom. I expected at any moment to leave the forest and enter the regions of a new kingdom.

The forest ended abruptly at the foot of the Mountains, opening to a large, white, featureless plain. A distant arm of the Lonely Mountains lay to the right, otherwise there was simply a vast expanse of snow and ice as far as the eye could see. The horizon seemed to melt into the sky, making it impossible to determine how far the plain continued. No trail existed in this desolate region; our only hope was to continue to travel and perhaps discover a trail or the borders of the next kingdom on the other side. I turned to Foucault and asked him what we should do. He put his hand on my shoulder and gently, but firmly, told me I must travel this last part of the journey on my own. Somehow, I was expecting this. I asked him if he would wait in this forest until I returned. He smiled in a very strange way and told me that I would see him again. I shook his hand, thanked him for all the help, guidance, and even torment he gave me in the past. "You are a worthy companion, Michel Foucault," I told him. I turned and stepped onto the plain.

Immediately a sharp wind tore at my face. I had to pull my jacket tightly around my head. Still, the wind seemed to cut right through my clothing making travel very slow and labored. The snow was not deep, though, but with every step forward my previous footprint was erased by drifting, shifting crystals of ice. I turned my back to the wind and felt some relief as my back pack blocked the wind. It was bitterly cold. Then the wind shifted, blowing from the right and it was all I could do to keep walking.

It was not easy. In the distance I could make out the source of the wind: a mountain glacier shaped like a giant angel. The wind seemed to be pushing me back towards the forest, demanding I return to the Kingdom, to safety and security. I could see still the deep green of the forest behind me. Foucault would still be there, waiting. Somehow I kept walking, my hands numb from the cold, my spirit sinking. The cold wind from the glacier tugged at my body, urging me back with strange, intense ferocity. I did not want to go on. I thought of the sparrows and smiled. I remembered the children in the chalet, those lives on the threshold of disappearing like so many in the Kingdom, and I was surprised by a deep resolve to continue, a force within urging me onwards. I had to try; my pace increased.

After a few hours the wind died down and the ground changed to bare rock with the occasional drift of snow. I was able to walk more easily now, but the horizon had changed from white to a strange darkness; no landmark that I could see appeared to break the horizon ahead. A terrible sense of foreboding came over me as I walked in the utter, eerie silence of the rocky landscape.

I was so surprised by the sudden chasm that opened before me I almost walked right off the precipice. As far as I could tell the land simply came to an end. The divide seemed to travel forever to my left and right, with nothing at all on the other side. I dropped a stone into the chasm, but did not hear the stone hit bottom; as far as I could tell the chasm was bottomless.

No rope, no bridge, no person could cross the abyss I faced. The horrible truth came to me, the awful conclusion to my journey screamed out: *There is no way out of this Kingdom.* I recorded in my journal how I felt at this abyss: "Trapped. Sad. Lonely. In the end, it's all worthless. I feel a sense of abandon, loss... my hopes are gone" (December 18, 1991). I had traveled all that way only to find that there is no other kingdom, there is no hope for the disappearing children and thus no hope for us all. Even if we fight the constant destining that pulls us back towards the center of the Kingdom, even if we could travel to the very margins of what is, there we find only despair and hopelessness for our efforts.

I thought of my comrades happy in the eastern regions of the Kingdom and I wanted to be with them. I thought of my students when I was still a Priest, and I wanted to be with them. I thought of the family I met in the mountains, and I wanted to be there. Then I thought of my own family and most of all I wanted to be home. But I was not home; I was all alone at the edge of the Kingdom, wretched, utterly spent, and without hope. Before me lay the night of a bottomless chasm, behind the great anonymous waiting to take me back.

Chapter 5

Possibilities for Change in
Science Education

At the Chasm of Despair

When you look long into an abyss, the abyss also looks into you.
—Friedrich Nietzsche, *Beyond Good and Evil* (1966, 89).

I don't know how long I had been asleep, but I woke suddenly, disturbed by a horrible dream. I imagined that I was falling, or rather sliding, almost imperceptibly into a deep, dark, quiet pit. I remembered in my dream looking up as the light around me constricted until all I could see was a small aperture of hope; this too closed until I was finally engulfed in the suffocation of nothingness. I then woke. Although it was still not yet light, I was too frightened to return to sleep, too terrified the dream might return.

Wrapped in the warm comfort of my sleeping bag, I poked my head out of the little tent and surveyed my situation. Around me the land carried the stillness before dawn with the dignity unique to barren places. I recalled where I was: my tent was pitched a few meters away from the chasm at the edge of the Kingdom. No visitor would come my way, no feature broke the monotonous rocky landscape, no bridge would carry me safely across the chasm out of the Kingdom. I was utterly alone.

I dressed and stepped outside. Careful to note the position of the chasm, I put on my travel sack and decided to take a walk. A confident stillness surrounded me, but my thoughts overwhelmed the silence. How long had I been at the edge of the chasm now? It was hard to say. A certain timelessness pervaded this region, infusing life with the peace of desolation. That morning I pondered my future. Snow on the plain towards the Lonely Mountains provided pools of fresh water and I had ample stores of food, thanks to the generosity of the family in the chalet. Why should I return? Every effort back in my former life seemed destined to serve the status quo of conformity, to serve the power of a King long since missing. So, what was the point of attempting change, or trying to make a difference? Are we not condemned already by the systems of power in which we are both trapped and trappers? The desolation of this question provided an odd comfort in the failure of the Quest, of *my* Quest. There was something there, in that question, that gave pause to the bitterness of my location. And from this question came another: If there is no way out of the Kingdom, no map that can be made, no workshops on how to take the journey out, then is any effort to find a cure for the dis-ease of our young people futile? Is hope naïve, are possibilities barren?

The chasm had an ominous presence and on that particular morning I felt drawn to look once again into the dark recesses of its innermost being. The predawn light was just sufficient for me to make my way to the edge of the Kingdom and the awaiting abyss. Like the mouth of some whale, the vast darkness of the chasm seemed to open before me, almost daring me to jump in. I stared into the void. No destination on the other side beaconed, no horizon was present: just a vast nothingness that appeared to extend forever. The phenomenon no longer unnerved me, so I sat on the edge, dangling my feet into the inky blackness. In fact—dare I confess this?—I new sensation was creeping into me spirit. For a few days I had noticed this new feeling, but was unable to identify it. Sitting at the edge of the Kingdom, I realized that morning what I was feeling: *I was bored.*

All of us need, I believe, times of refraction or recollection in our lives, time to restore energy and find once again what it means to find "the meaning of your own life" (Nietzsche, quoted in J. Miller 1993, 303). But refraction is but a pause in the repetition of living, a moment to find direction before continuing adventuring once again. I realized that morning I had strayed towards repetition of only what was, not recollecting forward (Kierkegaard 1983) to what might be. Perhaps the security of indecision provided some comfort after the failure of the Quest, perhaps I had become lazy, or perhaps the darkness of the chasm infected my spirit. I was bored, to be sure, but not willing or perhaps not able to do anything about my situation. Glancing at a nearby puddle of water beside the edge of the chasm, I caught a reflection of my face. A chill ran down my spine as I recognized my expression: I had the same look as the children fading away in the Kingdom. Had their disease infected me?

Then I thought of Foucault. It was very odd, I had not thought of him for since I left the forest—how long ago?—but the memory he was waiting for me returned with force. Then I felt a new feeling: *I was lonely*. You may be surprised I did not feel lonely sooner, but solitude often provides a comfortable home. I realized, though, that it was not comfort I was seeking, but the exact opposite: *I longed for the discomfort that comes from being with others*. Yet I knew with certainty no one would find me in the isolated, rocky wilderness I had discovered. A wretched unhappiness came over me; waves of grief racked my being. "Is anyone out there?" I yelled into the chasm. But any hope of a response to my call, even an echo, was smothered by the cold, dark and impersonal silence. My thoughts traveled beyond the Mountains behind me and on to the Kingdom sheltered within. There awaits the more gentle horror of definition; I realized at the edge of the abyss that the Kingdom could no longer be my home. There was no place for me to live, no where for me to go; bitterness grew as the hopelessness of my location overcame me. I knew the emptiness of the chasm was slowly but surely creeping into my spirit. I sat at this edge, cold and alone. I believe I sat there for a very long time.

Locations of Hope for Change in Science Education Curriculum-Discourses

Questioning builds a way.
—Martin Heidegger, *The Question Concerning Technology* (1977, 287).

The First Book: Foucault's Pedagogy

Then the first rays of the Sun crept over the eastern horizon, spreading warm, light fingers across the rocky landscape. Hungry, I reached into my travel sack for something to eat. Instead of food, the first thing I touched was one of the books I placed in the sack the morning I began my journey so many years ago. I turned to these works now in my despair of hope and possibilities for change. The first book I removed was by Foucault (1990), *The History of Sexuality, Volume 1*. A pang of sadness moved through me as I recalled my many travels with Foucault. The wrinkled cover and marked pages reminded me of days past when I frequented the pages of this work. I turned to a familiar passage, almost hearing the voice of Foucault once again in the words, "power is everywhere; not because it embraces everything, but because it comes from everywhere" (93).

Through my journeys in the Kingdom I observed and experienced the pervasive defining and determining of modernity that is power within the Kingdom. Charged with the task of making a difference in the lives of children in the Kingdom, the team I traveled with were unable to find a way through the mountains that encircle the Kingdom. Just when the team seemed to make progress in the journey, procedures of power assured the status quo. Through the dual functioning of who could speak and what could be said during the Quest, power remained mobile, anonymous, and effective in preventing change.

I thumbed through the book by Foucault, finding passages that resonated with my experiences in the Kingdom. Although Foucault was concerned with the fate of sexuality in the Great Conversation of modernity, I found in this work many direct parallels with the fate of the initiative to cure the dis-eased children in the Kingdom. Foucault suggests that in Europe during the eighteenth and nineteenth centuries human sexuality became a discourse in which "the sexual conduct of the population was taken both as an object of analysis and as a target of intervention" (26). In the Kingdom, a similar effect happened as controversy over the Quest grew. Every move of the team became subject to the scrutiny of professional groups and teachers until the Quest became a discourse—a curriculum-discourse—open to analysis. This led inexorably to interventionist strategies by the very organizers of the Quest, a procedure I called 'bureaucratization' in the previous chapter. Foucault quickly adds that a key interventionist strategy is silence, noting that silences form "an integral part of the strategies that underlie and permeate discourses" (27). Indeed, I found the timely silence of some participants in the curriculum-discourse of the Kingdom strategically important in enabling other voices in the curriculum-discourse to distract the team from its original direction.

I closed the book, stood up and stretched. The sun was above the horizon now, casting golden rays over the forbidding landscape. I tried looking into the abyss before me, but the inky blackness so far remained untouched by the early morning light. I continued reading, careful to note the precipice as I paced back and forth. In the first volume of *The History of Sexuality* Foucault observes how in the nineteenth century the discourse on sexuality came to focus on the child, strangely excluding the voice of children in the constellation of "parents, nurses, servants, educators and doctors" involved in the scientific study of sexuality (98). The result, notes Foucault, was an ironic turn towards increasing marginalization of other voices in the family, in particular the mother, as the "sexuality of the adults themselves was called into question" (99). The entire idea of family became increasingly complex, dictated more by scientific journals than the tradition of elder family members. I witnessed a similar effect of ironic turning during the Quest. The original vision for the Quest rose from the practical concerns of people close to the voices of children. But as controversy began to direct the journey of the team, the voices of children and those closest to the children became marginalized as other issues and voices occupied the center of the curriculum-discourse. This centering increased even when voices on the margins, the teachers, were eventually consulted. Ironically, consultation became another procedure of power, extending the defining reach of the existing curriculum-discourse. The teachers lost in this process the only voice left to them: a position of critique that comes precisely from being on the margins of a discourse. But power is relentless. As parents in the nineteenth century consulted with psychiatrists and newly published manuals on how to respond to the sexuality of their children, it was only a matter of time before the scientific study of sexuality would turn towards a focus on the parents, too, submerging these voices in the discourse of sexuality. In the Quest, power eventually extended to defining what participants central in the curriculum-discourse could say, a procedure I call 'ontological invasion' in Chapter 4, completing a mobile nexus of power relations dependent on situating voices at the center and at the margins of the curriculum-discourse.

The definition of who could speak in the curriculum-discourse limited what could be said; Foucault suggests this is due to the fact that in a discourse "power and knowledge are joined together" (100). Certainly the modification and legitimation of hierarchies, the active marginalization of voices, and the strategy of consultation served to direct the focus of the curriculum-discourse to knowledge of the techniques of travel, such as map-making, and away from the original vision of change. This re-direction towards technique in the curriculum-discourse was dependent on the production of public truths that the team was somehow watering down the Quest by engaging in something that had become 'Mickey Mouse'. The result of these public truths was the direction of the team to orthodox, well-traveled routes when, in fact, the initial vision was travel in precisely the opposite way. The knowledge of traditional routes of travel was promoted through the development of a 'public truth' that these routes were the best direction to go, but these routes led the team inevitably and surely back to the center of the Kingdom: The precise effecting of power in this curriculum-discourse.

And not just in this curriculum-discourse. I sat down, and thought back to my studies of curriculum-discourses when I lived in the Kingdom. Despite considerable investment in personnel and funds, almost every modern curriculum-discourse has proven to be incredibly resilient to change.[1] In the great need to reform science education, resilience to change presents a crisis in modernity. This crisis is approached in curriculum-discourses in the spirit of the Great Conversation as a technical-rational problem. But technical-rational approaches to curriculum change have proved hopelessly barren and so the crisis continues. In the Kingdom children are still disappearing, in science education curriculum-discourse technicality blocks possibilities for change. In both situations what prevents change are the adaptable, anonymous, far-reaching, and mobile procedures of power epidemic to the Great Conversation. We are, quite simply, trapped in a conversation that defines who may speak and what may be said through procedures of power that ensure the continued dominance of this conversation even though it has become no longer relevant to the situation of our present age.

To this desperate situation Foucault provides, through example, a completely different way of understanding the failure of reform in science education curriculum-discourses. Foucault demonstrates precisely in *The History of Sexuality* how the rise of the discourse on sexuality led to what he calls the "perversion" (36) of human sexuality:

> One had to speak of it as of a thing not simply condemned or tolerated but managed, inserted into systems of utility regulated for the greater good of all, made to function according to an optimum. Sex was not something one simply judged; it was a thing one administered. (24)

A whole "grid of observations" (26) resulted from this perversion as educational, medical, and penal institutions became fixated on "the question of sex" (70). Sexuality became an object of clinical investigation, a *scientia sexualis*, a subject of technologies of self until the modern person has become full of sexuality, but no longer sexy. The consequence of this development is the further alienation of humanity from itself, a perversion that Foucault, drawing from Nietzsche, suggests originates in the "will to knowledge" (73) that animates the Great Conversation of modernity and is expressed through procedures of power. Thus, Foucault presents a chilling prospect for curriculum studies: understanding why a curriculum-discourse does not change involves wrestling with the will to power that is the discourse; ultimately change is not a issue of technique, or even of power, change involves wrestling with the origins and activity of the perverse conversation of modernity itself.

Foucault suggests the trachealization of modernity can begin in discovering the procedures of power in discourses. What does the discovering of these procedures teach us? First, the events of the curriculum-discourse in the Kingdom were inevitable but not predictable. From the moment the team left on the Quest, their journey was destined to return them back to the center of the Kingdom. The team originally set out on a journey that seemed well planned. There was not any particular set of factors that could have been considered which would have guaranteed *a priori* the success of the Quest. Such attempts at analysis of the team's journey in the Kingdom are shallow and consequently destined to barrenness because they are founded on the structuralistic, technical-rational presuppositions of modernity which is the very conversation preventing change. A deeper, more profound, more difficult challenge is presented by the failure of the team in the Kingdom— and in other kingdoms—to find change in a discourse that is part of the Great Conversation of modernity; to find a post-modern vision for change. Without such a post-modern vision, the mission of the team was doomed from the start to slow, but inevitable, failure, exactly as curriculum change attempts before and any future attempts approached as a modern, technical-rational problem.

Foucault's work also suggests a consequence of the inevitaly of failure in curriculum change is the inability to predict the exact procedures of power destined to frustrate attempts at change. Of course, if the procedures of power were stable and uniform, one could propose a meta-theory of power which could then form a basis of subversion that might lead to change. But it is not that easy. Foucault's works suggest many procedures of power of particular discourses, but these procedures vary considerably depending on the discourse. For example, Foucault shows how procreative behavior was increasingly socialized through economic incitements and restrictions as a procedure of power in the modernization of sexuality, but socialization of behavior through economics is not a procedure presented in his discussion of the modern discourse of justice and systems of punishment or his interpretations of discourse of treating madness. The act of public confession figures as a prominent procedure of power in Foucault's understanding of prisons and punishment, while in the discourse of sexuality Foucault proposes that confession is a more private, yet still effective, procedure of power. Neither confession nor economic control of behavior seemed to play a role in the events of the science education curriculum-discourse in the Kingdom, although perhaps a different researcher than I might see these; but the procedure of consultation, a major procedure of power in the Kingdom, is not given attention in Foucault's interpretations. These few examples illustrate how procedures of power vary from discourse to discourse, perhaps even within the same discourse over time. From a Foucauldian perspective, power is a moving target where the procedures are always discovered after the discourse is in place, making a theory of power and the predictability of procedures impossible.

A cold wind started to blow across the plain and I shivered despite the warm rays of the Sun. I walked back to my tent, placed the book by Foucault on the sleeping bag and put on a sweater. There was enough light to see into the abyss and although I knew from my days at this edge what I would find, I went again to look over the precipice that extended around the Kingdom. Light illuminated the situation I faced. The rock plain continued vertically over the edge of the abyss, a vast grayness that formed a continual drop into an apparently bottomless chasm extending to the horizon.

As I gazed into the expanse, I realized that the sheer cliffs before me, the barren plain behind me, and the distant haze of the Lonely Mountains towards the center of the Kingdom held a certain, well, rugged charm. I thought of my colleagues on the team and wished they could be here, to share what I knew about the Kingdom. Then it suddenly occurred to me: Suppose the team *had* found a way through the mountains, through the forest and along the plain to the edge of the Kingdom, then what? I had traveled as far as one could go in the Kingdom, and I had not discovered a cure for the disease of children, either. The horror of the next thought overwhelmed me so much that I almost fell into the abyss: *What if there is no cure?* Suppose the children, indeed all of us, are completely, absolutely doomed to the status quo? Suppose there is no hope for change, suppose possibilities do *not* exist?

Unnerved, I decided to continue my walk. Alongside the abyss I fell into a rhythm of walking that freed my mind to consider further what Foucault had taught me. For the first time during my journeys, serious questions about Foucault's conception of power grew in my thinking. I could see Digeser's point (1992) that if power lies "at the bottom of all our social practices: politics, medicine, religion, psychiatry, work" (980) then essentially power "is everywhere. There's no escaping it" (980). Digeser observes that in all other conceptions of power there is "always the possibility for human relationships not to be mediated by power" (981). But Foucault, claims Digeser, does not define power in opposition to freedom: To Foucault there is no arena where power has no play. Foucauldian scholar James Bernauer (1990) agrees with this perspective on Foucault's concept of power, bluntly adding that if we accept Foucault's view of power then "one always exists within a specific deployment of power, and to nurture a wish to be outside of power is merely to cultivate a private fantasy" (150).

But it seemed to me the Foucauldian thesis that power is everywhere, inescapably constituting and constituted by discourse, presents two serious problems. First, it is difficult to establish the validity of Foucault's claims. The writings of Foucault are, of course, also a discourse. As a form of interpretation of our modern situation, Foucault's writings are, by the very thesis animating his writing, also a discourse mediated by power and thus must remain suspect and open to critique. Dreyfus and Rabinow (1982) invoke a medical metaphor to illustrate this point: "A doctor can stand outside a patient and treat him objectively, but a practitioner of interpretive analytics has no such external position. The disease he [sic] seeks to cure is part of an epidemic which has also affected him" (202). Thus, Foucault's conceptualization of power invokes a paradox: If what Foucault claims about power is valid, then it is possible his own work is part of a modern strategy of power in the discourse of philosophy, possibly leading us not towards an understanding of our modern situation but further away. The crux of this irony in Foucault's concept of power is what Foucauldian scholar Rainer Rochlitz (1992) claims to be the 'secret universalism' in Foucault's *oeuvre*: Power achieves a historical transcendence that is ultimately deterministic and thus completely modern.[2] If true, this criticism suggests a dilemma: How valid are Foucault's insights if they present a view of power that in scope and elaboration suggests a deterministic meta-theory of power, since the modern urge to present global, totalizing theories is precisely what Foucault claims to be fighting in his work? After all, if power is as totalizing as Foucault seems to suggest, how can his claims about power hold validity? Would these claims not also constitute part of the business of power and thus remain suspect and open to critique? How is Foucault able to exempt himself sufficiently from the effects of power to judge its effects?

This questioning led me to the second serious problem in Foucault's concept of power. If power is everywhere, constituting all aspects of the social order, are we not drawn into an endless vortex of nihilism? After all, it's one thing to see a situation clearly, quite another to propose what to do. This "dark realism" (Boyne 1990, 130) of the pervasive nature of power leaves us with a difficult, important question: "Where do we go from here" (130)? Or, perhaps more darkly, *Can* we go from here? I stopped and surveyed the expanse beside me, stretching endlessly to the horizon. During my travels, and especially along the Last Lonely Road, I felt I had come to know Foucault. Was my traveling companion really suggesting that every human action is completely predetermined to be a manifestation of procedures of power? Is it possible to speak of power, to work against power, without evoking defining metanarratives about power? Are we condemned to the pervasive, effective power of modernity? In the second great crisis of renewal in science education, can we speak in any way apart from the Great Conversation, or has Foucault simply elucidated some of the procedures of our entrapment, leading us to know more fully our hopeless situation? Here I was, at the edge of the Kingdom. Is my location a metaphor of what a study of the procedures of power teaches? The only direction of travel open to me was back towards the center of the Kingdom; indeed, this was the only direction for anyone, including the team, who might make the journey past the mountains. Then I came to know with complete certainty our modern situation: *There is no other kingdom, all we have is the kingdom we are in.* And if Foucault's elucidation of power is right, change in any discourse may well be beyond the reach of those in the discourse. I returned to my original assessment of the chasm at the edge of the Kingdom: We are hopelessly trapped. My elaboration of the procedures of power in the Kingdom seemed to only clarify the nature of this entrapment. From this assessment came a distinctly modern question: Now what?

Somehow, some way, there must be a way to help the children in the Kingdom, to find a cure for the disease. Yet I could not see a way out of the geography of the Kingdom and....

Excuse me! There is a knock on my door. I'm writing this section at my desk in my university office and I need to attend to this interruption. We will resume our conversation later.

(The First Interruption: Encouraging Beginning Voices)
I open the door to find Desireé, one of the students in an undergraduate science education methodology class I teach. I smile, greet her with a "Hi, Desireé," and invite her to sit down.

"So," I begin, "how can I help you?"[3]

She opens her notebook. "I wanted to ask you a question," she tells me. "You said in class today that there's been a declining interest among students in a career in science."

"Yes," I answer, "and my research with students (Blades 1992) also shows that students in secondary schools find their science classes boring and not relevant to their lives."

"O.K., but you also said that hope for change in all this lies with beginning teachers, like me." I nod agreement. Desireé then asks, "Well, my question is, how can a beginning teacher make such a difference? I mean, my friends doing their final practicum tell me that its all they can do to survive. Everyone knows your first few years are crazy and, well, I just wondered if...well..."

"If perhaps what I'm saying is out of touch with the realities of classroom life?" I venture.

She smiles. "Something like that."

It's a fair question. I was teaching these students they could make a difference in science education, that they were at the front lines, so to speak, of reform. And I believe it to be true. In fact, the possibility that beginning teachers could make a difference in the discourse of science education, and that I might play a role in encouraging this difference, was one of the reasons I left my high school classroom for a career at university. I thought of Desireé and her peers: Greg, Sherry, Jonathan, Steve, Kim...all of my students young, dedicated, eager teachers excited to teach children science. How could I encourage these beginning voices—give them courage—to truly make a difference? What could I say to Desireé; what could I say to my students?

I can begin by engaging Desireé, and her peers, in a conversation of critique.

"Remember in class how we explored stereotypes of scientists?" I ask. She nods. "What did the brainstorming exercise teach you?"

She laughs. "I was surprised," she confesses, "to find how many stereotypes of science *I* had. Our whole group laughed a lot as we shared stereotypes of scientists we had seen in films and movies. But," she adds, "I think the part of the lesson I liked the best was the way you showed us how the scientific method was not the straight-forward, rational access to truth we were taught in school."

"Why did you like this part the best?" I inquire.

"You see, Professor Blades... I hate to tell you this, but, well, even though I was good at it I *hated* science when I was in school. It was so, well, boring. Those things you shared about what students had to say about their science classes? That could have been my voice."

"That's O.K., Desireé," I respond, "most students tell me how much they hated their school science. Some, of course, also tell me they enjoyed their experience with school science. But I'm curious. What did you enjoy about our discussion about the scientific method?"

"What you said about science and other fields," she says decisively. She glances at her notes. "You said...wait, I have it here:

We have a wilderness of mystery to make our way through in the centuries ahead, and we will need science for this but not science alone. Science will, in its own time, produce the data and some of the meaning in the data, but never the full meaning. For getting a full grasp, for perceiving real significance when significance is at hand, we shall need minds at work from all sorts of brains outside the fields of science, most of all the brains of poets, of course, but also those of artists, musicians, historians, writers in general. (Thomas 1980, 150)

She closes her notebook. "You see," she continues, "this is a whole new idea to me. I always thought science and math were the most important subjects, at least in our school that's how it was. If you weren't good at science, well..."

"You felt like a failure?"

"Not really, more like you were made to feel not very smart. I was good at science, so I was O.K., but my best friend was good at art, but that didn't seem to count."

"Why not?"

"Because to get into university you needed science, and she also wanted to be a teacher. So, you can imagine how both of us felt when we found out that to become teachers we would have to take more science courses at university!

"And how do you feel now?"

"I can't believe it, but I actually like science now! It's fun."

"What changed your mind?"

"Well, I really enjoyed some of my university science classes— some of the profs are excellent—but I think my attitude changed when I realized in your class that science can be fun, and that science is not the most important way of knowing about life, just one way of knowing. Also, I'm looking forward to our class on environmental education. I think it's important we teach kids about how they can help heal the world."

"Desireé," I began, "although I'm no longer teaching in schools full time, I spend a lot of time there. In these schools I still see students having the same experience with science that you and your friend had when you were in school. You first asked me how you could make a difference in the lives of the children. I would say that if your students learn that science is something you *do*, a human activity full of fun, adventure, and limits like all human activity, important but not any more important that other types of human activity, then the children you teach will come to see science differently that you did and perhaps they will appreciate and understand science better. If you can do this, then you *will* have made a difference in science education."

Desireé ponders this thought for awhile, then rises to leave. "Thanks, Professor Blades. I see what you mean. Now I'm excited to teach children science!" She laughs. "Who knows? Maybe I'll make science my major!" She leaves the door open.

Maybe she will. Lots of students, when they realize how fun and exciting science can be, do change majors. Although this conversation interrupted my writing, I was glad to encourage Desireé, I always enjoy engaging my students in conversation, helping them to find a vision of what could be.

But I know the odds are against them. Once out in the schools these young teachers face an "institutional opposition or inertia" (Gruender and Tobin 1991, 6) reflected in a welcome by their experienced colleagues to the so-called 'real world' where the advice and examples of university professors are dismissed as the suspect ravings of ivory tower theorists on the fringes of educational practice. Educator Eric Wood (1990) reminds us that these beginning teachers have also experienced through their schooling a "10,000 hour 'apprenticeship of observation' and this apprenticeship is a powerful shaper of teacher belief and actions" (30). In the frenetic life of a new teacher, the siren of transmissional teaching—a conveyance of facts where students are required to depend without question on the authority of the teacher—will beckon through the examples of experienced colleagues and the remembered experiences of once being a child in school.

Desireé has left my office, but the interruption of her visit left questions behind. How can I encourage these beginning teachers to teach an authentic view of science as a human and social activity, to continue developing an STS approach to science education? In an age when teaching is increasingly becoming "not more than narrow technical skills" (P. Ryan 1989, 18) how might new teachers "enlist students as active, critical participants in the learning process" (Gruender and Tobin, 6)? Is there any way professors of education can support their students in the difficult task of retaining a voice of critique of what is once students graduate and (hopefully) find a classroom? Is the critique of science and science education offered in a methodology class enough? Is the development of this critique what beginning teachers need to make a difference in science education? Is it realistic to expect these voices alone can effect change in the long-established and quite resilient curriculum-discourses of science education? Might this critique find avenues for change through research partnerships between beginning teachers, university professors, experienced classroom teachers and children in schools?

The Second Book: Heidegger's Warning

Beside the door to my office is a book shelf. Glancing over the texts arrayed there, I find *The Opening of Vision* by the Heideggerian scholar David Levin (1988). I allow the book to open and notice that I have marked the following passage:

> Deep spiritual wisdom, deep enlightenment, lies hidden in the visionary being with which we are gifted in the innateness of childhood... But it is much harder for us, living in society, a world, a reality brought forth out of so much blindness, to see in that way. The historically given culture in which we live is itself more closed off from the presence of Being and its enchantment of vision. (58–59)

Where did this blindness come from? What has caused the loss of Being Levin speaks of? I glance at my desk and remember the narrative I am writing. I sit down and pick up my pen, transported back to the abyss at the edge of the Kingdom.

But as I stood before the vast chasm, the words by Levin continued to echo in my thinking. What does he mean by a loss of vision? I sat down, dangling my feet into the somber grayness before me. The afternoon Sun was warm and I felt sleepy. I surveyed the chasm once more. The horizon was not broken by the promise of anything different below than an infinite fall that disappeared to a blackness the sunlight could not reach. But today, inspired perhaps by Levin's comment, I continued to look.

At first, the haunting landscape of the precipice was as I found it every other time I looked over: a uniform wall of featureless gray rock. But this time I thought I noticed something different, a movement perhaps. I imagined that I saw a small sphere, like a black softball, moving along a straight path along the void. I found it hard to estimate the size of the object or its trajectory, but I recognized the object from pictures I had seen: It was the satellite *Sputnik*. As if in a dream, I followed the satellite until it was out of sight. I heard the now familiar moan as wind rushed into the abyss. But a new sound rose from the depths, the unmistakable sound of a baby crying. I looked for the source of the sound and somehow the light along the cliff face formed the shadow of a newborn child. And I knew the child was me, born only a few years before the launching of the first human-made satellite. An eerie series of visions appeared to me that afternoon. I saw scientists at the Wood's Hole Conference commissioned to work on science education reform in the United States in the interests of national defense. Then I could see myself as a young boy, holding a bucket of 20 or so garter snakes I had captured to study. I remembered my father built a cage for the snakes, assuring my mother the snakes could not possibly escape. I laughed out loud recalling the shriek from the kitchen as my mother discovered one of my snakes in a kitchen drawer!

Had I always been interested in science, or was a scientific interest nurtured in my upbringing? It was hard to say. Chemistry sets, electronic kits, microscopes and telescopes dominated my birthday gifts. I grew up in an era when all my friends, at least all my male friends, wanted to be scientists. I saw myself building models of Titan rockets, watching the original *Star Trek* series, reading novel after novel of science fiction. Then I watched the shadows narrate the landing of the Eagle spacecraft on the Moon. I felt again the thrill of the world as I watched, transfixed, as Neil Armstrong climbed out of the craft to stand on the Moon. A deep sigh came over me. Those were the days. If we could land people on the moon, I thought again, surely we could find a cure for the disappearing children in the Kingdom. After all, had I not grown up with the newly found cure for polio? Was not smallpox eradicated when I was a boy? Millions of children used to die from complications due to infections, but the development of powerful antibiotics before I was born enabled my generation to weather childhood diseases generally without harm.

My thoughts traveled back to my house back in the Kingdom. Through science and technology I could enjoy the quick convenience of a microwave oven, control over TV with my VCR, absolute fidelity in musical recording with my CD player, and ready access to information and production of text and graphics with my powerful microcomputer. I could enjoy relatively accurate weather predictions thanks to an application of satellite technology. Perhaps the modern promise of a better life through science and technology was true.

But the narration of the vision was not over. I saw with horror the use of napalm in the Vietnam War, the technologically sophisticated terror of carpet bombing and the perverse rape of the jungle by Agent Orange. With complete incredulity I watched myself as a young boy practicing with my classmates how to dive under our desks and cover our heads during routine drills for protection in the event of an attack by nuclear weapons. DDT, *Silent Spring*, Thalidomide children, Three Mile Island, Chernobyl—I witnessed the slow growth of crisis in a generation raised on faith in science and technology to progress. I did not want the next vision to appear, but I knew it was coming and somehow I could not turn my eyes away: I saw the sudden, tragic death of astronauts in the explosion of the space shuttle *Challenger*, a horrific exclamation mark to a text that spoke of the loss of faith in the promises of modernity. The promise of *Apollo* became the horror of *Challenger*; a deep sadness and sense of loss filled my soul. I stood up and turned away from the abyss, unable to bear the visions I found there, confused about the message these visions held. The words of the poet e. e. cummings came to visit as I stood along the edge of the abyss:[4]

pity this busy monster,manunkind,

not. Progress is a comfortable disease:
your victim(death and life safely beyond)

plays with the bigness of his littleness
—electrons deify one razorblade
into a mountainrange;lenses extend

unwish through curving wherewhen till unwish
returns on its unself.
                          A world of made
is not a world of born—pity poor flesh

and trees,poor stars and stones,but never this
fine specimen of hypermagical

ultraomnipotence. We doctors know

a hopeless case if—listen:there's a hell
of a good universe next door;let's go

I remember this poet once observed that we "can never be born enough" (Cummings 1969, 436). What did he mean in his poem that there's "a good universe next door"? How is finding this universe part of "a world of born?" I had been traveling a long time, but I felt no closer to helping the children in the Kingdom that when I first started my journeys many years ago.

It was way past lunch, and the break in the visions from the abyss allowed me the chance to realize I was hungry. I returned to my tent and reached into my travel sack, but instead of food I once again found one of the books I had brought with me on my journey. It was *The Question Concerning Technology* by Heidegger (1977). Heidegger begins this short book with the cryptic phrase that the "essence of technology is by no means anything technological" (287). But then he adds the explanation that "we shall never experience our relationship to the essence of technology so long as we merely conceive and push forward the technological, put up with it, or evade it" (287). Heidegger then proceeds to make a distinction between instrumental definition of technology as the application of scientific ideas, i.e., tools, equipment, etc. and an anthropological view of technology, that is, the means by which certain ends are achieved. Heidegger then asks a key question: Suppose technology was more than either of these two conceptions? By linking the bringing-forth (*poiesis*)[5] of something to technology, Heidegger deftly turns process into a question that dis-covers the essence of technology: What does technology itself bring forth, or reveal? Thus, Heidegger concludes that "technology is therefore no mere means. Technology is a way of revealing" (294).

What does technology reveal? Through the example of the construction of a hydroelectric plant on the Rhine river, Heidegger suggests "the essence of modern technology shows itself in what we call enframing (*Ge-stell*)" (304). The German verb *stellen* (to set upon) is also used, Heidegger notes, to mean "producing," or "presenting" (302). Then Heidegger reaches a profound insight. *Ge-stell* is an active process, a type of producing a particular revelation, that is, a particular way of seeing the world: A technological way. Heidegger calls this revealing *destining* (306). I note that I marked a passage that to me is the central point of Heidegger's claim:

> The essence of technology lies in enframing. Its holding sway belongs within destining. Since destining at any given time starts man [sic] on a way of revealing, man [sic], thus underway, is continually approaching the brink of possibility of pursuing and pushing forward *nothing but what is revealed in*

ordering, and of deriving all his standards on this basis. Through this the other possibility is blocked. (307, emphasis mine.)

In fact, Heidegger claims the destining of revealing of technology is "is in itself not just any danger, but *the* danger" (308, emphasis his). Heideggerian scholar Yong-Sik Kim (1991) explains the nature of this danger. Speaking about a technological way of seeing, Kim observes that in modernity

> the world is looked upon as just so much raw material waiting to be used up, to be shaped and transformed by labor. For modern human being, to be is to be re-presented, or posited (gestelit). Heidegger calls this new understanding of Being "*Ge-stell*," or the "enframing." He says in terms of his use of it to speak of the gathering-place that accomplishes in itself in techne as a bringing-forth that delineates, shapes, and reveals. When Being has withdrawn, ge-stell can but speak of a despoiling, structuring, a delimiting that brings everything, to appear only as a semblance of itself. It is as this enplaning, annihilating summons that modern technology holds sway. Ruled by this claim, human being is estranged from oneself in the modern age. (49–50)

It is dealing with this estrangement that was the life work of Heidegger: The struggle to recover Being by finding and maintaining a critical spirit towards those essences, such as modern technology, that continually threaten the closure of Being (Krell, 1977). But how do we find this critical spirit? How can we avoid the destining closure of being from modern technology? Heidegger quotes the German poet Hölderlin:

> But where the danger is, grows
> The saving power also. (310)

What does Heidegger mean by this? In her comparison of the work of Heidegger and Foucault, Jana Sawicki (1987) suggests Heidegger maintains the conviction change is possible because "all thinking in the modern age will not be reduced to technological thinking" (165). I marked my spot in Heidegger's text and stepped outside my tent, the thought of food long forgotten. Heidegger presents the situation of modernity with astounding clarity, but also suggests there also exists salvation from the defining entrapment of technicality. Where is this salvation? How might it begin?

I continued to read, pacing the ground between the chasm and my tent. Heidegger suggests in his book that through the "essential reflection upon technology" (317) we may yet reach a decisive confrontation between what is and what could be, leading to an opening for other possibilities. Exactly as the poet Cummings suggested, change is a matter of being re-born, a question of Being. And how does this journey to change Being begin? Heidegger calls us to *questioning* with the conclusion that "the closer we come to the danger, the more brightly do the ways into the saving power begin to shine and the more questioning we become" (317). Thus, questioning is not a technique to overcome technology, but a way of being that opens Being and, in so doing, may free us from the destining of technology.

Questioning. Question. I closed Heidegger's work and thought about the word 'question'. From the Latin *quaerere*, 'to ask', the word also means 'to seek,' from which we derive the English word, 'quest'. Thus, seeking and asking are bound in the word question, a word that also asks, what Quest-I-on? What Quest was I on? It was a good question! Well, I wanted to find a route out of the Kingdom; I had been on a quest to cure the children in the Kingdom of their horrible disease. Like the members of the team, I believed it was a matter of finding the correct route, of traveling the right roads so that the formula for curing the children would be discovered. Somewhere outside the Kingdom, we were convinced, the answers to our problems could be found. None of us imagined, least of all myself, that the Kingdom was surrounded by an uncrossable abyss, we simply had faith in... In what? I stopped pacing. In what?

A cold lump grew in my stomach and I began to feel sick. I knew where our faith lay and what our quest had become. It was all painfully clear. Sincerely concerned about the fate of our children in the Kingdom, everyone in the Quest, including myself, had slipped imperceptibly, comfortably, into technological thinking as we tried to find the correct route out of the Kingdom. We had assumed that curing the children was a matter of technique: Gather all the right people together, engage in the right Quest, travel in the right direction, and the children would be cured. Our Quest was founded on the technical search for The Answer, what I call the technical-rational approach to curriculum change in Chapter 2. But the destining of modernity revealed the futility of our Quest, leading the team to the status quo while blocking any other possibility. Then I knew what Foucault meant by the word power. I recorded in my journal that day:

> A discourse is clearly framed by the larger discourses in society. It's nearly impossible to move beyond technicality in curriculum change when our culture is destined to think in modern ways. It is also bigger than all of us, a great anonymous force that really *is* power—in a "powerful" way, so to speak. The question is: "Oh, great! Now what?" (Journal entry, June 22, 1992, emphasis in the entry.)

Completely ill, I looked once again in the abyss. The visions were still there, but this time I could see them all at once. They provided a panorama of my own careful definition: I became a thoroughly modern man, nurtured by faith in science and technology as a child, lacking a critical voice as a university student, and dedicated to modernity as a science teacher as I worked with evangelistic zeal to maintain the Great Conversation of modernity. I was not merely a participant in this conversation, I *was* this conversation and it was me. Then I knew the abyss I had reached at the edge of the Kingdom was mine. I had constructed it, or allowed its construction, I maintained it and invested in it; it was my Being: a vast wasteland of grayness that is wretched, torn, exhausted, and made colorless by the empty promises of modernity. I realized looking into my abyss that change is not, can never be, a question of technique. Change, true change that makes a difference in lives, must explore *questions of being*. I recoiled from this revelation in horror and terror. I had not expected my journey would turn out this way, that it would turn on myself. I did not want the fate of the children tied to the very discourse of a life—*my* life—to a conversation that included questions about who I am, why I live as I do and how else it might be.

I turned and ran as fast as I could from the abyss. Past my tent, onto the plain I ran in a cold sweat that came from fear. Finally, out of breath, I stopped right at the place where the snow began on the plain. I thought I saw, for a moment, the forest along the mountains in the distance. Foucault might still be waiting for me there. Somehow, that thought gave me courage. I knew why I had run, what I *really* feared the most: I was terrified of the personal responsibility of change, worried that even with an ontological turn to questions of change, there still might be the possibility that nothing will happen.

But Heidegger seemed confident that "questioning builds a way" (287). Drawing on Heidegger's work, David Levin (1988) also seems hopeful that change is possible. He suggests a point where questioning might begin:

> If we do not interpret enframing experientially, as, for example, something which actually *happens* in the field of our vision, we may miss an exceptional opportunity to work with ourselves and prepare for a vision which could participate in the advent of a different historical existence. (74, emphasis his.)

But how might we interpret the experience of *Das Ge-stell*? How can we investigate *how* we are enframed? Would such an investigation reveal possibilities for the other, reveal hope for change? I glanced up, convinced that I could see the forest as a thin green line highlighted by the clear light of the late afternoon.

I thought of my traveling companion Foucault. His elaboration of particular procedures of power through a Nietzschean investigation of "specific histories of technological practices" (Sawicki 1987, 168) allowed him to go beyond Heidegger's project by calling into question "modern notions of self, society, and history by showing how they have been constituted" (168). Sawicki notes that in this way Foucault is in the business, like Heidegger, of combating technological nihilism, although Foucault's historicities are

> designed to make the present seem less inevitable...not in the discovery of the essential features of the human situation, in the complete mastery of reality, or in releasement, but rather in "rebelling against the ways in which we are already defined, categorized and classified" by the dominating technologies of power. (169)

While Heidegger sought to fight against *Das Ge-stell* of modernity through a recovery of Being, Foucault adopts a more pragmatic stance: He invites us by example to dis-cover how this enframing works so that we can fight it.

But does this not present, once again, a dilemma? Earlier I raised concerns that Foucault's concept of power might not be valid, or possibly could be seen as a deterministic meta-theory. Foucault was, in fact, asked this very question: "Can you, too, not be criticized for seeing power everywhere, and, in the final analysis, of reducing everything to power?" (Foucault 1988, 104). In that interview

Foucault characteristically avoided the question, choosing instead to cite examples of what he termed the "problem of power" (104). In an earlier interview Foucault (1989h) claimed he was not a "theoretician of power" (254). He explains that "when I examine relationships of power, I create no theory of power. It is how relationships of power interact, are determining elements in every relationship which I want to examine" (254). In his examination of some of the implications of Foucault's thought to education, James Ryan (1991) suggests that Foucault refuses to grant power ontological status by consistently changing the question "What is power?" to questions about how power is exercised (110). This questioning has validity, suggest Foucauldian scholars Dreyfus and Rabinow (1982), precisely because Foucault admits to sharing our modern situation. They point out that Foucault "offers us, from the inside, pragmatically guided accounts" of the "organizing trends in our culture" (203). It is these accounts, suggests Leslie Thiele (1990) in an essay on the influence of Nietzshe's works on Foucault's thinking, that offer hope in our modern condition:

> Yes, our words and deeds, moral and political, are always suspect for their tainted origins and strategic implication; for there is no philosophical realm from which we might speak the truth to power. But no, we are not then left without any premise or purpose of our actions. There is indeed a legitimization for struggle, namely, the perpetuation and amelioration of the conditions that make struggle itself possible. (918)

Thiele describes Foucault's political project as "the valorization of struggle" (918) that is valid and hopeful since "it is the human condition to exist within a system of power; it is the human potential to incessantly resist its reach, relocate its boundaries and challenge its authority" (918).

This assumption of the human condition permeates Foucault's discourse on power, presenting an underlying stance of what might be called 'pessimistic hopefulness' in the face of modernity. The extent and effectiveness of power invokes a certain pessimism in the face of the task ahead of us, indeed it would be easy to become deterministic about power from a reading of Foucault's work. But this would be a superficial reading of Foucault, claims Bernauer (1990), since Foucault's work is also an invitation to "dissident thinking" (121) founded on the realization that "the other side of power's pervasiveness is precisely the omnipresence of the resistance it discovers" (150). Philosopher Gilles Deleuze (1988) agrees that Foucault also suggests hope in resistance since "power does not take life as its objective without revealing or giving rise to a life that resists power" (94). Foucault (1990) makes this observation in *The History of Sexuality, Volume 1*:

> just as the network of power relations ends by forming a dense web that passes through apparatuses and institutions, without being exactly localized in them, so too the swarm of points of resistance traverses social stratifications and individual unities. (96)

Foucault suggests, very cautiously, the strategic codification of these points of resistance makes "revolution possible, somewhat similar to the way in which the state relies on the institutional integration of power relationships" (96). But revolution is always a local event to Foucault. He assumes individual responsibility for action at points of resistance (Gordon 1980), although he suggests that helping other people "get their own struggles going in specific areas" (Foucault 1984c, 376) would be a post-modern ethical practice. Aside from this comment, Foucault preferred to demonstrate his ethics through personal involvement in prison reform and other areas involving human rights.[6] Change, in Foucauldian terms, is clearly a local event, a type of specific guerrilla warfare involving the relentless trachealization of discourses that attempt to define who can speak and what can be said, a call to a way of living Foucault calls 'critique'.[7] Foucault (1982) explains that by critique he refers to the act of

> showing that things are not as obvious as we might believe, doing it in such a way that what we accept as going without saying no longer goes without saying. To criticize is to render the too-easy gestures difficult. (34)

In other words, to continuously question, as philosopher G. B. Madison puts it, so as to fight the "distortions, systematic or otherwise, that constantly menace our conversations, the ones we pursue with our own self as well as those we pursue with others" so that we can "maintain the openness of the conversation and keep it going" (169).

I stood up, stretched and walked back to my tent to place the book by Heidegger back in my travel sack. The title of the third book I had brought had slipped my mind, and I was curious which one I had chosen. I also was beginning to feel very hungry. Returning to my tent, I thought about Heidegger's point that hope lies in the recovery of Being by maintaining a critical spirit towards that which continually threatens the closure of Being. This was very close to what Foucault meant by living critique, but Foucault has given us some advice as to *what* we could critique: the procedures of power that define who can speak and what can be said. I turned and looked over towards the edge of the abyss. When I first arrived at this location the chasm seemed to me a horrible barrier to change, a geographical enframing (*Ge-stell*) that prevented me from leaving the Kingdom of modernity. Is there another way of seeing this abyss? An idea began to form in my thinking. Maybe the chasm...

Another interruption! Please excuse me once again, there is *another* knock on the door to my office. I apologize—I feel like we will never finish our conversation!

(The Second Interruption: Challenging Experienced Voices)
Will pokes his head through the open door, knocking on the door frame. He is one of the graduate students I supervise. He often drops by and I always look forward to his provocative questions. "Gotta minute?"

"Sure Will," I reply. I put down my pen and with some reluctance leave my narrative for the moment. "So, how's the thesis proposal progressing?" I ask.[8]

"That's why I'm here," he explains. "I've run into a problem."

"What problem?" I ask.

"O.K., you remember I wanted to do my research on environmental education..."

"Right," I interject, "you were interested in developing a new environmental education program."

"Well, I *was*," Will confesses, "but lately I've been reading this book by Orr.[9] Now all I have are questions."

"Such as?" I invite.

"Well, Orr argues that our present environmental crisis "cannot be solved by the same kind of education that helped create the problems" (Orr 1992, 83).

"I agree with him," I add.

"I can see his point," Will tells me. "This week in my curriculum class we read a paper by W. Doll (1989) that says we need to 'challenge the modernist assumptions on which our present curriculum is founded' (252). Do you remember the book by Oelschlaeger I told you about?"

"You mean, *The Idea of Wilderness* (Oelschlaeger 1991)?"

"Yes," Will continues, "well, in that book he gives a good description of how our modern era was founded on the belief in the positive value of transforming wilderness."[10]

"After your recommendation I decided to read the book," I remark. "I remember Oelschlaeger described modernity as a historical movement as through 'science, technology, and liberal democracy modern people hoped to transform a base and worthless wilderness into industrialized, democratic civilization' (68)."

"Exactly. That book was a turning point for me," Will tells me. " I began to see how the modern project viewed wilderness as an object to exploit, not as what Cheney (1989) provokingly describes as a 'player in the construction of community' (128)."

"This is new to me, Will," I tell him. "Can you explain what you mean?"

"I'm still working through it," he admits, "but I like the idea of wilderness as a voice that can speak to us. Orr calls this having 'a dialogue with a place' (90)."

"What do you like about it?" I inquire.

"Well, Kohak (1984) argues that with the expansion of technology we have 'translated our concepts into artifacts, radically restructuring not only our conception of nature but the texture of our ordinary experience as well' (12). This restructuring took humanity from a biocentric (humans as only one element in an ecosystem dynamic) to an anthropocentric view (human-centered view of life). It seems to me that we need to recover a biocentric view (Guha, 1989) if we are to survive. At least, that's what I think Orr is saying in his book."

"But how can we achieve this new view, Will?" I ask.

"I'm not sure. I think part of this recovery involves a rethinking of wilderness, somehow listening to the narrative of nature, and realizing that we humans are not apart from nature but instead are part of it. I think this is what Orr means by a post-modern view of environmental education."

"I agree, I think this is what he argues."

"But this leaves me with a big problem!" Will tells me. "I was planning an environmental education program for the entire state..."

"...and?" I encourage.

Will sighs. Well, I'm beginning to think that maybe such a proposal is too technical..."

"Too modern?" I suggest.

"Exactly," Will responds. The more I read about post-modern environmental education and the further my studies in curriculum, the harder it is for me to see my project the same way."

"What do you mean?" I inquire.

"My studies in curriculum have opened a Pandora's box," he explains. "My whole awareness of educational issues has expanded. I used to think that changing the curriculum was simply a matter of developing a new program and giving it to teachers."

"Yet, did you not find that when you received programs for your classroom you changed them to fit your local situation?" I wonder out loud.

Will bursts out laughing. "All the time!" He says. "But I also changed them to what I thought was best for the kids. I guess my studies have shown me that the whole issue of curriculum and, in particular, curriculum change is more complex than I thought. In a way, I feel like my eyes have been opened now."

"Opened to what?" I inquire.

"To new ideas. I no longer take things for granted, like curriculum documents. I see the hidden curriculum of these documents and I know I'm more critically aware now of what goes on in schools. I think I understand what you call the agenda of modernity now."

"This brings us back to your thesis," I observe. "When you first arrived you mentioned you had a problem. What is that problem, Will?"

He smiles. "Just this: How can I develop a state-wide program that adopts a post-modern approach to environmental education?"

"I'm not sure that you can," I confess.

"I was afraid you'd say that!" Will laughs. So, now I have a whole new set of questions. What would a post-modern environmental education look like? What would we study? Would everyone have to study the same thing..."

"I don't see how they could," I respond. "Modernism maintains the belief in totalizing, colonizing discourse dependent on the assumption that concepts and theories can be 'abstracted from their paradigm setting and applied elsewhere' (Cheney, 120). A post-modern education would have to embrace some expression that the 'particular, the different are what's important, not the universal and the general' (Hutcheon 1991, 18)."

"But how could I encourage change in particular, local situations without some kind of general curriculum?" Will asks.

"Why not begin in your school setting?" I reply. "You're returning back to your classroom next year, right?"

"Yes, I only have a one year leave of absence."

"Suppose you were to infuse your biology or chemistry class, or both, with an environmental perspective? Instead of proposing a new curriculum, which seems to me fractionates our concerns about the environment further, why not research what you can develop in your own educational setting?"

"That research would have to involve my students," Will suggests.

"Absolutely," I agree. "You might wish to involve some fellow teachers in your research, perhaps a university professor."

"What would we research?"

"You mentioned earlier that a post-modern view of the environment would involve learning to listen to the narrative voice of wilderness. That suggests a provocative question: What would be the effect of a child's conception of the environment if that child learned to listen to the voice of wilderness?"

"Of course," muses Will, "the problem is, what is wilderness?"

"A key question," I add.

Will rises to leave. "You've given me a lot to think about," he says. "My view on teaching and environmental issues is totally different since I came to study at the university. It hasn't always been easy to have your head busted,[11] but all in all its been worth it. I think I'm going to drastically change my thesis proposal. Is it O.K. if I run it by you when I have a draft?"

"Anytime, Will," I call back. "You're always welcome."

Will goes to leave, but before he does he turns at the door and says, "You know, I won't be returning to my school the same person. I've seen a bigger view of education and after today I think I can see where I can make a difference in environmental education. I wish all teachers could have a chance to study for a year!"

"But its a two way street, Will," I tell him. "Before meeting you I was only somewhat interested in environmental education. The books and readings you have sent my way have changed my life, too. I can no longer look at development and so-called wilderness the same after our many conversations."

"That's good to know," he tells me. "Conversation is important, eh?"

"I believe that through conversation change may begin. Which is why I think you need to form a research partnership with your students and perhaps some of the teachers in your school."

"Interesting ideas, Dave. I'll have to think on that further. I'll see you later."

I call out good-bye as Will leaves. He'll be back with more questions as he finds his way and I know our conversations will enrich us both. His experience, and the experience of all our graduate students, encourages all of us to reflect on how schooling might be different. Their studies open a vista previously unknown to them, or provides a language to confirm their experiences and hunches about education. In their growing critique of the discourse of education these experienced voices reflect on their local situations and often discover active points of resistance in power and thus opportunities for change. Their vision for change is fundamentally practical; from their experience and their studies many graduate students work within the possible, choosing action-research projects that focus on changing particular situations. Over a year, or two, or more of graduate study students find hope and realize anew that their desire to make a difference in the world is possible.

What happens to these teachers when they return to the classroom? Do they lose their vision as their lives as teacher become increasingly intensified (Apple 1988)? Suppose teachers were given sabbaticals for study. What effect would these "time-outs" for reflection have on education? How can teachers take a more active role in educational research? Will's visits always seem to leave me with many questions. Why do we assume a centralized, single program of studies is best for a state, a province, or a nation? Why not encourage local centers of curriculum development where teachers, parents, and students work together in choosing the content and approach of the curriculum?

What is the role of professors of education in helping their colleagues teaching children find ways to change schooling? Should professors of education spend more time in schools? Would a partnership of experienced teachers with professors of education provide for a better education for undergraduate students of education? How can professors of education help teachers capture visions for how else schooling might be, visions that are not defined and constrained by the power of the existing discourse?

The Third Book: Nietzsche's Challenge

It's getting late. I decide to grab a cup of coffee from the faculty lounge and return to my office to tidy up before traveling home. As I come to my door I re-read a quote by Nietzsche (1969) I have posted:

> Why was I so frightened in my dream that I awoke? Did not a child carrying a mirror come to me? "O Zarathustra," the child said to me, "look at yourself in the mirror!" But when I looked in the mirror I cried out and my heart was shaken. (107)

I walk into my office pondering the words of Zarathustra and suddenly remember the third book I had brought along on my journey was also by Nietzsche: *On The Genealogy of Morals* (1967). I glance over to my desk at the unfinished narratives and sigh. Will I ever complete this story? I pick up my pen, transported once again to the barren wasteland and the chasm that has become my focal point for most of my final chapter.

The late afternoon sunlight was warm and deep shadows crossed the plain when I turned into my tent to retrieve the final book I had brought on my journey. I found Nietzsche often quite cryptic and wondered why I had brought this particular work along with me. The text was still fairly new, a testimony to how little I had explored Nietzsche's discussion of morals. I glanced at the first few pages and began to read.

Nietzsche writes with a deep, personal, humorous style I find inviting. In the preface to *On The Genealogy of Morals*, Nietzsche describes the agony of his journey to understand morals: "I saw the *great* danger to mankind [sic], its sublimest enticement and seduction—but to what? to nothingness?—it was precisely here that I saw the beginning of the end, the dead stop, a retrospective weariness, the will turning *against* life" (19, emphasis his). His description of the end of his inquiry reflected my discovery of the chasm of modernity in my search for change. I, too, had come to feel the dead stop Nietzsche describes. Nietzsche continues in his preface to share how asking questions, in his case questions about the value of morals, leads to new demands that open up understanding. He tells us that whoever

> *learns* how to ask questions here will experience what I experienced—a tremendous new prospect opens up for him, a new possibility comes over him like a vertigo, every kind of mistrust, suspicion, fear leaps up, his belief in morality, in all morality falters—finally a new demand becomes audible. Let us articulate this *new demand*. We need a critique of moral values. (20, emphasis his.)

I marked my page and stepped out of the tent, eager to look once more at the chasm before nightfall. It was not yet twilight, but deep shadows already obscured the place where I had once seen visions.

The chasm no longer frightened me, or even depressed me now that I knew both its origin and purpose. As the day came to an end I pondered the same question that I began the day with: The future. What should I do? How should I live? Now what? Nietzsche cites *cheerfulness* as "the reward of a long, brave, industrious, and subterranean seriousness" (21). Certainly I had been serious for too long! Long days agonizing by the chasm had worn on me, I could feel it. Cheerfulness seemed to me a very odd consequence to my labors, but Nietzsche assures us that it is possible to reach this condition. When we do, he explains, we will be able to "say with all our hearts, 'Onwards! our old morality is too part *of the comedy!*'" (21–22, emphasis his).

What comedy? There was nothing comic about the Quest others and I had taken. What was all our efforts destined to discover? Simply that all the roads out of the kingdom eventually lead to a chasm; a deep, uncrossable abyss of our own making. Our situation was not funny or even vaguely amusing. What was Nietzsche talking about?

I sat beside the abyss and read over Nietzsche's discussion of the genealogy of morals. In his first essay he argues that the concept of good and evil are not transcendent states of existence, but categories of behavior defined by "'the good' themselves, that is to say, the noble, powerful, high-stationed and high-minded, who felt and established themselves and their actions as good" (26). In his next essay Nietzsche makes a similar claim about responsibility, suggesting an origin in the relation between creditor and debtor. Then a passage in this essay about punishment captured my attention. Instead of elaborating a genealogy of the purpose of punishment, Nietzsche advances the ideas that

> the cause of the origin of a thing and its eventual utility, its actual employment and place in a system of purposes, lie worlds apart; whatever exists, having somehow come into being, is again reinterpreted to new ends, taken over, transformed and redirected by some power superior to it; all events in the organic world are a subduing, a *becoming master*. (77, emphasis his.)

Nietzsche then identifies what this becoming master is: "In all events a will to power is operating" (78). On summer vacation in 1953, Foucault was to read Nietzsche's words for the first time, and his life work was to forever travel in a new direction, inspired by Nietzsche's insight of power (Eribon 1991). In his essay, *Nietzsche, Genealogy, History* Foucault (1984d) applies Nietzsche's notion of a will to power to include a critique of a "rancorous, creative, destructive will to knowledge" (Megill 1985, 238) that was expressed by example in *The History of Sexuality, Volume 1* and other major works. By extending Nietzsche's will to power to include a will to knowledge, Foucault was able to formulate and extend the type of critique first articulated in Nietzsche's *On The Genealogy of Morals* to "matters of institutions, politics, and knowledge-production" (Deleuze 1988, x). In an interview Foucault (1989b) admits his entire project was greatly influenced by Nietzsche's *The Birth of Tragedy* and *The Genealogy of Morals*. When asked what he found interesting in these two works by Nietzsche, Foucault replied: "What I liked in Nietzsche is the attempt to bring up for discussion again the fundamental concepts of knowledge, of morals, and of metaphysics" (77). Deleuze (1988) argues that Foucault's work is profoundly Nietzschean in the way Foucault calls to question again knowledge, morals, and metaphysics through an exploration of power that develops into three major themes:

1. Power is not necessarily repressive.
2. It is practiced before it is possessed.

3. It passes through the hands of the mastered no less than through the hands
    of the masters. (71)

Deleuze concludes that Foucault, standing on the shoulders of Nietzsche's project, presents a question for a modern generation: "We should not ask: 'What is power and where does it come from?' but 'How is it practiced?'" (71) Foucault was not interested in a hermeneutic of power, instead Foucault chose to ask how power works to define the institutions and knowledge-forms we take for granted. Foucault's project is therefore a fundamentally practical and hopeful extension of Nietzsche's critique (Fink-Eitel 1992), a trachealizing of the violence of *Ge-stell*, so that, once our enframing is wrestled and laid bare, we can find ways to fight against our modern situation.

Foucault's *oeuvre* presents a challenge to modernity, an invitation built on the work of Heidegger and Nietzsche to fight against the will to power and the will to knowledge that animates the Great Conversation. Yes, we are trapped in a Kingdom, but the King is no longer present, what remains is a vast nexus of power/knowledge relations, mobile and effective; knowing this we are already able to fight against the totalizing, defining effects of power. It is perhaps in this fight, located through the strategic encouragement of points of resistance in the Kingdom, where change may be possible. I realized that if we can change the Kingdom then perhaps the conditions that have led to the dis-ease of the children will also change, and our children will no longer disappear. I felt giddy with hope, charged and excited by possibility.

I recollected conversations with my students I had enjoyed back in the Kingdom. Those entering the priesthood would be one location for working to change the Kingdom. I thought of Desireé and her peers: enthusiastic and energetic individuals that provide a locus for change by encouraging them to find and keep voices of critique. I thought of those already in the priesthood, Will and other experienced voices I knew. During retreats or timely Sabbaticals from their duties or through the opening of spaces for reflection perhaps these voices could also find ways to change the Kingdom from within. With Desireé or Will it was really a matter of designing the correct programs for these individuals, of giving these voices insight into how power/knowledge is expressed in the Kingdom, of providing a system of analysis...

My thinking was suddenly interrupted by a strange sound moving towards me across the abyss. I could not recognize the sound at first, and it was already becoming too dark to see if I could find the source of the sound. Then the sound reached me with perfect clarity: It was laughter! A deep, full laugh, full of fun and mischief, a totally infectious laughter that left me chuckling, too. I laughed because I knew that my plan for turning Foucault's work into systematic analysis, despite my honorable intentions, was simply the voice of modernity, *my* voice, my continuation in the Great Conversation. I laughed because, well, it struck me as humorous that after such a long journey I could slip so easily into the ways of the Kingdom. I could see now what Nietzsche meant by the Comedy: it was life, our continual struggle of Being against those forces that define our every act, thought, and word. Our situation was not hopeless, Foucault has taught us this, but our task in the face of *Ge-stell* is not easy and never will be easy. Standing at the edge of the chasm, I knew that the challenge ahead was to remain constantly in a state of critique, but critique tempered with cheerfulness that comes from the realization that in the enormity of the task of change one simply has to laugh. I had no particular strategy for change in the Kingdom, I could give no workshops on change, no maps can be written, there would be no books on steps to transform a curriculum-discourse. All I had were questions and a suspicion that hope for change in the Kingdom is located in developing conversations of critique within the lives of the experienced and beginning voices I met as well as with the voices without a voice that are hidden on the margins of a curriculum-discourse. What these conversations might be and where they may lead I simply could not say. In fact, I had no guarantees at all these conversations were even possible, that change was even possible—*but I could try*. I burst out laughing and a deep cheerfulness entered my being. I realized that day, facing an abyss that I unknowingly had helped to build and maintain, that I could try, that action was possible and hope not futile. The chasm I lived beside became that day more than a reflection of my modern situation, *but a challenge to return to the Kingdom and critique what is so that what might be may become possible.*

Perhaps it was the setting Sun, but as I glanced across the chasm it seemed as if the vast expanse before me was no longer present, an illusion that vanished before my eyes presenting instead a featureless plain where once an abyss had been. I turned around and in the lengthening twilight, the only feature I could make out was the dim outline of the Lonely Mountains that encircle the Kingdom. I knew I must head back. Anxious to be underway before nightfall, I quickly broke camp, packed and set out towards the mountains.

As I marched with determination across the rocky landscape I never once turned to see if the abyss was simply an illusion. It did not matter to me any more. What entered my soul was a cheerful resolve to find my way back to the Kingdom. The last rays of the Sun touched the peaks of the Lonely Mountains, presenting a pink beacon to guide my way. In no time at all I came to the snowy expanse on the plain and began the steady trip back. I grimly noted the wind was still against me and I braced myself for a long, difficult trip back to the forest in the growing darkness. After hours of dismal walking, a dark shape began to loom before me and I knew I had found the forest at the foot of the Lonely Mountains. Far off to my right was a point of light and I made my way steadily in that direction. It was a campfire. Hungry, tired, and more than a little cold, I walked towards the comforting campfire eager for company after my long sojourn at the edge of the Kingdom.

(The Third Interruption: Considering The Voice of Children)
As I approached the light of the campfire I was surprised to see a group of children! There was about twenty or so, ranging in age from the very young to older children ready to leave the Cathedral. I stopped and listened. The younger children were intent on keeping the fire going, the older children were discussing their experiences at the Cathedral. I could just make out what they were saying.[12]

One young woman, Sally,[13] thought her studies of chemistry were not relevant at all. When asked why, she responded, "I guess I'm just not mathematical. I like things that pertain more to everyday life and things I can relate to more." Everyone laughed around the campfire. She continued, "I just don't find it particularly interesting to learn about cyclohexanes and things like that. It just doesn't seem very relevant to me because I don't really come upon it or anything at any point in my life."

One of her friends disagreed, "I think it's important just at least to get acquainted with it even if you may not remember any of it in the future."

Another chimed in, "But not physics! It could go!" There was general agreement.

A young man named Dave commented, "Physics isn't very well set up. You have textbooks and what they do in the textbooks is physics and history and how they brought these formulas...they don't spend too much time on how these formulas work and how to derive them."

Naomi jumped in at this point, "Yeah, it's just a there kinda thing, they really don't make sense out of it. It's hard..."

Ernest interrupted her, "It's not hard, it's boring!"

"Like Biology," proposed another young woman.

Her friends did not agree, "I thought it was good!" Ellen told the group.

Ernest added, "The way they brought up issues like the environment, eugenics, and stuff."

The young man next to him had a different experience. He commented that, "If we had one disappointment in our curriculum that would be the lack of things that touch people as a whole, like the environment, health concerns; we just vaguely touched on the little diseases here and there." Students seemed to agree with this sentiment.

The conversation then shifted.

Christine interjected a concern, "It kinda bothers me," She said, "that you need two sciences to get into any real thing" after you leave the Cathedral. She noted that, "for some people who can't do sciences, they can't do chemistry or physics, then they're out of it!"

Cheryl said that she was interested in the Priesthood, so she had to take all three sciences but, she added, "Not that I wanted to, but I had to." Her friends were sympathetic.

Karen suggested that it would be a lot easier if they had a general science course and students were able to specialize if they chose to once they left the Cathedral. Everyone thought this was a good idea and the discussion turned once more to the type of subjects they would like to study in this new program.

I was shocked by their conversation, absolutely transfixed by what the students were saying. Before beginning my studies to be a Scholar I had served as a Priest, teaching children science in the Cathedral. I always assumed that generally my students at least enjoyed their classes and the topics they were studying. Certainly *I* found organic chemistry interesting! And who could doubt the value of knowing chemistry and physics? Yet these students seem to find their high school science boring and not relevant to their life. I was quite surprised at the high level of sophistication and insight these students demonstrated in their choices of what they would like to study. In general, students wished for courses of study in science that were more aligned with the everyday science needs of consumers and citizens. A greater emphasis on first aid and knowledge about disease, more studies in environmental science, household chemistry, and an understanding of science issues in the news would form the core of their studies (Blades 1992). The students also felt a well rounded science program would include topics in astronomy, modern physics, and the history and philosophy of science. They weren't afraid of difficult topics, such as black holes, quantum physics, or complex genetics; what these students wanted was courses relevant to them now and in their future, courses that involve "dynamic teaching from well-qualified teachers who develop science courses from the history and philosophy of science using an investigative approach" (15). Sadly, they concluded that the students following them will only dream of such an experience.

Questions formed in my thinking as I listened to the concerned wisdom shared by these students. I had been involved in several curriculum design committees yet, now that I thought about it, students were never involved in committee discussions. Why are the voices of children excluded from program decisions? Is this exclusion a deliberate function of the science education curriculum-discourse? Nietzsche first introduced the concept of exclusion as a strategic effect of power in *The Genealogy of Morals*, and Foucault certainly extended Nietzsche's insight by demonstrating how discourse marginalizes individuals. Concerning students, Foucault (1989a) observed that the student is caught

> inside a circuit which possesses a dual function. First a function of exclusion. The student is put outside society, on a campus. Furthermore, he [sic] is excluded while being transmitted a knowledge traditional in nature, obsolete, "academic" and not directly tied to the needs and problems of today. (65)

As I watched these students engage in their serious reflection, I marveled how the group most marginalized by the Cathedral was the exact group the Cathedral was supposed to be serving: our students.

During my travels with the team I found the exclusion of voices in a discourse a specific procedure of power that defines a discourse. This must mean that the "deliberate exclusion of these voices [students'] from discourses on curriculum change is not accidental but a function of present discourse practices" (Blades 1992, 16). I thought about how easy it was to assume children "had little to contribute to a conversation on curriculum, how simple to exclude them with a word, an act, an approach" (Blades 1995, 149).

It need not be so. Educators Ungerleider (1986) and Lock (1984) found students willing and able to be involved in curriculum decision-making. The voice of those "on the front lines of education," (Townsend 1990, 4) so to speak, should provide valuable insight into the needs and potentials for learning in classrooms within the Cathedral of our Kingdom. In his essay, *How Can Schooling be Improved?* educator Richard Townsend (1990) uses a medical metaphor to summarize the value of student voices in curriculum decisions, noting that when it comes to changing education, "who can tell the doctor where it hurts better than the patient her or himself?" (4). Indeed, Foucault (1989a) takes this one step further in his suggestion that the entire Cathedral system "can be put into question by the students themselves" (64).

I turned to leave the students and quietly stepped back into the surrounding trees, only to make a very loud cracking sound as I walked on a fallen tree branch. Immediately one of the students called out, "Who's there?" Some started to point in my direction and, not wanting to worry them, I decided to step into their light and conversation. I explained my situation and where I was headed. They were very accepting and invited me to join them. We talked almost until the morning light; mostly I simply listened to the deep experienced insights of these students about to leave the Cathedral. When I finally made camp and crawled into my sleeping bag, questions haunted my weariness and I found it hard to fall asleep. Farrell (1985) observes that the cyclical nature of attempts at educational reform has "little to do with how adolescents perceive or value schooling" (22). What would be the effect on the curriculum-discourse of science education if the voices of students were included? How might the integrity of student voices be safeguarded against the procedures of exclusion or consultation that are part of the defining activity of a curriculum-discourse? We have a lot of students enrolled in the study at the Cathedral—do these students present a location of resistance in the science education curriculum-discourse? How might this resistance be encouraged? Could students help generate conversations of critique Foucault suggests are avenues of hope for change in the *Ge-stell* of modernity? Could students play an active role in the kind of action-research I discussed with my graduate student Will? I remember falling asleep thinking that I have discovered many questions in my travels, but few answers.

Towards a Post-Modern Science Education Curriculum-Discourse

> To say that one can never be 'outside' power does not mean that one is
> trapped and condemned to defeat no matter what.
> —Michel Foucault, *Power/Knowledge* (1980, 142).

I could tell it was very late when I woke, for the Sun was already high in the sky. I had slept more soundly the previous night than at any time during my travels and I woke feeling rested and eager to break camp and get on my way. The students had long since cleared away any trace of their camp and for a moment I wondered if my encounter with them was a vision.

It was a beautiful day. I dressed quickly and broke camp, eager to be on my way. Beside my camping site was a clear pathway leading deep into the forest. I set out on this path wondering how long it would take me to find my way through the mountains.

The route was not familiar to me, but I was clearly rising in altitude and traveling directly into the range of mountains that encircle the Kingdom. At a height of perhaps a thousand meters the path turned sharply to the left, providing a last vista of the flank of the Lonely Mountains and the plain below. I could not see the chasm. I could just make out the glacier shaped like an angel on the mountains and I judged that I was traveling a little south of my first route through the mountains.

I decided this was a good spot to rest and have lunch. The encounter with the students came to me and I reviewed their questions. Questions. It was a single question that started me on my journey so many years ago. I laughed out loud at the audacity of Al's question, "Sir, why are we learning this crap?" Why, indeed. Good question, Al. But there are others. My conversations with Foucault, Heidegger and Nietzsche initiated a critique of the procedures of power in a particular science education curriculum-discourse. This critique then moved to consider the practical concerns of change as my conversations widen to include students, such as Desireé, Will, and those I met in the forest. At every moment, however, I knew our conversation of critique would be in danger of an enticing subduction into the comfortable defining of the Great Conversation of the Kingdom.

I finished my lunch, picked up my backpack and headed deeper into the forest and mountain pass, sorry to leave behind the beauty of sunlight on the mountain glacier. How would I be able to work against the power of modernity? How might my conversation of critique remain not comfortable? As I hiked the impression of an angel reminded me of the account of Jacob wrestling with an angel that opened the fourth chapter of this book. I recalled the final verse of the passage: "Your name shall no longer be called Jacob, but Israel; for you have striven with God and with men and have prevailed" (Creation House 1984, 50: Genesis 32: 29). Something did not make sense in that verse. Did Jacob not wrestle an angel, not "with men"? The Hebrew word angel (*'ish*) also means a 'person', thus my midrash that on that key night in the transformation of Jacob that the real adversary Jacob faced was himself. Why then does the giving of a new name to Jacob refer to Jacob wrestling "with men"? The Hebrew word for men in the text is *A'Nashim,*[14] literally the 'breathed into ones', or people in general. Jacob's blessing came after he had struggled not only with himself, the Bible suggests, but also with others.

As I hiked I thought about the meaning of this subtle change in wording in the Biblical passage. Jacob became someone else, *Israel,* but this change was not something he could do completely alone. He needed to wrestle, with God, with himself, *and with others* to complete his transformation. It is the act of wrestling that brings a new name, a new being and, in Jacob's case, the courage to cross the river and claim his inheritance.

I could relate to Jacob. In my life the chasm was my angel; I wrestled at the edge of the Kingdom with my modernity, my contribution to the Great Conversation; my struggle was a trachealization of the procedures of power in a curriculum-discourse that became a trachealization of the discourse of my being. That discovering of being was not possible without a wide range of conversations: with Foucault, Heidegger, and Nietzsche, with professors and students at the University, and with those directly involved in the science education curriculum-discourse. My journey back to the Kingdom would not be possible without the call to continue engaging these voices and the voices of beginning teachers, experienced teachers, and students as we wrestle together the discourse that seeks to define who may speak and what may be said in science education. I started to whistle a tune, a song I had heard once back in the Kingdom. As I walked through the forest that afternoon I realized I was not the same person that left the team at the crossroads long ago. Cheerfulness had entered my being and I had the courage to enter the Kingdom. I knew the task of change involves questions of being, but that change in being *is* possible. That afternoon I made my last entry in my journal:

> I sense a distancing from where I once was. The whole event has been moving, jarring, stretching and transformational. I wish I could express the deep contentment I feel now. I'm relaxed, happy, and looking forward. (Journal entry, January 4, 1992)

The path I had taken led to a crossroads. I recognized the location. Ahead, the path served to traverse the mountain range. To my left was the familiar route the children had taken Foucault and me on our journey out of the forest to the plain below. To my right I could just see the winding path that led to the chalet that offered such hospitality to us on our journey and a wider pathway leading through the mountains. This path led to the main roads of the Kingdom. I knew I did not have to go back but I caught an image of the parents who welcomed us to their chalet. They could not hide their fear for their children, a fear we all held as children continued to disappear across the land. No, I did not have to go back but I knew I would. I knew I *could* go back because *I was no longer one of the King's subjects.* Foucault had taught me that the King is no longer present and my experience at the abyss taught me that I no longer have to live as if the King still existed. Aware of some of the procedures of power, modernity had a less defining grip on my being and I knew change was possible still. I chose the right path.

The short pass through two large mountains was still well marked by cairns and soon the trail led to hills that slowly descended to the valley of the Kingdom. At the end of the pass the forest gave way to a spectacular view of the valley below. There, waiting for me, was Foucault and two companions I immediately recognized as Heidegger and Nietzsche.

It was good to see Foucault again and I was glad to get to know a little better the two philosophers that influenced Foucault's work. We spent the afternoon chatting in the cheerful warmth of the afternoon sun. This was not serious talking, but the casual joking and spontaneous changes in topics of people parted too long. We talked about everything and anything, from my experiences at the chasm to a recent popular recording in the Kingdom.

I was interested to find out that a recording by the poet Leonard Cohen had become popular in the Kingdom. Although I had been a long time fan of Cohen's work, his poems set to music had never captured a wide base of public attention. My companions assured me this recording was quite different. I examined a copy they had brought and read the opening lines of the title song, *The Future*[15]

Give me back my broken night
my secret room, my secret life
it's lonely here,
there's no one left to torture

From this dark and deeply sarcastic introduction Cohen continues later:

Give me back the Berlin wall
give me Stalin and St. Paul
I've seen the future, brother:
it is murder.

The poet then paints an apocalyptic vision in a haunting chorus:

Things are going to slide in all directions
Won't be nothing
Nothing you can measure anymore
The blizzard of the world
has crossed the threshold

and it has overturned
the order of the soul
When they said REPENT
I wonder what they meant

I looked to my companions, shocked by the words. Other songs on the album held a similar nihilistic edge, as Cohen sarcastically suggests we're all waiting for a miracle that may never come while the barkeeper of the world is shouting, "Closing time!" I wondered if the popularity of the songs was partially due to their dark message. Perhaps the citizens of the Kingdom truly felt the future was murder. I shivered, even though warm. Was the situation really as desperate as Cohen portrays in this album? I thought of the dire predictions of environmentalists that we have only a few decades to turn around the present rate to planetary degradation. The rise of STS science education may be an important response to this new crisis, but science education curriculum-discourse is still enframed by technicality. I glanced at Foucault and recalled that children were still disappearing. Perhaps Cohen's words were prophetic after all.

In the midst of the sarcastic nihilism of Cohen's latest work one poem, *The Anthem*,[16] stands alone in its vision of hope and promise:

The birds they sang
at the break of day
Start again
I heard them say
Don't dwell on what
has passed away
or what is yet to be.

Ring the bells that still can ring.
Forget your perfect offering.
There is a crack in everything.
That's how the light gets in.

I smiled and thanked Cohen in my heart for the timely reminder that in the midst of the Great Conversation there are bells that can still ring. The interrupting voice of children, beginning and experienced teachers, philosophers and poets still call out to be heard. We can help the clear chime of these voices to sound throughout a curriculum-discourse by opening spaces where discourse finds resistance.

To find these spaces we must forget our perfect offerings. There is no ideal science education curriculum-discourse, no generalizable formula for changing a discourse, no method that works in every situation. What happened in Alberta to Science 10, 20, and 30 is the relentless defining of *Das Ge-stell*, the effects of an anonymous Great Conversation that includes us all.

But Cohen proposes that there is a crack in everything, including power. Where power is exercised, so too resistance can be found. By dis-covering the procedures of power in a curriculum-discourse we already are aware of how power operates and thus can enter into a life of critique. In the science education curriculum-discourse power defined who may speak and what could be said, but its exercise also revealed critical voices on the margins of the discourse and penetrating questions that were not asked. The procedures of power may change from discourse to discourse, even within the same discourse over time, but because of Foucault's example we can say now that we are on to power: It has lost anonymity.

By a constant trachealization of power where it exists the cracks in enframing (*Ge-stell*) appear, and that's how the light gets in. Thus illuminated, we can begin to see our way out of the darkness, from the modern to the post-modern. Change *is still possible*, though a night of our own making is falling there is still time.

At the beginning of Chapter 4 Jacob taught us that change is difficult, a constant wrestling that may involve injury but also promises great blessing. Wrestling is hard work; our opponent shifts and changes so much that the match promises to be a difficult one. As the text hints, we need to include others in the match, the contest is ours to share and together we may prevail.

I glanced at my companions and then stood up. Before me was the great valley of the Kingdom, quiet as twilight approached. At the chasm I had longed for the discomfort that comes from being with others and now the invitation to find this discomfort was only a short trip away. I was unable to find a cure for the disappearing children because I could not find a route out of the Kingdom, trapped by the chasm we all helped to create and maintain. My despair at the abyss led me to consider how else the Quest could be, and I discovered the importance of questions. What quest was I on now? I thought of the conversations of critique possible in the location of the lives of beginning and experienced teachers and through listening to the interrupting voices of children. I no longer believed a route out of the Kingdom was possible, but I now held the conviction we can change the Kingdom itself. Perhaps if the conditions that allow the Kingdom to exist were to change, that which causes our children to disappear may also change. I did not know, but it was worth a try. I looked at the valley below. Like Jacob, I reached the point where I was willing to cross the border, to find the blessing. I cannot make this blessing on my own, however. Foucault, Heidegger, and Nietzsche travel with me and I know they have much, much more to teach. But to find the blessing, *our* blessing others must join me in the struggle to encourage conversations of critique towards a post-modern science education curriculum-discourse. I turn to you who have so patiently lived with/in the conversation of this text, and to whom I have shared my discoveries and journey. There is much to do and the children are waiting. I'm ready now to travel back into the Kingdom and I extend an invitation that we travel together: Let's go.

Notes

Chapter 1

1   "One small step for man" was a common misquote of Armstrong due, at least initially, to the poor transmission of the communication signal from the moon. Armstrong actually said, "One small step for *a* man."

2   For example, see science writer N. P. Ruzic's *Where The Winds Sleep.* Garden City, New York: Doubleday, 1970.

3   This comment appears in the editorial of *The Edmonton Journal,* (22 July, 1969: 2) a major daily newspaper in the province of Alberta, Canada. Similar comments were made in editorials world-wide; the *Edmonton Journal* was selected as an example because it was in this province of Canada that the events described in this book take place. This reference demonstrates that the sentiments outlined in Chapter 1 existed in Alberta.

4   From the article, "Johnson Says Feat Shows 'We Can Do Anything'." 1969. *New York Times,* 21 July: 15.

5   These quotes appear on page 10 of the July 21, 1969 edition of the *New York Times* in an article by W. E. Farrell: "The World's Cheers For American Technology Are Many."

6   This optimistic hope was reported by the Southam News Service and presented on page 29 of the July 22, 1969 issue of *The Edmonton Journal.*

7   For example, the Physical Science Study Committee (PSCS) had completed a new secondary school physics program. Other courses of study such as secondary school biology programs developed by the Biological Sciences Curriculum Study (BSCS) and secondary school chemistry programs developed through the Chemical Bond Approach (CBA) and the Chemical Education Materials Study (CHEM Study) were at various stages of design and implementation in schools before the Wood's Hole Conference.

8   This is the consensus of many curriculum scholars, such as Eisner (1979), Giroux, Penna, and Pinar (1981), Pinar, Reynolds, Slattery and Taubman (1995), and Schubert (1993).

9   This dramatic headline appeared on the front page of the major Canadian newspaper, *The Globe and Mail.* Similar headlines appeared throughout the world.

10   From the article, "Russian Launches First Satellite." 1957. *The Globe and Mail,* 5 October: 1.

11   From the article, "More Likely to See Red Earth Satellite Than U.S. Versions." 1957. *Toronto Globe and Mail,* 5 October: 9.

12   This essay was written by H. Schwartz and was reprinted on page 6 of the October 9, 1957 edition of *The Globe and Mail.* Entitled, "Soviet Science Far Advanced in Many Fields," the essay articulated what many suspected: America had slipped behind the Soviets in scientific development.

13   From the article, "Reds Say Sputnik II Raised by New Source of Power." 1957. *The Globe and Mail,* 5 November: 1–2.

14   For further discussion on the intent of the new science programs to encourage students towards a career in science, see Champagne and Hornig (1986), Matthews (1989), and Nadeau and Désautels (1984).

15   For example, in addition to existing high school science programs (see Note 7 of Chapter 1), the early sixties saw the publication of Science—A Process Approach (SAPA), Elementary Science Study (ESS), Science Curriculum Improvement Study (SCIS), Minnemest, COPES, and many others.

16   For a discussion of the intent and development of the Nuffield Science programs, see Layton (1984) and Waring (1979).

17   Studies of the adoption of these programs into Canadian schools have been conducted by MacKeracher (1985) and Tomkins (1977).

18   To speak of *The* Enlightenment would be to betray a Euro-centric perspective that ignores advances in science, philosophy, and art over many centuries that are part of the rich history of India, communities in Africa and Asia, and Moslem and Jewish communities. I thus I refer to this era in Western European history (and by extension, to colonies in the New World) as the 'European Enlightenment'. Durant (1961) provides a good overview of the European Enlightenment.

19   For a good discussion of this assumption, see Stenhouse (1985).

20   For example, during the years 1983–1984 over 120 national studies of educational progress were published in the U.S. (Victor and Kellough 1993, 11).

21   The word 'science' is interpreted widely to refer to health sciences, physical and biological sciences, and applied sciences. Canadian government publications from 1969 to 1985 reveal a steady increase in students graduating with science-related degrees until the mid-seventies. Numbers plateau during the latter seventies until the early eighties when most university science areas began to experience a steady decline in their numbers of graduates. Notable exceptions are the fields of forestry and engineering; these areas enjoyed steady increased enrollment until the late eighties. DeBoer (1991) reports a similar phenomenon in the United States during the latter seventies.

22   See DeBoer (1991), Kyle, Shymansky, and Alport (1982), and National Science Foundation Panel on School Science (1980).

23   This perception is well documented. See Beardsley (1992), Blades (1992), Jones and Hutchings (1993), and Kass and Blades (1992) or talk to any high school student today. Media portrayals of scientists have no doubt played a major role in helping to shape this perception.

24   Carson's book documents some of the devastating effects of indiscriminate pesticide use on wildlife. The publication of *Silent Spring* caused a furor with the general public in the U.S. and Canada which was influential in banning the use of DDT and partly responsible for the creation of the U.S. Environmental Protection Agency. Nader's book was not particularly anti-science, but rather a "criticism of corporate interests for misusing technology for short-sighted economic gain" (Smith 1990, 74).

25   I am indebted to Borgmann (1992) for his insightful term, "sullenness." The growth of an anti-science sentiment is examined very well by Holton (1992), Passmore (1975), B. Smith (1990), and Stenhouse (1985). The journal *Skeptical Inquirer* features scholarly articles and research devoted to fighting the current anti-science sentiment.

26   Bev Savan's excellent book, *Science Under Siege* (Savan 1988) is a highly readable examination of myth of scientific objectivity and the 'dark side of science'.

27   For example, refer to the December, 1988 issue of *National Geographic*; January, 1989 issue of *Time*; April, 1990 issue of *Discover*; May 3, 1990 edition of *Rolling Stone*; and September 17, 1990 issue of *Maclean's*.

28   See Aikenhead (1983), Bybee (1985), Cox (1980), Roberts (1983), Yager (1984), and Zeidler (1984).

29   For examples of this declaration, refer to Duschl (1990), Hurd (1989), Klopfer and Champagne (1990), and Yager (1984).

30   These questions are drawn from the work of Blades (1986), Duschl (1990), Keeves (1992), Matthews (1992), and Science Council of Canada (1984b).

31   This discussion began to appear among science education publications in the mid-eighties and continues to this day. For further details, see: Aikenhead (1983, 1994), Blades (1986), Bybee (1987) Fensham (1988b, 1993), Hurd (1985, 1989), Jenkins (1990), Ramsey (1993), Rosenthal (1989), Yager (1981, 1984, 1992), and Zeidler (1984).

32   For a discussion of these initiatives, see American Association for the Advancement of Science (1989), Bybee (1992), Hurd (1991a), and O'Neil (1992).

Chapter 2

1   For a summary of the content of these courses, please refer to Appendix A.

2   At the University exemplary classroom teachers are able to spend one or two years sharing their pedagogical expertise by teaching undergraduate courses in education. For example, a skilled teacher of senior high school biology would be invited to teach for a year or two undergraduate education courses on methods of teaching high school biology.

3   This discussion paper, *Proposals for an Industrial and Science Strategy for Albertans—1985 to 1990* (Government of Alberta 1984) suggested strong support for the idea of science renewal among science-related industries (see 24–25). As we shall see, this paper is ironic in the light of how the curriculum-discourse evolved.

4   This general title is used in an earlier work (Blades 1994) for all individuals who were working as employees of Alberta Education at the time. Various individuals involved in the science education curriculum-discourse were interviewed. Only individuals granting permission to use their interview comments are quoted in this work and only those who were significantly involved in the curriculum-discourse were interviewed. To protect the anonymity of these individuals, general titles, such as 'Secondary School Science Teacher' or 'Career Associate with Alberta Education' are used to identify the role or occupation of the person interviewed. Some individuals have the same title; in these cases different interview dates signify different individuals.

5   Career Associate with Alberta Education, quoted in Blades (1994). Interview: 19 November, 1991.

6   Various ad hoc interest groups formed during this time. The Alberta Science Education Consultants Council was the largest and perhaps most influential. Submissions made by various groups reveal a general concern that renewal was needed, but no real consensus on how renewal might be achieved. In almost every case, science educators, teachers, professors of education and others involved in these discussions realized it was time to address the serious concerns about the relevancy and usefulness of existing science courses, especially at the high school level.

7   The phrase, 'technical-rational' is commonly used to describe Tyler's approach. See Aoki (1985), Eisner and Vallance (1974), Giroux, Penna, and Pinar (1981), and House (1979).

8   Further examples of this technical approach to curriculum change are presented in the works by Joyce and Hersh (1983), Hunkins (1980), Oliva (1982), and Zais (1976a, 1976b).

9   This decision was announced in *Essential Concepts, Skills and Attitudes for Grade 12* (Alberta Education 1987d, see 12–14).

10   Career Associate with Alberta Education, quoted in Blades (1994). Interview: 18 October 1991.

11   Theory is all well and good, but this doesn't keep things from existing.

12   This change in credits was due to the decision by personnel with Alberta Education to allocate 3 credits each to Biology 20, Chemistry 20, and Physics 20 instead of the previous 5 credits each.

13   Letter to science teachers by the Edmonton Regional Chemistry Council, March 13, 1989.

14   Beatty, quoted in Blades (1994). Interview: 11 June, 1991. Blades notes these comments are cited with the permission of Dr. Dave Beatty.

15   Ibid.

16   Mr. Dinning's response was a good summary and presentation of the intent, direction and activity of the proposed changes.

17   Northern Alberta Institute of Technology; SAIT is the Southern Alberta Institute of Technology.

18   Titles of these letters, editorials and articles indicate the discontent in Alberta. Some examples include: *Alberta students won't be able to compete* (Andrews 1989), *Board wants changes delayed* (Ross 1989b), *Science changes worry* (Lau 1989), *Science curriculum change no help to students* (Blackman 1989), *Science friction: proposed changes under fire* (Ross 1989c).

19   Dinning, quoted in Blades (1994). Interview: 15 May, 1992. These comments are cited with the permission of Mr. Jim Dinning, then Government Minister of Education in the Province of Alberta.

20   Bing Masley. (1989). Alberta Education's new science curriculum (cartoon). Medicine Hat, Alberta: *The Medicine Hat News,* 25 November, 1989: A4. Reprinted by permission of the artist and publisher. All rights reserved.

21   For examples, see the work of Carroll (1986), Crandall (1983), R. Doll (1986), Fullan (1977), Joyce and Hersh (1983), and Tessmer and Harris (1990).

22   Shirley E. Forbes. (1990). Letter of the day. *Edmonton Journal,* 8 February, 1990: A15.

23   Seconded Associate with Alberta Education, quoted in Blades (1994). Interview: 10 October, 1991. The general title 'Seconded Associate' refers to teachers who, still employed with their school boards, elect to serve with Alberta Education, often for a period of two years. When their term is completed, these Associates return to their classroom teaching responsibilities. This general title is used to protect the anonymity of those seconded teachers working at Alberta willing to be interviewed about their involvement in the evolution of Science 10, 20, and 30.

24 Seconded Associate with Alberta Education, quoted in Blades (1994). Interview: 21 October, 1991.

25 Government administered final exams worth 50% of course standing are required for all 30 level academic courses in Alberta. An exam for Science 30 had been discussed at Alberta Education, but up to this point not publicly.

26 Member of the University Community, quoted in Blades (1994). Interview: 29 May, 1992.

27 Ibid.

28 Seconded Associate with Alberta Education, quoted in Blades (1994). Interview: 27 April, 1992.

29 Member of the University Community, quoted in Blades (1994). Interview: 29 May, 1992. In an interview a Seconded Associate with Alberta Education shared the same opinion (Seconded Associate with Alberta Education, quoted in Blades (1994). Interview: 27 April, 1992).

30 Seconded Associate with Alberta Education, quoted in Blades (1994). Interview: 21 October, 1991.

31 Member of the University Community, quoted in Blades (1994). Interview: 29 May, 1992.

32 Ibid. This was confirmed in an interview with a Seconded Associate with Alberta Education (Seconded Associate with Alberta Education, quoted in Blades (1994). Interview: 27 April, 1992).

33 Ibid.

34 Interview with a Seconded Associate with Alberta Education, quoted in Blades (1994). Interview: 27 April, 1992.

35 The more the change, the more it's the same thing.

36 This is not her real name. Students choose pseudonyms in this study to protect their anonymity.

37 Alberta Education (1990d).

38 Some significant challenges to technical-rational approaches to curriculum change were advanced from Neo-Marxist approaches to education during the late seventies (see Note 7, Chapter 3) and in the past two decades, but

these challenges do not represent mainstream educational discourse.

Chapter 3

1   Appendix B provides a brief biography of Michael Foucault.

2   For information on Nietzsche's influence on Foucault's thinking, see Dreyfus and Rabinow (1982), Eribon (1989), Foucault (1989b) or the brief note appearing in Appendix B.

3   From a post-modern perspective, this classification should remain elusive. The role of the author in post-modern writing is discussed in the next chapter.

4   A reference work that lists, by author, citations of these authors among major sociological journals. There are *hundreds* of citations of Foucault's work recorded in the *Citation Index*.

5   Ball, Stephen. 1990. *Foucault and education: Disciplines and knowledge.* New York: Routledge.

6   Hermeneutics is the philosophy of interpretation. A major goal in hermeneutic analysis is discovery of meaning.

7   Social-critical theory develops from attempts to reconceptualize Marx's ideas on social progress. Some of the characteristics of social-critical theory in the social sciences are: Critical view of rationalism, rejection of positivism in social sciences, belief in theory development through dialectic criticism, and redefinition of culture as essentially political, dynamically open to domination by the ideology of capitalism (Giroux 1983). Habermas, Adorno, Marcuse and other social-critical theorists founded the Institute for Social Research in Frankfurt, Germany in 1923. This so-called 'Frankfurt School' was destined to have an influential role in the development of social-critical theories.

8   τραχηλιζω = Trachelizo, from the passage: πάντα δὲ γυμνὰ καὶ τετραχηλισμένα τοῖς ὀφθαλμοῖς αὐτοῦ πρὸς ὃν ἡμῖν ὁ λόγος, "but all things are *naked and laid bare* to the eyes of him with who is our account" (Hebrews 4:13b), Zondervan 1978, *New International Version Bible*, 1578, emphasis mine). The term was commonly used in Greek wrestling. During a match exposing the trachea of an opponent—

trachealizing the person wrestled—led to an automatic victory for the wrestler.

9 Derrida founded deconstructionism in France and was one of Foucault's students. For a discussion of their conflict and eventual resolution, see Eribon (1991, 116–122).

Chapter 4

1 The acronym BCE stands for "Before the Common Era," essentially the same as the Christian designation BC.

2 אִישׁ, from the text by Sinai Publishing (1984, 73).

3 To read about the meeting of Jacob and Esau after twenty years of separation, refer in the Bible to Genesis, Chapter 33.

4 For further discussion of this point, see Mercer (1990), Rosenau (1992), and Vattimo (1988).

5 Derrida uses the word 'eidetically' to refer to the generation of abstract representations believed to capture the essence of reality. The addition of 'vulnerable' suggests such abstractions, common to phenomenological inquiry, are suspect.

6 For further discussion of the idea of 'metanarratives' see Lyotard (1984), Mercer (1990), and Milner, Thomson, and Worth (1990).

7 In our Kingdom, priests can be either gender.

8 A map of the Kingdom tracing the travels of the team is provided in Appendix C. This map is *not* the map I originally brought with me on my journey, however; it is the map that I produced at the end of the Quest. Readers may find it convenient to consult this map from time to time to trace the route of the Quest.

9 Secondary School Teacher, quoted in Blades (1994). Interview: April 29, 1992.

10 Career Associate with Alberta Education, quoted in Blades (1994). Interview: April 24, 1992.

11   Seconded Associate with Alberta Education, quoted in Blades (1994). Interview: October 21, 1991.

12   Ibid. This perspective was also shared by a Career Associate with Alberta Education (see note 10 of Chapter 4).

13   Seconded Associate with Alberta Education, quoted in Blades (1994). Interview: October 10, 1991.

14   Career Associate with Alberta Education, quoted in Blades (1994). Interview: November 7, 1991.

15   Seconded Associate with Alberta Education, quoted in Blades (1994). Interview: October 21, 1991.

16   Seconded Associate with Alberta Education, quoted in Blades (1994). Interview: October 10, 1991.

17   Ibid.

18   Ibid.

19   Member of the University Community, quoted in Blades (1994). Interview: May 29, 1992.

20   Career Associate with Alberta Education, quoted in Blades (1994). Interview: October 29, 1991.

21   Member of the University Community, quoted in Blades (1994). Interview: May 29, 1992.

22   Member of the Publishing Community, quoted in Blades (1994). Interview: April 29, 1992.

23   Seconded Associate with Alberta Education, quoted in Blades (1994). Interview: October 10, 1991.

24   Member of the University Community, quoted in Blades (1994). Interview: May 29, 1992.

25   Mr. Jim Dinning, Minister of Education, quoted in Blades (1994). Interview: May 15, 1992.

26   Career Associate with Alberta Education, quoted in Blades (1994). Interview: October 17, 1991.

27   Seconded Associate with Alberta Education, quoted in Blades (1994). Interview: October 17, 1991.

28   Career Associate with Alberta Education, quoted in Blades (1994). Interview: October 17, 1991.

29   Ibid.

30   Ibid.

31   Member of the Publishing Community, quoted in Blades (1994). Interview: April 29, 1992.

32   Ibid.

33   Secondary School Science Teacher, quoted in Blades (1994). Interview: April 29, 1992.

34   Ibid.

35   Ibid. This is the impression held by this teacher.

36   Ibid.

37   Ibid.

38   Career Associate with Alberta Education, quoted in Blades (1994). Interview: November 19, 1991.

39   Ibid.

40   Ibid.

41   Seconded Associate with Alberta Education, quoted in Blades (1994). Interview: October 10, 1991.

42   Ibid.

43   Seconded Associate with Alberta Education, quoted in Blades (1994). Interview: October 21, 1991.

44   Ibid.

45   Ibid.

46   Seconded Associate with Alberta Education, quoted in Blades (1994). Interview: October 10, 1991.

47   Career Associate with Alberta Education, quoted in Blades (1994). Interview: October 17, 1991.

48   Ibid.

49   Ibid.

50   Ibid.

51   Ibid.

52   Secondary School Science Teacher, quoted in Blades (1994). Interview: April 27, 1992.

53   Ibid.

54   Mr. Jim Dinning, Minister of Education, quoted in Blades (1994). Interview: May 15, 1992.

55   Career Associate with Alberta Education, quoted in Blades (1994). Interview: October 29, 1991.

56   Member of the Publishing Community, quoted in Blades (1994). Interview: April 29, 1992.

57   Ibid.

58   Ibid.

59   Ibid.

60   Ibid.

61   Career Associate with Alberta Education, quoted in Blades (1994). Interview: April 24, 1992.

62   Ibid.

63   Seconded Associate with Alberta Education, quoted in Blades (1994). Interview: October 21, 1991.

64   Career Associate with Alberta Education, quoted in Blades (1994). Interview: October 17, 1991.

65   Interview with a Career Associate with Alberta Education, November 19, 1991.

66   Ibid.

67   Ibid.

68   Seconded Associate with Alberta Education, quoted in Blades (1994). Interview: October 21, 1991.

69   Ibid.

70   Seconded Associate with Alberta Education, quoted in Blades (1994). Interview: October 10, 1991.

71   Career Associate with Alberta Education, quoted in Blades (1994). Interview: April 24, 1992.

72   Seconded Associate with Alberta Education, quoted in Blades (1994). Interview: October 21, 1991.

73   Career Associate with Alberta Education, quoted in Blades (1994). Interview: November 19, 1991.

74   Storytellers note: See Chapter 2, page 67 for an example of the type of posters produced at this time. In the allegory, 'posters' broadly refers to newspaper headlines, cartoons, and covers of magazines.

75   Mr. Jim Dinning, Minister of Education, quoted in Blades (1994). Interview: May 15, 1992.

76   Ibid. This perception was shared by a Career Associate with Alberta Education, quoted in Blades (1994). Interview: April 24, 1992.

77   Member of the Publishing Community, quoted in Blades (1994). Interview: April 29, 1992.

78   Seconded Associate with Alberta Education, quoted in Blades (1994). Interview: October 17, 1991.

79   Seconded Associate with Alberta Education, quoted in Blades (1994; emphasis his). Interview: October 10, 1991.

80   Member of the University Community, quoted in Blades (1994). Interview: May 29, 1992.

81   Seconded Associate with Alberta Education, quoted in Blades (1994). Interview: April 27, 1992.

82   Member of the University Community, quoted in Blades (1994). Interview: May 29, 1992.

83   Ibid.

84   Ibid.

85   Ibid.

86   Seconded Associate with Alberta Education, quoted in Blades (1994). Interview: April 27, 1992.

87   Ibid. Also confirmed in an interview with a Seconded Associate with Alberta Education, quoted in Blades (1994). Interview: October 21, 1991.

88   Seconded Associate with Alberta Education, quoted in Blades (1994). Interview: April 27, 1992.

89   Ibid.

90   Member of the Publishing Community, quoted in Blades (1994). Interview: April 29, 1992.

91   Member of the University Community, quoted in Blades (1994). Interview: May 29, 1992.

92   Career Associate with Alberta Education, quoted in Blades (1994). Interview: October 29, 1991.

93   Ibid.

94   Career Associate with Alberta Education, quoted in Blades (1994). Interview: April 24, 1992.

95   Career Associate with Alberta Education, quoted in Blades (1994). Interview: October 17, 1991.

96   Seconded Associate with Alberta Education, quoted in Blades (1994). Interview: October 21, 1991.

97   Mr. Jim Dinning, Minister of Education, quoted in Blades (1994). Interview: May 15, 1992.

Chapter 5

1   This resilency to change in education is documented widely; for example, see Blades (1992, 1995), Cuban (1982, 1984, 1990), Fensham (1988a, 1993), Fullan (1993), Hurd (1991b), and Sarason (1990).

2   Rochlitz is not the only scholar to express concern about the 'hidden universalism' in Foucault's work.   See Habermas (1992), Kurzweil (1983), Megill (1985), Poster (1989) and Roth (1992) for a similar critique.

3   The conversation that follows is somewhat metaphorical and is drawn from my experience teaching undergraduate students courses in science education methodology and comments students have made in their evaluations of my courses. "Desireé" is a fictional name. Our conversation is quite typical of the many I have in my office.

4   "pity this busy monster,manunkind,", copyright 1944, © 1972, 1991 by the Trustees for the E. E. Cummings Trust, from *Complete Poems: 1904–1962* by E. E. Cummings, Edited by George J. Firmage, 554. Reprinted by permission of Liveright Publishing Corporation.

5   Heidegger (1977) notes that *poiesis* is a Greek term used in Plato's *Symposium* to mean "to bring forth," related to what an artist or craftsperson produces and reflected in our modern word 'poetic'. The *ability* of the artisan or craftsperson to bring something forth is called in Greek *techne*, from which our word technology derives.

6   For examples of Foucault's work for human rights, see Eribon (1991) and Miller (1993).

7   Foucault uses the word 'critique' to mean an active engagement with power, an effort to uncover the violence of power as the first act towards freedom. For further discussion of this view of critique, see Poster (1989) and Miller (1993).

8   Similar to the conversation with Desireé, the conversation that follows is drawn from my experiences with students engaged in graduate study in education. The name "Will" is metaphorical.

9   Orr, David. 1992. *Ecological literacy: education and transition to a postmodern world.* Albany: State University of New York Press.

10   See Chapter 3 of *The Idea of Wilderness* (Oelschlaeger 1991).

11   A common idiom used by our graduate students to describe the effects of their study of curriculum.

12   The following comments are verbatim comments from children I interviewed as part of a research paper. For a description of the research methodology and findings see Blades (1992).

13   Names of students participating in the interviews have been changed to protect the anonymity of the students. In most cases, the students chose their own pseudonyms.

14   אֲנָשִׁים from the text by Sinai Publishing (1984, 73).

15   "The Future" written by Leonard Cohen
       Copyright 1993 Leonard Cohen Stranger Music, Inc.
       Used by permission. All Rights Reserved.

16   "Anthem" written by Leonard Cohen
       Copyright 1993 Leonard Cohen Stranger Music, Inc.
       Used by permission. All Rights Reserved.

Appendix A

Summary of Topics in Biology 10, Chemistry 10, and Physics 10

Biology 10 (Alberta Education 1984)

Major Units	Topics of Study
Cell Biology	<ul><li>cell theory, Leeuwenhoek, Hooke</li><li>structure of eukaryote cells, cell organelles, differences between plant and animal cells</li><li>organization of cells into tissues, organs, and systems</li></ul>
Taxonomy	<ul><li>morphological comparisons, basis of groupings</li><li>use of dichotomous keys in classification</li><li>viruses, bacteria, unicellular and colonial eukaryote cells</li><li>fungi, photosynthetic plants: ferns, gymnosperms, angiosperms (structure and function)</li><li>porifera and coelenterata, worms</li><li>mollusks and echinoderms, arthropods</li><li>chordates</li></ul>

Chemistry 10 (Alberta Education 1977a)

Major Units	Topics of Study
Experimental Technique	<ul><li>qualitative and quantitative measurement, use of S. I. system, significant figures</li><li>laboratory safety, scientific method</li></ul>
Classification of Matter	<ul><li>chemical and physical properties of matter</li><li>mixtures and pure substances</li><li>metals and non-metals</li><li>ionic or molecular substances</li></ul>

Atomic Theory	• history of atomic theory
	• structure of the atom
	• use of the periodic table of elements
Chemical Reactions	• IUPAC rules for naming chemical substances and writing formulas for them
	• the concept of the 'mole'
	• balancing chemical equations, stoichiometry
	• classifying chemical reactions
	• Law of conservation of mass
	• importance of chemical reactions and their effects (environmental, economic, etc.).

Physics 10 (Alberta Education 1977b)

Major Units	Topics of Study
Physics and the Work of Physicists	• physics studies the interactions between matter and energy
	• physicists ask questions about nature, historical treatment of these questions form the early Greeks
The Use of Mathematics to Describe Natural Phenomenon	• complexity of motion
	• motion in a straight line, distance-time graphs
	• uniformly accelerated motion
	• acceleration and speed-time graphs
	• graphic analysis to describe instantaneous and average speed
	• use of algebra describe uniform acceleration
New Insights on Describing Motion from the 16th Century	• the climate of the 16th century
	• contributions of Galileo; thought experiments, falling bodies and uniform motion
	• the derivation of the d/T^2 for uniform acceleration
	• significance of Galileo's work
The Importance of Direction in Describing Motion	• the importance of reference points
	• the term velocity, graphic representation of velocity
	• use of algebraic equations for scalar motion, vector analysis

The Contributions of Newton's Descriptions of Motion

- dynamics
- vector addition rule
- Newton's three laws of motion, inertia, mass as a property of matter, differences between mass and weight, unbalanced forces, $F = ma$
- the Newton as a unit of force

Appendix B

Michel Foucault: A Brief Biography

Michel Foucault (1926–1984) was born in Poitiers, France. His early education was through the local state system, later in a Catholic school he received his baccalauréat and, with study at the École Normale Supérieure in Sorbonne, he received his Licence de Philosophie in 1948.

The intellectual climate of post-World War II France was dominated on one hand by the existentialism of Sartre and Camus, and the spirit of phenomenology advanced by Merleau-Ponty, and on the other hand the political ascendancy of Marxism. Having been a student of the Marxist-structuralist Althusser, and "owing him much" (Foucault, 1989i 14), Foucault was initially attracted to Marxist interpretations of history; Foucault even became a member of the Communist Party of France (PCF) for a few months. He describes this time in his life as "defined by Husserl in a general way, Sartre more precisely and Merleau-Ponty even more precisely" (1989, 42). But Foucault began to experience a growing unease with Marxism for political, ideological and scientific reasons which led to what he calls an "empty space" (42) in his life.

Foucault decided on a career in psychology. In 1950 he took his Licence de Psychologie and in 1951 split from the PCF. A year later he obtained a diploma in psychopathology, enabling him to research into psychiatric practice and mental illness. Foucault's first publication was a monograph written in 1952 entitled, *Maladie Mentale et Personnalité* (Mental Illness and Personality). In this work one can see themes that will be developed much further in Foucault's later works and the influence of Heidegger and Merleau-Ponty on his thinking. During the years 1952–1955 Foucault began to write on the philosophy of psychology and, in his words, 'conversed' (*parlera*) with the works of Nietzsche (see Eribon 1989). Nietzsche presented Foucault with a new perspective by "bringing up for discussion again the fundamental concepts of knowledge, of morals, and of metaphysics" (Foucault 1989b, 77).

Foucault left France in 1958 to be an assistant at the University of Uppsala in Sweden. During the time Foucault taught and studied in Sweden he observed that despite Sweden's reputation as a freer country than France (i.e., less social restrictions), a certain kind of freedom may have as many restrictive effects as a directly restrictive society. Foucault felt this was a very important experience in shaping his thinking. During his three years at Uppsala Foucault was able to finish and edit his doctoral thesis, which he titled, *L'Historie de la Folie* (A History of Madness). From Uppsala, Foucault accepted a position as Director of the French Center in Warsaw, Poland where he was able to experience first-hand the impositions of an oppressive society; he stayed only one year. The following year he became Director of the French Institute of Hamburg, Germany. While in Germany, Foucault became acquainted with the social-critical theorists of the Frankfurt School; this experience was to be influential in the development of Foucault's concept of power.

By 1961 Foucault had returned to France to teach and study at the University of Clermont-Ferrand. That same year, Foucault submitted his thesis for the degree of Doctor of Letters: *Historie de la Folie à L'Âge Classique* (Published in English under the title *Madness and Civilization*). In his thesis Foucault proposes that a historicity of madness can be approached as a study of the relationship between power and knowledge. He continued his study of the power-knowledge relationship after his appointment as Professor of Philosophy at the University of Clermont-Ferrand.

Over the next two decades Foucault entered the intellectual discourse of France (and in the late sixties, other nations as well) with the publication of many articles, interviews, essays, and major books. In 1968 Foucault accepted an appointment to the chair of philosophy at the prestigious Collège de France in Paris. Key works published by Foucault prior to 1968 include: *Naissance de la Clinique: Une Archaeologie du Regard Médical* (Birth of the Clinic: An Archaeology of Medical Perception), 1963 and *Les Mots et Les Choses* (Released in English with Foucault's choice of the title *The Order of Things*), 1966. In both works, Foucault adapts Nietzsche's notion of a genealogy of ideas into an 'archeology' of the development of scientific knowledge and power; first in the medical field of psychopathology and later in the "established order of things' (Foucault 1973, xix) in present discourses of science.

The political events of 1968 (such as the Paris student revolts, assassination of Robert Kennedy and Martin Luther King, Jr., and the Russian invasion of Czechoslovakia) led to a shift in Foucault's thinking. He began to believe in a more concretely political role for intellectuals. Considering his earlier works as "a very imperfect sketch" (1973, 16) of how power/knowledge is structured in discursive formation, Foucault admits his works prior to 1968 were written in a "happy state of semi-consciousness, with a great deal of naiveté and a little innocence" (Foucault 1989g, 57). His attempts to clarify his thinking and correct what he calls "inaccuracies and carelessness contained in previous books" led to the publication of *L'Archéologie du Savoir* (The Archeology of Knowledge) in 1969. This work represents a maturing of Foucault's understanding of the relationship between power/knowledge and discursive practice and lays out a research approach which Foucault would follow in his later studies: Of prisons, *Surveiller et Punir—Naissance de la Prison* (Discipline and Punishment—The Birth of the Prison), 1975; and Foucault's comprehensive study of the history of sexuality, *Historie de la Sexualité I: La Volanté de Savoir* (History of Sexuality I: The Turn of Knowledge), 1976; *Historie de la Sexualité II: L'Usage des Plaisirs* (History of Sexuality II: The Use of Pleasure), 1984; Foucault's third volume on the History of Sexuality, *Le Souci de Soi* (Concern for the Self) was in progress when he died from a septicemia that infected his brain (*supperation cérébrale*, Eribon 1989, 350) on the 25th of June, 1984.

For further information and good overviews of the life of Michael Foucault I recommend the works by J. Hug (1985), Didier Eribon (1989, 1990), and Jim Miller (1993).

Appendix C

General Map of the Kingdom

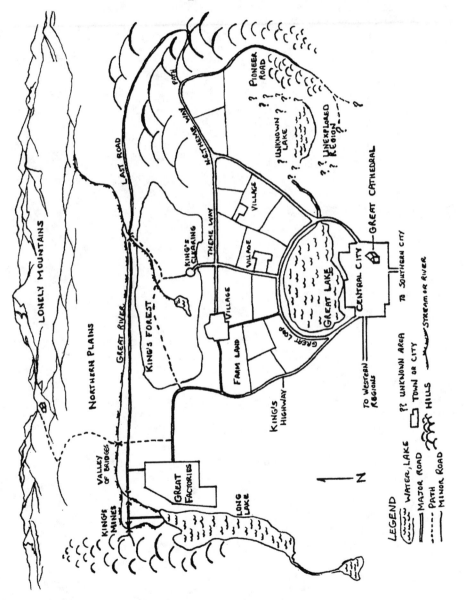

References

Aiken, Henry D. 1956. *The age of ideology*. New York: Mentor Books.

Aikenhead, Glen. 1980. *Science in social issues: Implications for teaching*. Ottawa, Ontario, Canada: Science Council of Canada.

———. 1983. Teaching science today, relevant to 2001 A.D. *Teacher Education* 23: 58–75.

———. 1994. The social contract of science: Implications for teaching science. In *STS education: International perspectives on reform*, edited by Joan Solomon and Glen Aikenhead, 11–20. New York: Teachers College Press.

Aikenhead, Glen S. and Reg W. Fleming. 1975. *Science, a way of knowing*. Saskatoon, Saskatchewan, Canada: University of Saskatchewan.

Alberta Education. 1977a. *Curriculum guide for senior high school chemistry*. Edmonton, Alberta, Canada: Alberta Education.

———. 1977b. *Curriculum guide for senior high school physics*. Edmonton, Alberta, Canada: Alberta Education.

———. 1984. *Biology 10-20-30 curriculum guide*. Edmonton, Alberta, Canada: Alberta Education.

———. 1986a. *Instructional program review and development: policy, guidelines and procedures manual*. Edmonton, Alberta, Canada: Alberta Education.

———. 1986b. *Secondary education action plan*. Edmonton, Alberta, Canada: Alberta Education.

Alberta Education. 1987a. *General Science Subcommittee (10-20-30) terms of reference.* Edmonton, Alberta, Canada: Alberta Education.

———. 1987b. *General Science 10, 20, 30 Subcommittee minutes (3–4 March 1987).* Edmonton, Alberta, Canada: Alberta Education.

———. 1987c. *General Science 10, 20, 30 Subcommittee minutes (8–9 April 1987).* Edmonton, Alberta, Canada: Alberta Education.

———. 1987d. *Essential concepts, skills and attitudes for Grade 12.* Edmonton, Alberta, Canada: Alberta Education.

———. 1987e. *Proposed directions for senior high school programs and graduation requirements.* Edmonton, Alberta, Canada: Alberta Education.

———. 1988a. *Interim program of studies: Science 10-20-30 (7 September 1988).* Edmonton, Alberta, Canada: Alberta Education.

———. 1988b. *Curriculum Design Branch three-year plan: 1988–1991.* Edmonton, Alberta, Canada: Alberta Education.

———. 1988c. *General Science 10, 20, 30 Subcommittee minutes (25 January 1987).* Edmonton, Alberta, Canada: Alberta Education.

———. 1988d. *General Science 10, 20, 30 Subcommittee minutes (27 October 1988).* Edmonton, Alberta, Canada: Alberta Education.

———. 1989a. *The science programs for Alberta's high school students: A brief report.* Edmonton, Alberta, Canada: Alberta Education.

———. 1989b. Science, technology, society and curriculum. *InFocus* February 1989: 5.

Alberta Education. 1989c. *Program implementation/support schedules for ECS–Grade 12*. Edmonton, Alberta, Canada: Alberta Education.

———. 1989d. *Draft program of studies: Science 10-20-30*. Edmonton, Alberta, Canada: Alberta Education.

———. 1989e. *Science 10 textbook, introductory chapter: Synopsis of comments—Science 10/20/30 Subcommittee members/Alberta Education (20 March 1989)*. Edmonton, Alberta, Canada: Alberta Education.

———. 1990a. *News release, 26 January 1990*. Edmonton, Alberta, Canada: Alberta Education.

———. 1990b. *Backgrounder: Directions for senior high science programs—issues and actions*. Edmonton, Alberta, Canada: Alberta Education.

———. 1990c. *A guide to curriculum planning in science*. Edmonton, Alberta, Canada: Alberta Education.

———. 1990d. *Science.10 draft course of studies, 31 August 1990*. Edmonton, Alberta, Canada: Alberta Education.

———. 1991. *Science 10: Discussion draft course of studies*. Edmonton, Alberta, Canada: Alberta Education.

Alberta Medical Association. 1989. *News release, 27 June 1989*. Edmonton, Alberta, Canada: Alberta Medical Association.

Alberta Science Education Consultants Council. 1984. *Secondary school science in Alberta: A focus to the future*. Edmonton, Alberta, Canada: Alberta Science Education Consultants Council. Photocopy.

American Association for the Advancement of Science. (1989). *Science for all Americans: Project 2061*. Washington, D.C.: Author.

Andrews, G. E. 1989. Alberta students won't be able to compete. *Calgary Herald*, 25 July: A6.

Aoki, Ted T. 1985. *Toward curriculum inquiry in a new key*. Curriculum Praxis: Occasional Paper Series, No. 2. Edmonton, Alberta, Canada: University of Alberta, Department of Secondary Education.

————. (1988). Toward a dialectic between the conceptual world and the lived world: Transcending instrumentalism in curriculum orientation. In *Contemporary curriculum discourses,* edited by William F. Pinar, 402–416. Scottsdale, Arizona: Grosuch Scarisbrick.

Apple, Michael W. 1988. *Teachers and texts*. New York: Routledge.

Armstrong, George. 1989. Sabotage in schools. *The Alberta Science Teacher* 9 (3): 10–13.

Atkin, J. Myron. 1989. Can educational research keep pace with educational reform? *Phi Delta Kappan* 71 (3): 200–205.

Author Group. 1977. *ALCHEM*. Edmonton, Alberta, Canada: Karitann.

Bacon, Francis. 1942. *Essays and New Atlantis,* edited by Gordon Haight. New York: Walter J. Black. Original edition, 1597.

Ball, Stephen J. 1990. Introducing Monsieur Foucault. In *Foucault and education: Disciplines and knowledge,* edited by Stephen J. Ball, 1–8. New York: Routledge.

Beardsley, Tim. 1992. Teaching real science. *Scientific American* 267 (4): 98–108.

Berman, Morris. 1989. *Coming to our senses*. New York: Bantam Books.

Bernauer, James W. 1990. *Michel Foucault's force of flight: Towards an ethics for thought.* London, England: Humanities Press International.

Bexon, Sandy. 1989. New curriculum threatens fine arts options. *Calgary Herald,* 29 October: D6.

Bjerg, Jens and Henning Silverbrandt. 1980. Roskilde University Center—a Danish experiment in higher education. *Journal of Curriculum Studies* 12 (3): 245–261.

Blackman, W. J. 1989. Science curriculum change no help to students. *Calgary Herald,* 15 May: A6.

Blades, David W. 1986. *The effects of an integrated approach to science education on the development of critical thinking abilities of grade ten secondary school students.* Master's thesis, University of Victoria, Victoria, B.C., Canada.

———. 1990. *The 5th corner: Deconstruction, hope and possibilities for change in science education.* Paper presented at the 1990 Bergamo Conference on Curriculum Theory and Classroom Practice, 17–20 October, Bergamo Conference Center, Dayton, Ohio.

———. 1992. Conversations form the margins: Grade 12 students' perceptions of their senior high school science program and possibilities for change. *Alberta Science Education Journal* 25 (1): 8–18.

———. 1994. *Procedures of Power and Possibilities for Change in Science Education Curriculum-Discourse.* Ph.D. dissertation, University of Alberta, Edmonton, Alberta, Canada.

———. 1995. Procedures of power in a curriculum-discourse: Conversations from home. *JCT: An Interdisciplinary Journal of Curriculum Studies* 11 (4): 125–155.

Bollnow, Otto Friedrich. 1987. *Crisis and new beginning.* Translated by Donald and Nancy Moss. Pittsburgh: Duquesne University Press. Original edition, Heidelberg: Quelle and Meyer Verlag, 1966.

Borgmann, Albert. 1992. *Crossing the postmodern divide.* Chicago: University of Chicago Press.

Boyne, Roy. 1990. *Foucault and Derrida: The other side of reason.* Boston: Unwin Hyman.

Brouwer, Wytze. 1985. *Rethinking the rationality of science.* University of Alberta Curriculum Praxis Occasional Paper. Edmonton, Alberta, Canada: Department of Secondary Education.

Bruner, Jerome S. 1960. *The process of education.* Cambridge, Massachusetts: Harvard University Press.

Buck, George. H. and John Osborne. 1990. Progress in education: A deconstructionist view. *Journal of Educational Thought* 24 (3): 178–186.

Bump, Jerome. 1985. Metaphor, creativity, and technical writing. *College Composition and Communication* 36 (4): 444–453.

Butt, Richard and Eric Mokosch. 1984. *Scientific enlightenment for a technological age.* Lethbridge, Alberta, Canada: University of Lethbridge.

Bybee, Roger W. 1985. The Sisyphean question in science education: What should the scientifically and technologically literate person know, value, and do—as a citizen? In *Science, Technology, Society: 1985 yearbook of the National Science Teachers Association*, edited by Roger W. Bybee, 79–93. Washington, D.C.: National Science Teachers Association.

———. 1987. Science education and the science-technology-society (S-T-S) theme. *Science Education* 71 (5): 667–683.

Bybee, Roger W. 1992. Science-technology-society in science curriculum: The policy—practice gap. In *Handbook of Science, technology and society: Volume 1. A theoretical and conceptual overview of science, technology and society education,* edited by M. O. Thirunarayanan, 74–85). Tempe, Arizona: Arizona State University.

Bybee, Roger W. and Teri Mau. 1986. Science and technology-related global problems: An international survey of science educators. *Journal of Research in Science Teaching* 23: 599–618.

Byfield, Mike. 1989. APEGGA slams science course. *Calgary Sun,* 11 July: 22.

Byfield, Ted. 1989a. Here's why Alberta should fire its Minister of Education. *Alberta Report* 16 (26): 44.

———. 1989b. Cage those education monkeys! *Calgary Sun,* 28 May: 12.

Byfield, Virginia. 1989a. The science fight goes political. *Alberta Report* 16 (28): 30–31.

———. 1989b. Whom do you trust on Science Ed? *Alberta Report* 16 (37): 44.

Campbell, Phill. 1986. *Proposal for change—senior high school science.* Edmonton, Alberta, Canada: Alberta Education.

Caputo, John D. 1987. *Radical hermeneutics: Repetition, deconstruction, and the hermeneutic Project.* Bloomington, Indiana: Indiana University Press.

Carroll, Paul. 1986. Change: Nightmare or euphoric dream? *The Ontario Journal of Educational Administration* 1 (3): 19–21.

Carson, Terrance R. 1986. Closing the gap between research and practice: conversation as a mode of doing research. *Phenomenology + Pedagogy* 4 (2): 73–85.

Central Office of Information. 1988. *Education reforms in Britain.* London, England: Central Office of Information.

Champagne, Audrey and Leslie E. Hornig. 1986. Critical questions and tentative answers for the school science curriculum. In *This year in science education 1986: The science curriculum,* edited by Audrey Champagne and Leslie E. Hornig, 1–12. Washington, D.C.: American Association for the Advancement of Science.

Cheney, Jim. 1989. Postmodern environmental ethics: Ethics as bioregional narrative. *Environmental Ethics* 2 (Summer): 117–134.

Cherryholmes, Cleo H. 1985. Theory and practice: On the role of empirically based theory for critical practice. *American Journal of Education* 94 (1): 39–70.

———. 1987. A social project for curriculum: Post-structural perspectives. *Journal of Curriculum Studies* 19 (4): 295–316.

———. 1988a. An exploration of meaning and dialogue between textbooks and teaching. *Journal of Curriculum Studies* 20 (1): 1–21.

———. 1988b. *Power and criticism: Poststructural investigations in education.* New York: Teachers College Press.

Committee on High-School Biology Education. 1990. *Fulfilling the promise: Biology education in the nation's schools.* Washington, D.C.: National Academy Press.

Common, D. L. 1981. Two decades of curriculum innovation and so little change. *Education Canada* 21 (3): 42–48.

Connelly, F. Michael and D. Jean Clandinin. 1990. Stories of experience and narrative inquiry. *Educational Researcher* 19 (4): 2–14.

Connelly, F. Michael, Robert K. Crocker, and Heidi Kass. 1985. *Science education in Canada: Volume 1*. Toronto: OISE Press.

———. 1989. *Science education in Canada: Volume 2*. Toronto, Ontario, Canada: OISE Press.

Cox, David C. 1980. *Unified science education and the paradigms of science*. Halifax, Nova Scotia, Canada: Atlantic Institute of Education.

Crandall, David P. 1983. The teacher's role in school improvement. *Educational Leadership* 41 (3): 6–9.

Creation House. 1973. *New American Standard Bible*. Carol Stream, Illinois: Creation House.

Crichton, Michael. 1990. *Jurassic Park*. Toronto: Ballantine Books.

Crocker, Robert K. 1982. Implementing curriculum change: experience from two science projects. *Morning Watch* 9 (3): 28–35.

Crowell, Sam. 1989. A new way of thinking: The challenge of the future. *Educational Leadership* 47 (1): 60–63.

Cuban, Larry. 1982. Persistent instruction: the high school classroom, 1900–1980. *Phi Delta Kappan* 64 (2): 113–118.

———. 1984. *How teachers taught: Constancy and change in American classrooms 1890–1980*. New York: Longman.

———. 1990. Reforming again, again, and again. *Educational Researcher* 19 (1): 3–13.

Cummings, E. E. 1955. Three statements. In *20th Century poetry & poetics,* edited by Gary Geddes, 435–438. Toronto: Oxford University Press.

Cummings, E. E. 1991. pity this busy monster,manunkind,. In *Complete Poems: 1904–1962,* edited by George J. Firmage, 554. New York: of Liveright.

Curtis, Bruce. 1988. Policing pedagogical space: "Voluntary" school reform and moral regulation. *Canadian Journal of Sociology* 13 (3): 283–304.

Dalgleish, Oakley. 1957a. Funds for research. *The Globe and Mail,* 9 October: 6.

———. 1957b. Reassessing our values. *The Globe and Mail,* 6 November 6: 6.

DaSilva, Tomaz Tadeu. 1988. Distribution of school knowledge and social reproduction in a Brazilian urban setting. *British Journal of Sociology of Education* 9 (1): 55–79.

Deane, Philip. 1957. Eisenhower undisturbed by Red satellite; casts doubts on accuracy of Soviet rockets. *The Globe and Mail,* 10 October: 1–2.

DeBoer, George E. 1991. *A history of ideas in science education: Implications for practice.* New York: Teachers College Press.

Deleuze, Gilles. 1988. *Foucault.* Translated and edited by Sean Hand. Minneapolis: University of Minnesota Press. Original edition, Les Éditions de Minuit, 1986.

DeLuna, Phyllis. 1989a. Universities place conditions on accepting Science 30. *ATA News* 23 (13): 6.

———. 1989b. Teachers weigh new science program. *ATA News* 23 (13): 6.

———. 1989c. Alberta education postpones senior high science program. *ATA News* 23 (16): 3.

Derrida, Jacques. 1982. *Margins of philosophy*. Translated by Alan Bass. Chicago: The University of Chicago Press. Original edition, Les Édition de Minuit, 1972.

Digeser, Peter. 1992. The fourth face of power. *The Journal of Politics* 54 (2): 977–1007.

Doll, Ronald. C. 1986. *Curriculum improvement: Decision making and process*. Toronto: Allyn and Bacon.

Doll, William E. 1989. Foundations for a post-modern curriculum. *Journal of Curriculum Studies* 21 (3): 243–253.

Dreyfus, Hurbert L. and Paul Rabinow. 1982. *Michel Foucault: Beyond structuralism and hermeneutics*. Chicago: University of Chicago Press.

Durant, Will. 1961. *The story of philosophy*. Toronto: Washington Square Books.

Duschl, Richard A. 1988. Abandoning the scientistic legacy of science education. *Science Education* 72 (1): 51–62.

———. 1990. *Restructuring science education*. New York: Teachers College Press.

Eamon, John. 1989. Minister defends science change. *Grande Prairie Herald Tribune*, 25 September: 3.

Eisner, Elliot W. 1979. *The educational imagination*. New York: Macmillan.

Eisner, Elliot W. and Elizabeth Vallance. 1974. *Conflicting conceptions of curriculum*. Berkeley, California: McCutchan Publishing.

Elliott, Olive. 1989. Better science programs a must for schools. *The Edmonton Journal*, 6 February: C2.

Eribon, Didier. 1989. *Michel Foucault*. Paris: Flammarion.

———. 1991. *Michel Foucault*. Translated by Betsy Wing. Cambridge, Mass.: Harvard University Press. Original edition, Paris: Flammarion, 1989.

Faculty of Science, University of Alberta. 1991. Science 30. *Faculty of Science Express* 1 (5): 1.

Farrell, Edmund J. 1985. Making connections: Academic reform and adolescents' priorities. *English Journal* 74 (4): 22–28.

Farrell, William E. 1969. The world's cheers for American technology are many. *New York Times*, 21 July: 10.

Feather, Frank. 1989. *G-forces: Reinventing the world*. Toronto: Summerhill Press.

Fensham, Peter J. 1988a. Physical science, society and technology: A case study in the sociology of knowledge. *Australian Journal of Education* 32 (3): 375–386.

———. 1988b. Approaches to the teaching of STS in science education. *International Journal of Science Education* 10 (4): 346–356.

———. 1993. Academic influence on school science curricula. *Journal of Curriculum Studies* 25 (1): 53–64.

Fink-Eitel, Hinrich. 1992. *Foucault: An introduction*. Translated by Edward Dixon. Philadelphia: Pennbridge Books.

Foucault, Michel. 1972. *The archeology of knowledge and the discourse on language*. Translated by A. M. Sheridan Smith. New York: Pantheon Books. Original edition, Paris: Éditions Gallimard, 1969.

Foucault, Michel. 1973. *The order of things: An archaeology of the human sciences.* New York: Vintage Books. Original edition, Paris: Éditions Gallimard, 1966.

———. 1977. *Pouvoir/Savoir.* New York: Pantheon Books.

———. 1979. *Discipline and punish: The birth of the prison.* Translated by Alan Sheridan. New York: Vintage Books. Original edition, Paris: Éditions Gallimard, 1975.

———. 1980. *Power/Knowledge: Selected interviews and other writings 1972–1977.* Translated by Colin Gordon, Leo Marshall, John Mepham, and Kate Soper, edited by Colin Gordon. New York: Pantheon Books.

———. 1982. Is it really important to think? (Thomas Keenan, Trans.). *Philosophy & Social Criticism* 9 (1): 31–40.

———. 1983. On the genealogy of ethics: An overview of a work in progress. In Dreyfus, Hubert L. and Paul Rabinow, 1983. *Michel Foucault: Beyond structuralism and hermeneutics,* 229–254. Chicago: University of Chicago Press.

———. 1984a. *The Foucault reader.* Edited by Paul Rabinow. New York: Pantheon Books.

——— 1984b. Truth and power. In *The Foucault Reader,* edited by Paul Rabinow, 51–75. New York: Pantheon Books.

———. 1984c. Politics and ethics: An interview. In *The Foucault Reader,* edited by Paul Rabinow, 373–390. New York: Pantheon Books.

———. 1984d. Nietzsche, genealogy, history. In *The Foucault Reader,* edited by Paul Rabinow, 76–100. New York: Pantheon Books.

Foucault, Michel. 1988. On power. In *Michel Foucault: Politics, philosophy and culture, interviews and other writings 1977– 1984,* translated by Alan Sheridan (and others), edited by Lawrence D. Kritzman, 96–109. New York: Routledge.

―――. 1989a. Rituals of exclusion. In *Foucault live,* translated by John Johnston, edited by Sylvère Lotringer, 63–72. New York: Columbia University, Semiotext(e).

―――. 1989b. An historian of culture. In *Foucault live,* translated by John Johnston, edited by Sylvère Lotringer, 73–88. New York: Columbia University, Semiotext(e).

―――. 1989c. What calls for punishment?. In *Foucault live,* translated by John Johnston, edited by Sylvère Lotringer, 279– 292. New York: Columbia University, Semiotext(e).

―――. 1989d. Foucault responds to Sartre. In *Foucault live,* translated by John Johnston, edited by Sylvère Lotringer, 35– 43. New York: Columbia University, Semiotext(e).

―――. 1989e. The archaeology of knowledge. In *Foucault live,* translated by John Johnston, edited by Sylvère Lotringer, 45– 56. New York: Columbia University, Semiotext(e).

―――. 1989f. The order of things. In *Foucault live,* translated by John Johnston, edited by Sylvère Lotringer, 1–10. New York: Columbia University, Semiotext(e).

―――. 1989g. The birth of the world. In *Foucault live,* translated by John Johnston, edited by Sylvère Lotringer, 57–61. New York: Columbia University, Semiotext(e).

―――. 1989h. How much does it cost for reason to tell the truth? In *Foucault live,* translated by John Johnston, edited by Sylvère Lotringer, 233–256. New York: Columbia University, Semiotext(e).

Foucault, Michel. 1989i. The discourse of history In *Foucault live,* translated by John Johnston, edited by Sylvère Lotringer, 11– 33. New York: Columbia University, Semiotext(e).

———. 1990. *The history of sexuality. Volume I: An introduction.* Translated by Robert Hurley. New York: Vintage Books. Original edition, Paris: Édition Gallimard, 1976.

Fowler, Robert H. 1990. *Politics and ideology in curricular decision-making: The case of British Columbia 1979–1982.* Paper presented at the 1990 Conference on Curriculum Theory and Classroom Practice, 17–20 October, Bergamo Conference Center, Dayton, Ohio.

Fraser, Nancy and Linda J. Nicholson. 1990. Social criticism without philosophy: An encounter between feminism and postmodernism. In *Feminism/postmodernism,* edited by Linda J. Nicholson, 19–38. New York: Routledge.

Freedman, Joe. 1989a. *The Science 10 controversy explained.* Red Deer, Alberta. Photocopy.

———. 1989b. The new science courses are pulp. *Red Deer Advocate*, 12 August 12: 5A.

Freedman, Kerry and Thomas S. Popkewitz. 1988. Art education and social interests in the development of American schooling: Ideological origins of curriculum theory. *Journal of Curriculum Studies* 20 (5): 387–405.

Fullan, Michael. 1977. Research on curriculum and instruction implementation. *Review of Educational Research* 47 (1): 335– 397.

———. 1982. *The meaning of educational change.* Toronto: OISE Press.

———. 1991. *The new meaning of educational change.* Toronto: OISE Press.

Fullan, Michael. 1993. Innovation, reform and restructuring strategies. In *Challenges and achievements in American education: 1993 yearbook of the Association of Supervision and Curriculum Development,* edited by Gordon Cawelti, 116–133. Alexandria, VA: Association of Supervision and Curriculum Development.

Gagné, Robert Mills and Leslie J. Briggs. 1974. *Principles of instructional design.* Toronto: Holt, Rinehart, and Winston.

Galbraith, Bernie. 1983. *Science process skills and the Alberta science curriculum: A position paper.* Edmonton, Alberta, Canada: Alberta Education.

Gane, Mike. 1986. Introduction: Michel Foucault. In *Towards a critique of Foucault,* edited by Mike Gane, 2–14. New York: Routledge & Kegan Paul.

Gaskell, Jim. 1980. World trends in science education: A report from Halifax. *B.C. Science Teacher* 21 (4): 25–26.

Gay, Peter. 1988. *Freud: A life for our time.* New York: W. W. Norton & Co.

Gibran, Kahlil. 1977. *The Prophet.* New York: Alfred A. Knopf.

Gillan, Garth. 1987. Foucault's philosophy. *Philosophy and Social Criticism* 12 (2–3): 145–155.

Giroux, Henry A. 1983. *Theory and resistance: A pedagogy for the opposition.* South Hadley, Massachusetts.: Bergin and Garvey.

———. 1985. Teachers as transformative intellectuals. *Social Education* 49 (5): 376–379.

Giroux, Henry A., Anthony N. Penna, and William F. Pinar. 1981. Introduction and overview to the curriculum field. In *Curriculum and Instruction,* edited by Henry A. Giroux, Anthony N. Penna and William F. Pinar, 1–9. Berkeley, California: McCutchan.

Goddard, Robert. 1989. The management of change: Getting started. *The Monograph* 40 (2): 14–16.

Goodwin, Irwin. 1988. Five years after 'A Nation at Risk' US schools still seek better grades. *Physics Today* November, 1988: 50–52.

Gordon, Colin (1980). Preface. In *Power/Knowledge: Selected interviews and other writings 1972–1977,* translated by Colin Gordon, Leo Marshall, John Mepham, and Kate Soper; edited by Colin Gordon, vii–x. New York: Pantheon Books.

Government of Alberta. 1984. *Proposals for an industrial and science strategy for Albertans—1985 to 1990.* Edmonton, Alberta, Canada: Government of Alberta.

Government of Alberta. 1985. *Secondary education in Alberta.* Edmonton, Alberta, Canada: Ministry of Education.

Government of Canada. 1988. *Science and technology in Canada.* Ottawa, Ontario, Canada: Department of Science and Technology.

Greene, Maxine. 1986. Towards possibility: Expanding the range of literacy. *English Education* 18 (4): 231–243.

———. 1987. Sense-making through story: An autobiographical inquiry. *Teaching Education* 1 (2): 9–14.

———. 1988. *The dialectic of freedom.* New York: Teachers College Press.

Gruber, David F. 1989. Foucault and theory: Genealogical critiques of the subject. In *The question of the other: Essays in contemporary continental philosophy,* edited by Arlene B. Dallery and Charles E. Scott, 189–196. Albany, New York: State University of New York Press.

Gruender, C. David and Kenneth G. Tobin. 1991. Promise and prospect. *Science Education* 75 (1): 1–8.

Grumet, Madeline R. 1981. Autobiography and reconceptualization. In *Curriculum and instruction,* edited by Henry A. Giroux, Anthony N. Penna and William F. Pinar, 139–144. Berkeley California: McCutchan.

———. 1987. The politics of personal knowledge. *Curriculum Inquiry* 17 (3): 317–329.

Guba, Egon G. and Yvonna S. Lincoln. 1982. *Effective evaluation.* London, England: Jossey-Bass.

Guha, Ramachandra. 1989. Radical American environmentalism and wilderness preservation: A third world critique. *Environmental Ethics* 2 (Summer): 71–83.

Guinness, Os. 1979. *The dust of death.* Downers Grove, Illinois: InterVarsity Press.

Gutting, Gary. 1989. *Michel Foucault's archeology of scientific reason.* New York: Cambridge University Press.

Habermas, Jürgen. 1982. *Knowledge and human interests.* Translated by Jeremy J. Shapiro. Boston: Beacon Press. Original edition, Frankfurt am Main: Suhrkamp Verlag, 1968.

———. 1992. *The philosophical discourse of modernity.* Translated by Frederick G. Lawrence. Cambridge, Massachusetts: MIT Press. Original edition, Frankfurt am Main: Suhrkamp Verlag, 1985.

Hansard Education News. 1989. *Oral question period, June 13, 1989.* Edmonton, Alberta, Canada: Government of Alberta.

Heidegger, Martin. 1977. The question concerning technology. In *Martin Heidegger: Basic writings,* translated and edited by David Krell, 287–317. New York Harper & Row.

Helgeson, Stanley L., Patricia E. Blosser, and Robert W. Howe. 1977. *The status of pre-college science, mathematics, and social science education: 1955–1975: Volume 1 Science Education.* Ohio, Ohio State University: Center for Science and Mathematics Education.

Hellfritz, Claudia. 1990. Dialogue on science education in Alberta. *The Pegg* (January, 1990): 6.

Hershel, Abraham J. 1955. *God in search of man: A philosophy of Judaism.* New York: Farrar, Straus, and Giroux.

Hodson, Derek. 1988. Toward a philosophically more valid science curriculum. *Science Education* 72 (1): 19–40.

Hoffer, Eric. 1951. *The true believer.* New York: Harper and Row.

Holton, Gerald. 1992. How to think about the 'anti-science' phenomenon. *Public Understanding of Science* 1 (1): 103–128.

House, Ernest R. 1979. Technology versus craft: a ten year perspective on innovation. *Journal of Curriculum Studies* 11 (1): 1–15.

Hug, J. 1985. *Michel Foucault: Une histoire de la vérité.* Paris: Syros.

Hugo, Victor. 1887. *Les Misérables.* New York: Thomas Y. Crowell & Co.

Hunkins, Francis P. 1980. *Curriculum development: Program improvement.* Toronto: Charles E. Merrill Publishing.

Hurd, Paul DeHart. 1961. *Biological education in American secondary schools 1890–1960.* Washington, D.C.: American Institute of Biological Sciences.

Hurd, Paul DeHart. 1964. Toward a theory of science education consistent with modern science. In *Theory into action in science curriculum development*, National Science Teachers Association, 5–15. Washington, D.C.: National Science Teachers Association.

––––––. 1975. Science, technology, and society: New goals for interdisciplinary science teaching. *Science Teacher* 42 (2): 27–30.

––––––. 1985. A rationale for a science, technology, and society theme in science education. In *Science, technology, society: 1985 yearbook of the National Science Teachers Association,* edited by Roger W. Bybee, 94–101. Washington, D.C.: National Science Teachers Association.

––––––. 1986. Perspectives for the reform of science education. *Phi Delta Kappan* 67 (5): 353–358.

––––––. 1989. Problems and issues in science-curriculum reform and implementation. In *High-school biology: today and tomorrow*, Committee on High-School Biology Education, 291–312. Washington, D.C.: National Academy of Sciences.

––––––. 1991a. Closing the educational gaps between science, technology, and society. *Theory Into Practice* 30 (4): 251–259.

––––––. 1991b. Why we must transform science education. *Educational Leadership* 49 (2): 33–35.

––––––. 1994. New minds for a new age: Prologue to modernizing the science curriculum. *Science Education* 78 (1): 103–116.

Hutcheon, Linda. 1991. Theories of culture, ethnicity, and postmodernism. *Aurora* 15 (1): 15–18.

Hutchins, R. M. 1952. *The great conversation.* Toronto: Encyclopaedia Britannica.

Huyssen, Andreas. 1990. Mapping the postmodern. In *Feminism/postmodernism,* edited by Linda J. Nicholson, 234–277. New York: Routledge.

International Council of Associations for Science Education. 1992. *The status of science-technology-society reforms efforts around the world.* Edited by Robert E. Yager. Arlington, Virginia: National Science Teachers Association.

Jacknicke, Kenneth and Pat M. Rowell. 1987. Alternative orientations for educational research. *Alberta Journal of Educational Research* 33 (1): 62–72.

Jacobs, Louis. 1984. *The book of Jewish belief.* New York: Behrman House.

Jenkins, E. W. 1992. School science education: towards a reconstruction. *Journal of Curriculum Studies* 24 (3): 229–246.

Jenkins, Frank. 1990. *STS science education: Unifying the goals of science Education.* Edmonton, Alberta, Canada: Curriculum Support Branch, Alberta Education.

Johnson, Mauritz. 1981. Definitions and models in curriculum theory. In *Curriculum and instruction,* edited by Henry A. Giroux, Anthony N. Penna, and William F. Pinar, 69–85. Berkeley, California: McCutchan.

Johnson, Neil A. 1987. The pervasive, persuasive power of perceptions. *The Alberta Journal of Educational Research* 33 (3): 206–228.

Johnson, Paul. 1991. *The birth of the modern.* New York: Harper Collins.

Jones, Carolyn and Ben Hutchings. 1993. Science's 'nerd' image turns students off. *Weekend Australian,* 8–9 May: 1–2.

Joyce, Bruce R. 1969. *Alternate models of elementary education.* Toronto: Blaisdell Publishing.

Joyce, Bruce R. and Richard Hersh. 1983. *The structure of school improvement.* New York: Longman.

Kass, Heidi and David W. Blades. 1992. *A post-modern perspective on the marginalization of student voices in science education curriculum-discourse.* Paper presented at the 1992 Fourth Annual Conference, International Consortium for Research in Science and Mathematics Education, 3–4 February, San Juan, Puerto Rico.

Keeves, John P. 1992. Science education: Towards the future. In *The IEA study of Science III: Changes in science education and achievement, 1970 to 1984,* edited by John P. Keeves, 1–23. New York: Pergamon.

Keeves, J. P. and C. Morgenstern. 1992. Attitudes towards science: measures and effects. In *The IEA study of Science III: Changes in science education and achievement, 1970 to 1984,* edited by John P. Keeves, 122–140. New York: Pergamon.

Kennedy, Edward. 1979. Biomedical science in an expectant society. In *The biological revolution,* edited by Gerald Weissmann, 11–19. New York: Plenum Press.

Kidder, Louise H. 1981. *Research methods in social relations.* New York: Holt, Rinehart and Winston.

Kierkegaard, Søren. 1983. Repetition. In *Fear and Trembling/Repetition,* translated and edited by Howard V. Hong and Edna H. Hong, 125–232. Princeton, New Jersey: Princeton University Press. Original edition 1843.

Kim, Yong-Sik. 1991. *The nihilisitic challenge to curriculum and pedagogy.* Ph.D. dissertation, University of Alberta, Edmonton, Alberta, Canada.

Kline, Meredith. 1970. Genesis. In *The new Bible commentary revised,* edited by Donald Guthrie, Alec Motyer, Alan M. Stibbs and Donald J. Wiseman, 79–114. Grand Rapids, Michigan: Wm. B. Eerdmans.

Klopfer, Leopold E. and Audrey B. Champagne. 1990. Ghosts of crisis past. *Science Education* 74 (2): 133–154.

Kohak, Erazim. 1984. *The embers and the stars.* Chicago: University of Chicago Press.

Krell, David F. 1977. General introduction. In *Martin Heidegger: Basic writings,* translated and edited by David F. Krell, 3–35. New York: Harper & Row.

Kubish, Glen and Virginia Byfield. 1990. On senior high science, a compromise. *Alberta Report* 17 (5): 26.

Kurz, Dorothy. 1983. The use of participant observation in evaluation research. *Evaluation and Program Planning* 6: 93–102.

Kurzweil, Edith. 1983. Michel Foucault and culture. *Current Perspectives in Social Theory* 4: 143–179.

Kyle, William C.; James A. Shymansky; and Jennifer M. Alport. 1982. Alphabet soup science. *The Science Teacher* 49 (8): 49–53.

Langford, Cooper. 1989. Science curriculum weak: Engineers. *Fort McMurray Today*, 5 October: 1.

Lather, Patti. (1986). Research as praxis. *Harvard Educational Review* 56 (3): 257–257.

Lau, Michael. 1989. Science changes worry. *Red Deer Advocate*, 23 June: 1B.

Layton, David. 1973. *Science of the people: The origins of the school science curriculum in England.* New York: Science History Publications.

Layton, David. 1984. *Interpreters of science: A history of the Association for Science Education.* Portsmouth, England: John Murray.

―――. 1994. STS in the school curriculum: A movement overtaken by history? In *STS Education: International perspectives on reform,* edited by Joan Solomon and Glen Aikenhead, 32–46. New York: Teachers College Press.

Levin, David M. 1988. *The opening of vision: Nihilism and the post-modern situation.* New York: Routledge.

―――. 1989. *The listening self.* New York: Routledge.

Lewington, Jennifer. 1992. Breathing life into an old subject. *The Globe and Mail,* 16 January: A1, A4.

Leithwood, Kenneth A. 1986. *Planned educational change.* Toronto: OISE Press.

Lock, Corey R. 1984. Involving students in curriculum development. *Clearing House,* 57 (4): 261–262.

Lovelock, James. 1991. *Healing Gaia.* New York: Harmony Books.

Luke, Carmen; Suzanne De Castell and Alan Luke. 1983. Beyond criticism: The authority of the school text. *Curriculum Inquiry* 13 (2): 111–127.

Lyotard, Jean-François. 1984. *The post-modern condition: A report on knowledge.* Translated by Geoff Bennington and Brian Massumi. Minneapolis, Minnesota: University of Minnesota Press. Original edition, France: Les Éditions de Minuit, 1979

MacDonald, James B. 1988. Theory-practice and the hermeneutic circle. In *Contemporary curriculum discourses,* edited by William F. Pinar, 101–113. Scottsdale, Arizona: Grosuch Scarisbrick.

Macdonald, Peter. 1990. Taking a few steps back. *Alberta Report* 17 (10): 32.

Macdonald, Peter and Virginia Byfield. 1989a. The death of science. *Alberta Report*, 16 (26): 23–24.

———. 1989b. 'Dumbing down' high schools. *Alberta Report* 16 (27): 28–34.

———. 1989c. Quelling the science fire. *Alberta Report* 16 (33): 28.

MacKeracher, Dorothy. 1985. Science education in a changing society. In *Science education in Canada, Volume 1: Policies, Practices, & Perceptions,* edited by F. Michael Connelly, Robert K. Crocker and Heidi Kass, 82–107. Toronto: OISE Press.

Madison, G. B. 1988. *The hermeneutics of postmodernity.* Indianapolis, Indiana: Indiana University Press.

Marshall, James D. 1989. Foucault and education. *Australian Journal of Education* 33 (2): 99–113.

———. 1990. Foucault and educational research. In *Foucault and education: Disciplines and knowledge,* edited by Stephen J. Ball, 11–28. New York: Routledge.

Marshall, S. J. 1962. The improvement of science education and the administrator. In *The new school science,* American Association for the Advancement of Science, 2–12. Washington, D.C.: American Association for the Advancement of Science.

Matthews, Michael R. 1989. A role for history and philosophy in science teaching. *Interchange* 20 (2): 3–15.

Matthews, Michael R. 1992. History, philosophy and science teaching: The present rapprochement. *Science & Education* 1 (1): 11–48.

McFadden, Charles P. 1990. Paradigm shifts: A revolution in science teaching? *Crucible* 21 (5): 16–17.

McGeachy, Frank. 1989. The death of science in Alberta. *The Alberta Science Teacher* 9 (3): 2–3.

McLaren, Digby J. 1990. Preface. In *Planet under stress: The challenge of global change,* edited by Constance Mungall and Digby J. McLaren, xiii–xv. Toronto: Oxford University Press.

Megill, Allan. 1985. *Prophets of extremity: Nietzsche, Heidegger, Foucault, Derrida.* Berkeley, California: University of California Press.

Mercer, Kobena. 1990. Welcome to the jungle: Identity and diversity in postmodern politics. In *Identity, community, culture, difference,* edited by Jonathan Rutherford, 43–71. London, England: Lawrence & Wishart.

Miles, Matthew B. and A. Michael Huberman. 1984a. *Qualitative data analysis.* London, England: Sage Publications.

———. 1984b Drawing valid meaning from qualitative data: Toward a shared craft. *Educational Researcher* 13 (5): 20–29.

Miller, Jim. 1993. *The passion of Michel Foucault.* New York: Simon & Schuster.

Miller, John P. and Wayne W. Seller. 1985. *Curriculum: Perspectives and practice.* New York: Longman.

Milner, Andrew; Philip Thomson; and Chris Worth. 1990. Introduction. *Postmodern conditions,* edited by Andrew Milner, Philip Thomson and Chris Worth, ix–xv. New York: Bergamon.

Mueller, George E. 1969. In the next decade: A lunar base, space laboratory. *New York Times,* 21 July: 14.

Murphy, P. J. 1986. Managing situations: The politics of curricular change. *Comment on Education* 17 (1): 12–18.

Nadeau, Robert and Jacques Désautels. 1984. *Epistemology and the teaching of science*. Ottawa, Ontario, Canada: Science Council of Canada.

National Science Foundation Panel on School Science. 1980. The state of school science: A review of the teaching of mathematics, science, and social studies in American schools, and recommendations for improvements. In *What are the needs in precollege science, mathematics, and social studies education? Views from the field,* National Science Foundation, 79–120. Washington, D.C.: National Science Foundation.

National Science Teachers Association. 1964. *Theory into action in science curriculum development.* Washington, D.C.: National Science Teachers Association.

Newton, Earle. 1991. The challenge of change. *The Medium* 31 (1): 3–7.

Nietzsche, Friedrich. 1966. *Beyond good and evil: Prelude to a philosophy of the future.* Translated by Walter Kaufmann. New York: Vintage Books. Original edition 1886.

———. 1967. *On the genealogy of morals.* Translated by Walter Kaufmann. New York: Vintage Books. Original edition 1887.

———. 1969. *Thus Spoke Zarathustra.* Translated by R. J. Hollingdale. London, England: Penguin Books. Original edition 1885.

O'Neil, John. 1992. Science Education: Schools pushed to broaden access, overhaul practice. *ASCD Update* (September) 1992.

Oelschlaeger, Max. 1991. *The idea of wilderness.* London, England: Yale University Press.

Oliva, Peter F. 1982. *Developing the curriculum.* Toronto: Little, Brown & Company.

Orr, David. 1992. *Ecological literacy: Education and the transition to a postmodern world.* New York: State University of New York Press.

Palmer, Roger. 1989a. *Who decides what students should learn in school...and how?* Edmonton, Alberta, Canada: Alberta Education, Student Programs and Evaluation Division.

———. 1989b. *High quality science programs for all Albertans.* Edmonton, Alberta, Canada: Alberta Education.

Panwar, Raja. 1989. This is not watered-down science. *Red Deer Advocate,* 12 August 12: 5A.

———. 1991. Alberta's senior high science programs. *Alberta Science Education Journal* 24 (2): 8–11.

Panzeri, Allen. 1989. Health care threatened if science curriculum is diluted, AMA warns. *Edmonton Journal,* 28 June: D15.

———. 1990a. Dinning passes science test. *Edmonton Journal,* 27 January: A8.

———. 1990b. Pop-science content seen as key to new curriculum. *Edmonton Journal,* 12 March: B3.

———. 1990c. Dinning proves deft in thorny portfolio. *Edmonton Journal,* 14 April: G1, G3.

Passmore, J. A. 1975. The revolt against science. In *The structure of science education,* edited by P. L. Gardner, 41–59. New York: Longman.

Pedersen, Jon E. 1992. STS issues in science : A new paradigm. In *Handbook of Science, Technology and Society: Volume 1. A Theoretical and conceptual overview of science, technology and society education,* edited by M. O. Thirunarayanan, 179–184. Tempe, Arizona: Arizona State University.

Pinar, William F. 1988. Autobiography and the architecture of self. *Journal of Curriculum Theorizing* 8 (1): 7–35.

Pinar, William F.; William M. Reynolds; Patrick Slattery; and Peter M. Taubman. 1995. *Understanding curriculum: An introduction to the study of historical and contemporary curriculum discourses.* New York: Peter Lang.

Popkewitz, Tom S. 1988. What's in a research project: Some thoughts on the intersection of history, social structure, and biography. *Curriculum Inquiry* 18 (4): 379–400.

Poster, Mark. 1989. *Critical theory and poststructualism: In search of a context.* London, England: Cornell University Press.

Rabinow, Paul. 1984a. Introduction. In *The Foucault Reader,* edited by Paul Rabinow, 3–29. New York: Pantheon Books.

———. 1984b. *The Foucault reader.* Edited by Paul Rabinow. New York: Pantheon Books.

Rajchman, John. 1985. *Michel Foucault: The freedom of philosophy.* New York: Columbia University Press.

Ramsey, John. 1993. The science education reform movement: Implications for social responsibility. *Science Education* 77 (2): 235–258.

Rifkin, Jeremy. 1983. *Algeny.* New York: Penguin Books.

Roberts, Douglas A. 1983. *Scientific literacy—towards balance in setting goals for school science programs.* Ottawa, Ontario, Canada: Science Council of Canada.

Rochlitz, Rainer. 1992. The aesthetics of existence: Post-conventional morality and the theory of power in Michel Foucault. In *Michel Foucault: Philosopher,* translated and edited by Timothy J. Armstrong, 248–259. New York: Routledge, Chapman and Hall.

Rosenau, Pauline Marie. 1992. *Postmodernism and the social sciences*. Princeton, New Jersey: Princeton University Press.

Rosenthal, Dorothy B. 1989. Two approaches to science-technology-society (S-T-S) education. *Science Education* 73 (4): 581–589.

Ross, Elsie. 1989a, 'Diluted' science program draws fire. *Calgary Herald*, 28 June: B6.

———. 1989b. Board wants changes delayed. *Calgary Herald*, 21 March: B3.

———. 1989c. Science friction: Proposed curriculum changes under fire. *Calgary Herald*, 14 July: C8.

———. 1989d. Council will evaluate new science courses. *Calgary Herald*, 3 August: B3.

———. 1990. Educators fear credit crunch. *Calgary Herald*, 9 February: A5.

Roth, Jeffrey. 1992. Of what help is he? A review of *Foucault and Education*. *American Educational Research Journal* 29 (4): 683–694.

Russell, Bertrand. 1952. *The impact of science on society*. London, England: George Allen & Unwin.

Ryan, Brendan P. 1989. Schooling for technological change—Two nations once again. *Interchange* 20 (3): 17–34.

Ryan, James. 1991. Observing and normalizing: Foucault, discipline, and inequality in schooling. *Journal of Educational Thought* 25 (2): 104–119.

Sarason, Seymour B. 1982. *The culture of the school and the problem of change*. (2nd ed.). Boston: Allyn and Bacon.

Sarason, Seymour B. (1990). *The predictable failure of educational reform*. Oxford, England: Jossey-Bass.

Sartre, Jean-Paul. 1969. *The age of reason*. Translated by Eric Sutton. London, England: Heron Books. Original edition 1945.

Savan, Bev. 1988. *Science under siege*. Toronto: CBC Enterprises.

Sawicki, Jana. 1987. Heidegger and Foucault: escaping technological nihilism. *Philosophy and Social Criticism* 13 (2): 155–173.

Schwab, Joseph J. 1978. Education and the structure of the disciplines. In *Science, curriculum, and liberal education*, edited by Ian Westbury and Neil J. Wilkof, 229–272. Chicago: University of Chicago Press.

Science Council of Canada. 1984a. *Summary of Report 36: Science for every student*. Hull, Québec, Canada: Canadian Government Publishing Center.

———. 1984b. *Report 36: Science for every student*. Hull, Québec, Canada: Canadian Government Publishing Center.

Shelley, Mary S. 1988. *Frankenstein*. New York: Dilithium Press. Original edition 1831.

Shubert, William. 1993. Curriculum reform. In *Challenges and achievements of American education: 1993 Yearbook of the Association for Supervision and Curriculum Development*, edited by Gordon Cawelti, 80–115. Alexandria, Virginia: Association for Supervision and Curriculum Development.

Sinai Publishing. 1984. *The Holy Scriptures*. Tel Aviv, Israel: Sinai Publishing.

Smith, Bruce L. R. 1990. *American science policy since World War II*. Washington, D.C.: Brookings Institute.

Smith, Herbert A. 1980. A report on the implications for the science community of three NSF-supported studies of the state of precollege science education. In *What are the needs in precollege science, mathematics, and social studies education? Views from the field,* National Science Foundation, 55–78. Washington, D.C.: National Science Foundation.

Solomon, Joan. 1991. Teaching about the nature of science in the British National Curriculum. *Science Education* 75 (1): 95–103.

————. 1994. Conflict between mainstream science and STS in science education. In *STS Education: International perspectives on reform,* edited by Joan Solomon and Glen Aikenhead, 3–10. New York: Teachers College Press.

Soltis, Jonas F. 1984. On the nature of educational research. *Educational Researcher* 13 (10): 5–10.

Southam Environment Project. 1989. Our Fragile Future. *Edmonton Journal,* 7 October 7: Special supplement.

Stenhouse, David. 1985. *Active philosophy in education and science.* London, England: George Allen & Unwin.

Stevenson, Hugh A. 1973. Ten years to know-where. In *The failure of educational reform in Canada,* edited by Douglas Myers, 50–59. Toronto: McClelland and Stewart.

Suzuki, David. 1989a. *Inventing the future: Reflections on science, technology, and nature.* Toronto: Stoddart Publishing.

————. 1989b. Facing up to our eco-crisis is not 'gloom and doom'. *The Edmonton Journal,* 3 December: C5.

Suzuki, David. 1992. 'Beneficial' technology can have negative side. *The Star Phoenix,* 8 August: D12.

Taba, Hilda. 1962. *Curriculum development: Theory and practice.* New York: Harcourt, Brace & World.

Tanner, Daniel and Laurel N. Tanner. 1980. *Curriculum development: Theory into practice.* New York: Macmillan Publishing.

Teachers cautiously approve new science curriculum. 1990. *ATA News*, 12 February: 1.

Tenzin Gyatso. 1990. *Freedom in exile.* New York: Cornelia & Michael Bessie.

Tessmer, Martin and Duncan Harris. 1990. Beyond instructional effectiveness: Key environmental decisions for instructional designers as change agents. *Educational Technology* 30 (7): 16–21.

Thiele, Leslie Paul. 1990. The agony of politics: The Nietzschean roots of Foucault's thought. *American Political Science Review* 84 (3): 907–925.

Thomas, J. R. 1989. City's high school education fails grade. *Calgary Herald*, 10 July: A6.

Thomas, Lewis. 1980. *Late night thoughts on listening to Mahler's Ninth Symphony.* London, England: Bantam Books.

Tomkins, George S. 1977. Tradition and change in Canadian education: Historical and contemporary perspectives. In *Precepts, policy and process: Perspectives on contemporary Canadian education,* edited by Hugh A. Stevenson and J. Donald Wilson, 1–20. London, Ontario, Canada: Alexander, Blake Associates.

Townsend, Richard C. 1990. How can schooling be improved? *Orbit* 21 (3): 2–4.

Tri-Partite Committee on Inservice Education. 1980. *Inservice education for implementation of new and revised programs.* Edmonton, Alberta, Canada: Alberta Education. Photocopy.

Turney, David. 1976. Sisyphus revisited. In *Perspectives on curriculum development: 1776–1976,* edited by O. L. Davis, Jr., 223–239. Washington, D.C.: Association for Supervision and Curriculum Development.

Tyler, Ralph W. 1949. *Basic principles of curriculum and instruction.* Chicago: University of Chicago Press.

————. 1981. Specific approaches to curriculum development. In *Curriculum and Instruction,* edited by Henry A. Giroux, Anthony N. Penna, and William F. Pinar, 17–30. Berkeley, California: McCutchan.

Ungerleider, Dorothy. 1986. The organic curriculum. *Academic Therapy* 21 (4): 465–471.

United Nations Environment Program. 1990. *The state of the environment, 1990.* New York: UNICEF House.

University of Alberta Faculty of Science Ad Hoc Committee on the Proposed Revisions to the High School Programs. 1989. *Report on the Proposed Revision to the High School Science Program.* Edmonton, Alberta, Canada: University of Alberta Faculty of Science.

Vattimo, Gianni. 1988. *The end of modernity.* Translated by Jon R. Snyder. Baltimore, Maryland: John Hopkins University Press. Original edition, Garzanti Editore, 1985.

Victor, Edward and Richard D. Kellough. 1993. *Science for the elementary school.* New York: Macmillan publishing.

Visvanathan, Shiv. 1987. From the annals of the laboratory state. *Alternatives* 12: 37–59.

Von Braun, Werner. 1970. Introduction. In *Where the winds sleep,* N. P. Ruzic, i. Garden City, New York: Doubleday and Company.

Waring, Mary. 1979. *Social pressures and curriculum innovation: A study of the Nuffield Foundation science teaching project.* London, England: Methuen.

Webster, Norman. 1986. That moment in space. *The Globe and Mail,* 29 January: A6.

Wereley, Ian. 1989. Physics and the new Alberta science curriculum. *Alberta Science Teacher* 9 (2): 16–18.

Westbury, Ian and Neil J Wilkof. 1978. Introduction. In *J. J. Schwab: Science, curriculum, and liberal education,* edited by Ian Westbury and Neil J Wilkof, 1–40. Chicago: University of Chicago Press.

Wilford, John Noble. 1971. *We reach the moon.* New York: W. W. Norton and Company.

———. 1986. Faith in technology jolted, but there is no going back. *New York Times,* 29 January: A7.

Wilson, John. 1991. Is science falling on deaf ears? *The Globe and Mail,* 21 August: A.16.

Wise, Arthur E. 1977. Why educational policies often fail: The hyperrationalization hypothesis. *Curriculum Studies* 9 (1): 43–57.

Wood, Eric. 1990. Reforming teaching: Is it possible? *Education Canada* 30 (4): 28–35.

World Commission on Environment and Development. 1987. From one Earth to one world. In *Our Common Future,* Gro Brundtland, Chairman, 2–23. New York: Oxford University Press.

Yager, Robert E. 1981. What are "The Basics" in general biology? *The American Biology Teacher* 43 (3): 154–156.

Yager, Robert E. 1984. The major crisis in science education. *School Science and Mathematics* 84 (3): 189–197.

———. 1992. Forward. In *The status of Science-Technology-Society reforms efforts around the world,* edited by Robert E. Yager, iii. Arlington, Virginia: National Science Teachers Association.

Yager, Robert E. and John E. Penick. 1986. What students say about science teaching and science teachers. *Science Education* 68 (2) 143–152.

Yager, Robert E. and Stuart O. Yager. 1985. Changes in perceptions of science for third, seventh, and eleventh grade students. *Science Education* 22 (4): 347–358.

Zais, Robert S. 1976a. *Curriculum: Principles and foundations.* New York: Thomas Y. Crowell.

———. 1976b. Conceptions of curriculum and the curriculum field. In *Curriculum and instruction,* edited by Henry A. Giroux, Anthony N. Penna and William F. Pinar, 31–49. Berkeley California: McCutchan.

Zeidler, Dana L. 1984. Moral issues and social policy in science education: Closing the literacy gap. *Science Education* 68 (4) 411–419.

Zeitlin, Irving M. 1987. *Ideology and the development of sociological theory.* Englewood Cliffs, New Jersey: Prentice Hall.

Zondervan Bible Publishers. 1978. *New international version of The Holy Bible.* Grand Rapids, Michigan: Zondervan Bible Publishers.

Zukav, Gary. 1979. *The Dancing Wu Li Masters.* New York: Bantam Books.

Index

—A—

A Nation At Risk, 34

AAAS. *See* American Association for
the Advancement of Science

Aikenhead, Glen, 24
*Science in Social Issues
Implications for Teaching*, 38

Alberta Education, 43
consultation with science
teachers, 73, 75
curriculum reform process, 49–50
curriculum, meaning of, 86
debate over the new science
programs, 67
feedback on initial science
programs, 54
final version of the science
programs, 77
program credit system, 43
reaction to criticism of new
science programs, 64
science program credit
allocations, 53, 54, 68
STS initiative, 44
technical-rational approach to
curriculum change, 52–53, 69,
86
thematic approach in science
education, 73, 75

Alberta Medical Association
criticism of new science
programs, 65–66

Alberta Report
criticism of Alberta Education,
63, 64
criticism of Alberta's Minister of
Education, 63
criticism of new science
programs, 63–64
praise for Alberta's Minister of
Education, 72
reaction to by Alberta Education,
64

Alberta Science Teacher, 62
criticism of new science
programs, 59

Alberta, Canada
Freedman, Joe, criticism of new
science programs by, 66, 67
newspaper criticisms of new
science programs, 60
review of secondary education, 48
science education reform, 3
secondary school education, 43
significance of STS initiatives in,
39, 47, 48
teacher criticisms of new science
programs, 59–60, 61–62,
134–35

ALCHEM, 36, 46

Algeny. *See* Rifkin, Jeremy

allegories and metaphors. *See also*
The Quest, Chapter 4
curriculum understanding and, 128
in post-modern writing, 127–29
trachealizing discourse, use of,
129

alphabet soup science programs. *See*
science education curriculum
reforms

AMA. *See* Alberta Medical
Association

American Association for the
Advancement of Science, 37
Project 2061, 73
STS programs, influence on, 37

Aoki, Ted, 50

APEGGA. *See* Association of
Petroleum Engineers, Geologists
and Geophysicists of Alberta

Apollo 11
  criticisms of, 25
  hope for peace, 10
  moon landing, 9
  optimism in science, 9, 190
  support of modernity, 11, 20
Association of Petroleum Engineers,
  Geologists, and Geophysicists of
  Alberta
  criticism of new science
    programs, 64–66
Atomic Energy Commission, 13
  science education curriculum
    reforms and, 13, 15

—B—

*Basic Principles of Curriculum and
  Instruction. See* Tyler, Ralph
Bernauer, James, 183, 197
Blades, David, 25, 31, 41, 63, 79,
  89, 127, 141, 185, 210, 211
Borgmann, Albert, 87, 92, 130
Bruner, Jerome
  The Process of Education, 12, 18
  Wood's Hole Conference, 11

—C—

Caputo, John, 124, 126
  Radical Hermeneutics, 127
Carson, Rachel
  Silent Spring, 26, 190
Challenger, 27
  Apollo 11 and, 190
  failure of modern technology, 28
change
  being and, 167, 175, 193, 195
  conversion and, 95
  critique and, 5
  despair of possibilities, 174
  discomfort and, 176
  freedom and, 95
  possibility of, 170, 193
  post-modern vision of, 181
  questioning and, 194, 195

  resistance and, 198, 203, 207,
    217
  technical thinking blocking
    possibilities of, 95
  wrestling with self and, 122–23,
    174, 214
Cherryholmes, Cleo, 69, 96, 102
  discourse analysis and Foucault,
    103
  on Foucault's concept of truth,
    117
  power and textbooks, 102
Cohen, Leonard, 216
  The Anthem, 217
  The Future, 216–17
Compte, Auguste
  positive philosophy of, 17
conversation
  change and, 97, 198, 202
  change in being and, 214
  critique and, 5, 97, 98, 208
credit crunch, 154. *See* Alberta
  Education, science program credit
  allocations
critique
  defined by Foucault, 5, 97. *See
    also* Foucault, Michel, critique
    defined by
  possibilities for change and, 97,
    218
  post-modern conversations of, 5,
    188
Cuban, Larry
  resilience of schooling to change,
    83
  review of attempts of educational
    change, 83
cummings, e. e.
  being reborn, 191
  *pity this busy
    monster,manunkind*, 191
curriculum change. *See also*
  technicality
  barren history of, 83–84, 180
  barrenness of technical-rational
    approaches, 181

failure of, in science education,
82–84
Foucauldian approach to
understanding, 180
possibility of, 89
questions and, 213
students, role in decisions, 141
technical-rational approach, 2,
51, 84
technical-rational approach steps,
51
technical-rational approach,
barrenness of, 96
technical-rational approach,
factors, 70
technical-rational models,
dominance of, 51–52, 89
Tyler's technical-rational model,
51
curriculum reform, science education.
See also science education
curriculum reforms
beginning teachers involvement
in, 185–88
graduate students, involvement
in, 199–203
student involvement in, 209–12
curriculum renewal in science
education. *See* science education
curriculum reforms
curriculum-discourse, 178. *See also*
discourse
defined, 42
reflected in texts, 42

—D—

deconstruction
defined, 108
Foucault and, 107
questioning as, 93
Deleuze, Gilles
on Foucault's concept of power,
99
on Nietzsche and Foucault, 206

Derrida, Jacques
deconstruction and, 108
Foucault and, 108
nihilism and, 108
on communication of meaning,
124
destining. *See also* enframement; Ge-
stell; modernity
of modernity, 195
Dinning, Jim. *See* Minister of
Education, Alberta
discourse
definition of, 41
midrash as, 121
power and, 99
practice of and boundaries, 42
practice of and technicality, 194
production of knowledge, 153,
154
public truths defining, 156
trachealization of, 107, 108, 198
Doll, William
on post-modernism and curriculum
reform, 199
Dreyfus, Hubert, 197
on Foucault's concept of power,
99
on pervasiveness of power, 183
on the effects of power, 100

—E—

education, research in
conversations of critique as, 118
document collection, 58–59, 99,
104–6
ethics, 114–18
events matrix chart, 58–59
Foucauldian approach, 109
interviewing, 109–13
participant-observation, 56, 112,
115
post-modern view of, 97
purpose of, 96–97
role of the researcher, 117
student involvement in, 202

teacher-based, 202
validity, 112–14
Eisenhower, U.S. President
reaction to *Sputnik*, 14
science education curriculum
reforms and, 15
Eisner, Elliot, 19
enframement. *See also* destining; Ge-
stell
of being, 195
of modernity, 8
procedures of power and, 184
environment
eco-crisis, 30
environmental education. *See*
Oelschlaeger, Max; Orr, David
public concerns, 30
sustainable development of, 31

—F—

Feather, Frank
G-Forces, 31
Fensham, Peter, 37
on academic influence in
curriculum development, 86
on STS world-wide, 37
on the difficulty of curriculum
change in science education,
82–83
Foucault, Michel, 3, 88, 133, 158.
See also Biography, Appendix B
archaeology of knowledge, 106
archeology of discourse, 107
concept of power, 3, 4, 93–94,
95, 99, 148–50, 157, 162,
166, 177, 206
concept of power, criticisms of,
166, 183–84
concept of power, paradox in, 183
concept of power, response to
critics, 196
concept of power, sovereignty
and, 163–66, 215
concept of truth, 117
critique, defined by, 198

Discipline and Punish, 100
History of Sexuality, Volume 1,
133, 177, 178–82, 180, 197,
206
hope for change, 197
influence in educational research,
102–4
influence in sociological
research, 102
influence of Nietzsche on, 206
knowledge and power, 107, 154,
179
local theory of change, 198
new method of research, 102
Nietzsche, Genealogy, History,
206
nihilism and, 184
on hermeneutics, 106
on intellectuals, 117, 139
on knowledge (savoir), 153
on political action, 88
on silence in discourse, 138
on student voices, 141
on students and power, 164
pessimistic hopefulness, 197
research approach, 106
research project, 3, 101, 108,
196, 206
resistance and change, 197
truth and power, 157
work, definition of, 154
freedom
change and, 95, 122
deconstruction and, 108
from modernity, 4
limitations of and power, 2
Fullan, Michael
structuralist approach, 70–72
*The New Meaning of Educational
Change*, 70
view of curriculum change, 85

—G—

Gage Publishing, 54, 56
Visions 1, 55

Ge-stell, 110, 199, 208, 217. *See also* Heidegger, Martin
   deconstruction and, 93
   defined, 192
   destining and, 192
   discovery and change, 129
   essence of technology, 88
   limiting possibilities, 89
   post-modern writing and, 126
G-Forces. See Feather, Frank
Great Conversation, The. *See* The Great Conversation
Greene, Maxine, 7, 129
Grumet, Madeleine, 8, 116

—H—

Habermas, Jürgen, 107
Heidegger, Martin, 88. *See also* Ge-stell
   hope for change, 193
   on destining, 5
   on technology, 192
   The Question Concerning Technology, 56, 191–94
Huberman, Michael
   on events matrix charts, 58, 59
   on interviewing, 111
Hurd, Paul DeHart, 13
   call for STS science education, 35
   on curriculum reform in science education, 23, 87
   on the lack of change in science education, 39, 84

—I—

ICASE. *See* International Council of Associations for Science Education
International Council of Associations for Science Education, 37
International Organization for Science and Technology Education, 37

IOSTE. *See* International Organization for Science and Technology Education

—J—

Johnson, Paul, 11, 17

—K—

Kass, Heidi
   on curricular knowledge, 41
   on student views of scientists, 25
Kierkegaard, Søren
   recollection, 5
   recollection, importance of, 129, 176

—L—

Levin, David
   hope for change, 195
   on destining, 89
   on the modern loss of vision, 189
   The Opening of Vision, 89, 188
Lovelock, James
   Gaia hypothesis, 30
   hope for the future, 32
   on sustainable development, 32
Lyotard, Jean-François, 92
   challenge to Ge-stell, 129
   post-modernism and the author, 126

—M—

Madison, G. B., 17, 92, 123, 198
   description of deconstruction, 108
   on Derrida's deconstructionism, 108
metanarratives, 128
   defined, 125
   power and, 125
metaphors. *See* allegories and metaphors

midrash
  defined, 121
  metaphorical style and, 121, 127
  wrestling and, 122
Miles, Matthew
  on events matrix charts, 58, 59
  on interviewing, 111
Minister of Education, Alberta
  changes to initial science
    education proposal, 68
  delays in implementing new
    science programs, 62
  formation of a Minister's
    Advisory Committee, 67, 68
  public praise for, 74
Minister's Advisory Committee. *See*
  Minister of Education, Alberta,
  formation of a Minister's
  Advisory Committee
modernity
  agenda of, 201
  assumptions of, 2
  crisis in and curriculum change,
    87
  destining and, 194
  erosion of faith in science and
    technology in, 27, 190
  failure of, 26, 130
  Foucault's challenge to, 207
  foundations of, 11, 123, 130, 201
  in popular fiction, 18
  metaphysical foundations, 17
  promises of, 1, 17, 91–92, 91,
    190
  scientific discovery and, 18
  technological risks, 26, 136
  wrestling against, 214
  writing and, 124

—N—

Nader, Ralph
  Unsafe at Any Speed, 26
narratives
  change and, 8
  purposes of, 7

NASA
  funding of science education, 15
National Defense Education Act, 15
National Science Foundation (U.S.)
  reports on American science
    education, 22
  STS programs, influence on, 37
  support of Post-World War II
    reforms, 15
National Science Teacher
  Association, 37, 51
NDEA. *See* National Defense
  Education Act
newspapers. *See* Alberta, Canada,
  newspapers
Nietzsche, Friedrich
  comedy and, 208
  influence on Foucault, 100
  on cheerfulness, 205
  on good and evil, 205
  On The Genealogy of Morals,
    100, 204, 205–7, 206, 211
  on the importance of questioning,
    204
  The Birth of Tragedy, 206
  will to power, 100, 180, 206
NSF. *See* National Science
  Foundation (U.S.)
NSTA. *See* National Science Teacher
  Association
Nuffield Science Foundation (Britain)
  science education reform and, 16

—O—

Oelschlaeger, Max
  on modernity, 200
  on wilderness, 32
  The Idea of Wilderness, 199
On The Genealogy of Morals. See
  Nietzsche, Friedrich
Orr, David
  Ecological Literacy, 199
  on a post-modern vision of
    education, 200

on post-modern environmental
education, 199, 200

—P—

*Physical Science, Society and
Technology* (Australia), 37
PLON (Netherlands), 36
positivism. *See also* The Great
Conversation
in science education curriculum
reforms, 18
post-modern. *See also* post-
modernism
disruption, 126
education, local nature of, 201
writing, 4, 123–27
post-modernism
avoidance of definition, 124
break from modernism, 125
project, 92
questioning, 1
The Great Conversation and, 92
theory and, 99
writing, as wrestling, 129
power. *See also* Foucault, Michel,
concept of power
adaptability of, 159–62, 182
and curriculum change in science
education, 178
anonymous nature of, 166
apparatus of, 159
curriculum change in science
education and, 101
defining nature of, 165, 179, 180
discourse and, 100
enframing nature of, 4, 153, 162,
168–70
exclusion of students voices, 211
Marxist view of, 99, 148
mobility of, 162
modernity as, 177
procedures of, 95, 110, 114, 129,
134, 166, 177, 180, 184
procedures of and hope for
change, 104

procedures of, bureaucratization,
136–37, 178
procedures of, consultation, 145–
50, 179
procedures of, destining, 198
procedures of, hierarchies, 134–
36, 179
procedures of, marginalization,
139–45, 178, 179
procedures of, production of
knowledge, 150–55
procedures of, production of truth,
155–57
procedures of, silence, 137–39,
178
public truths and, 156, 179-180
resistance and, 197, 207
trachealization of, 181, 218
Process of Education, The. See also
Bruner, Jerome
as modernistic guide to curriculum
reform, 18
Project Classroom Earth, 27
public truths. *See* discourse, public
truths in; power, public truths and

—R—

Rabinow, Paul, 197
on Foucault's concept of power,
99
on pervasiveness of power, 183
on the effects of power, 100
research. *See* education, research in
resistance. *See* change, resistance
and; power, resistance and
Rifkin, Jeremy
Algeny, 31
Rosenau, Pauline, 91, 125

—S—

Sarason, Seymour
*The Culture of the School and the
Problem of Change*, 70

*The Predictable Failure of
    Education Reform*, 84
SATIS. *See* Science and Technology
    in Society
SCC. *See* Science Council of Canada
Schwab, Joseph J., 20
    *Education and the Structure of the
        Disciplines*, 19
Science
    concerns in popular fiction, 26
    dark side of, 28
    Frankenstein, metaphor of, 26
    human activity of, 187
    myth of objectivity and, 28
    student views of. *See* students
Science 10. *See also* Science 10, 20,
    and 30
    defined, 44
    initial proposal for, 45–47
    topics, final version, 80–81
    topics, initial proposal, 46
Science 10, 20, and 30
    as a response to second crisis in
        science education, 45
    as rigorous science education, 77
    controversy over, 59–67
    development of science literacy,
        79
    failure of, 81–82
    major goal of, 45
    outline of initiative, 44–47
    revised program after
        controversy, 80–81
    sub-committee meetings, 52–54
    technical-rational assumptions in
        the development of, 85–87
    vision for, 80
Science and Technology in Society
    (Britain), 36
Science Council of Canada
    effect on STS science education in
        Alberta, Canada, 48
    recommendations for science
        education reform, 22
    study of science education, 21

science education. *See also* science
    education curriculum reforms
    post-World War II crisis in, 13
    second crisis since World War II,
        35
science education curriculum reforms
    alphabet soup programs, 16
    Canadian adoption of American
        programs, 16
    effect of *Sputnik*, 15. *See also*
        Sputnik, effect on science
        education
    export of programs world-wide,
        16
    in the U.S., 23
    lack of impact on instruction, 23
    national security and, 13, 189
    orientation towards males, 15
    questions about the direction of,
        35
    science disciplines orientation,
        15, 44
Science for All movement (Australia),
    37
Science in a Social Context (Britain),
    36
Science in Society (Britain), 36
science literacy
    defined, 34
    in the U.S., 34
    promoted by the AAAS, 73
    world-wide, 34
science teachers
    apprenticeship to transmissional
        teaching, 188
    criticisms of new science
        programs in Alberta. *See*
        Alberta, Canada, teacher
        criticisms of new science
        programs
    questions concerning, 188
Science, A Way of Knowing, 47
science, technology and society. *See*
    STS science education
Secondary Education in Alberta, 49
Silent Spring. See Carson, Rachel

Smith, Bruce, 13
  drift from science, 26
  Vietnam war and the drift from
    science, 26
Sputnik. See also science education
  curriculum reforms, effect of
  Sputnik
  effect on science education, 1, 15,
    35, 189
  reaction in the West, 14
  Russian technological
    superiority, 14
  Sputnik II, reaction in the West,
    14
spy in the sky. *See Sputnik*
Stenhouse, David, 23
structuralism
  defined, 69
  determined hope for change, 84–
    85
  in curriculum change models, 69–
    72
  in technical-rational models, 69
  interpretation of evolution of
    Science 10, 20, and 30, 80
  serving the status quo, 83, 181
STS approach. *See* STS science
  education
STS science education
  compared to post-*Sputnik*
    reforms, 36
  defined, 35, 36
  in Alberta, Canada, 38, 44, 48
  in Canada, 38
  progress world-wide, 37
  purpose, 36
students
  decline in attitude towards
    science, 24, 25
  negative views of scientists, 25
  post-secondary enrollment in
    science, 23
  views of their science education,
    79, 185, 209–12

Suzuki, David
  children and hope for change, 32–
    33
  on the activity of science, 28
  witness to environmental
    degradation, 29

—T—

teachers. *See* science teachers
technicality. *See also* curriculum
  change, technical-rational
  approaches; modernity
  as a mode of thinking, 87
  as destining, 89
  closure of being and, 193
  curriculum change and, 2
  destining and, 153
  determinism and, 96
  Heidegger's warning concerning,
    125, 192
  limiting possibilities, 89, 180
  possibilities for change and, 97
  science education enframed by,
    217
  seduction of, 110, 194, 200, 207
technical-rational approach. *See*
  curriculum change, technical-
  rational approaches
technoptimism, 31
  belief in human ability, 31
  environmental concerns and, 32
The Great Conversation, 178, 207,
  217. *See also* modernity
  belief in progress, 91
  European Enlightenment and, 17
  logos and, 16
  modern science and, 17
  post-modern abandonment of, 92
  restriction of vision in, 89. *See
    also* Levin, David
  second call for renewal in science
    education, 33
The History of Sexuality, Volume 1.
  See Foucault, Michel

The Question Concerning Technology. See Heidegger, Martin

Third National Assessment of Science Education (U.S.), 24

truths, public. See Power, public truths and

Tyler, Ralph
  Basic Principles of Curriculum and Instruction, 50
  influence on curriculum change theory, 51
  modernism in change theory of, 51
  on curriculum change, 50

—U—

U.S. Department of Defense
  funding of science education, 15

U.S. National Survey of Science and Mathematics Education, 34

U.S. Office of Naval Research
  science education curriculum reforms and, 13

universalism
  in Foucault's concept of power. *See* Foucault, Michel, concept of power, paradox in

University of Alberta Faculty of Science
  criticism of new science programs, 60–61
  reaction to revised science programs, 74, 78

Unsafe at any Speed. See Nader, Ralph

—V—

violence
  the failure of change as, 88

Visions 1. See also Gage Publishing
  final version, 78
  problems in text development, 62, 68, 75
  Teachers' Guide, 116

—W—

wilderness. *See also* Oelschlaeger, Max
  environmental education, importance of, 200
  post-modern environmental education and, 202
  transformation of and modernity, 169, 199

Wood's Hole Conference, 11, 189. *See* also *The Process of Education* and *Sputnik*, 15
  effect on science education, 12
  modernistic premises, 11

wrestling. *See* change, wrestling with self and

—Y—

Yager, Robert, 24
  on the STS reform movement, 37

DAVID W. BLADES is Associate Professor at the University of Alberta. He received his Ph.D. in Secondary Education from the University of Alberta. His paper on power and curriculum change was awarded a Tetuso Aoki Award in 1993 by *JCT: An Interdisciplinary Journal of Curriculum Studies*. A Killam Scholar and award-winning teacher, he has published and presented widely on the topics of curriculum change and science education.

Studies in the Postmodern Theory of Education

General Editors
Joe L. Kincheloe & Shirley R. Steinberg

Counterpoints publishes the most compelling and imaginative books being written in education today. Grounded on the theoretical advances in criticalism, feminism and postmodernism in the last two decades of the twentieth century, Counterpoints engages the meaning of these innovations in various forms of educational expression. Committed to the proposition that theoretical literature should be accessible to a variety of audiences, the series insists that its authors avoid esoteric and jargonistic languages that transform educational scholarship into an elite discourse for the initiated. Scholarly work matters only to the degree it affects consciousness and practice at multiple sites. Counterpoints' editorial policy is based on these principles and the ability of scholars to break new ground, to open new conversations, to go where educators have never gone before.

For additional information about this series or for the submission of manuscripts, please contact:

Joe L. Kincheloe & Shirley R. Steinberg
637 West Foster Avenue
State College, PA 16801